Plants and Animals
of the Pacific Northwest

Plants and Animals
OF THE
Pacific Northwest

AN ILLUSTRATED GUIDE TO THE NATURAL HISTORY OF WESTERN OREGON, WASHINGTON, AND BRITISH COLUMBIA

By Eugene N. Kozloff

UNIVERSITY OF WASHINGTON PRESS
SEATTLE AND LONDON

Printed in the United States of America

Library of Congress Cataloging in Publication Data

Kozloff, Eugene N
Plants and animals of the Pacific Northwest.

Bibliography: p.
Includes index.
1. Zoology—Northwest, Pacific. 2. Botany—Northwest, Pacific. I. Title.
QH104.5.N6K69 574.9′795 75–40875
ISBN 0–295–95449–3

Preface

THROUGHOUT a fairly long career of teaching biology in the Northwest, I have enjoyed improving my knowledge of the plant and animal life of the region. For a number of years, I offered a course on natural history that was sufficiently nontechnical to be understood by anyone interested in the subject. Eventually, I decided to develop a little book that would serve the needs of amateurs, students, and perhaps even some professional biologists concerned with the terrestrial fauna and flora.

From the beginning, I wanted the guide to be reasonably thorough in its coverage of the material selected for inclusion. I knew this would not be possible if the geographic area under consideration were too large. I thought it best to concentrate on the lowland portions of Oregon, Washington, and British Columbia that lie west of the Cascade Mountains. From Roseburg and Eugene, Oregon, to well north of Vancouver and Nanaimo, British Columbia, the vegetation and animal life include many common denominators. To put it another way, if one learns the trees, shrubs, common wildflowers, and birds of a coniferous forest or grove of oaks at the southern end of the Willamette Valley, he will find most of them in comparable situations in British Columbia. The southwestern sector of Oregon, occupied largely by the Siskiyou Mountains, is characterized by many species whose distribution does not extend farther north. I have therefore excluded this area. The guide will be helpful there, but one will just have to consult other books as well.

Before deciding whether a particular plant or animal should be described in this book, I asked myself the following questions. Is it at least fairly common and widely distributed? Have I seen it more than just once or twice? Is its occurrence in our area "freakish," or limited to one or just a few localities? Will it be reasonably obvious to someone who is not a specialist trained to pick out minute and esoteric novelties?

It would be impractical, of course, to include everything that happens to be important or abundant. Early in the course of getting things together I decided to minimize the treatment of birds and mammals, and to forget about grasses, mushrooms, insects, spiders, and some other things. I had misgivings about this, but it seemed best to concentrate on groups that I could discuss in satisfying detail. The birds of western North America, and of our region in particular, are the subject of a number of practical guides. Relatively few mammals are sufficiently distinctive to be recognized easily in the field. I would have liked to include at least ten or fifteen kinds of grasses and mushrooms, but when I started to compile lists I did not know where to stop. I am grateful to authors of some excellent handbooks for lifting a heavy burden from my shoulders.

The exclusion of spiders and all but a few insects is difficult to justify, but the number of important kinds that clamor for attention is so large that it is easier to look the other way and hope that someone else will round them up. The problem of what to do with weeds and other plants that have escaped from cultivation has been a constant annoyance. As this is a guide to the general natural history of our region, I have concentrated on native species. But certain introduced species just nagged at me until I made room for them.

Although I have stressed some of the unique aspects of the flora of bogs, I have summarily excluded all but a few of the numerous kinds of grasslike plants that grow in wet places, as well as strictly submerged vegetation, fishes, and other purely aquatic animals. Our freshwater fauna and flora are so marvelously varied that my decision to leave them alone will come as no surprise to any who have studied in this field. The subject needs to be developed more fully in a separate book, instead of being dealt with superficially here.

What we have left is a guide that covers over 400 species of plants and animals and that illustrates nearly all of them. It is substantially complete for trees, shrubs, and vines, and has enough wildflowers to keep a budding botanist busy for a while. I have included most of the ferns and fern allies that one is likely to find west of the Cascades, a few birds and mammals, and all of the reptiles and amphibians that may reasonably be expected. I am particularly happy to have been able to describe and illustrate a wide selection of mosses, liverworts, and lichens, as well as some of the more common snails, slugs, millipedes, centipedes, and certain other invertebrates. It is difficult to get information on most of these groups, except in specialized treatises.

As in my book *Seashore Life of Puget Sound, the Strait of Georgia, and the San Juan Archipelago* (Seattle: University of Washington Press, 1973), I have organized this guidebook around certain habitats and biotic assemblages that are abundantly represented in our region. I am well aware of the overlaps that exist between a coniferous forest and a grove of oaks, or between a brushy area and a weedy field. There are some real advantages, however, to this approach, for it brings together the descriptions of species that are most likely to be found in a particular situation. Many users of this book will begin their attempts to identify the common animals and plants by leafing through the illustrations. To the extent that it was practical, I have grouped the color pictures in a way that will make this easier.

The usefulness of this book has been enhanced by frank and constructive criticism from several colleagues. Melinda Denton read the portions of the manuscript dealing with higher plants. Besides weeding out errors and ambiguities, she kept me informed of recent changes in scientific names and showed me how to improve the text in many places. Richard Snyder generously shared his extensive knowledge of vertebrates of this region, correcting what I had written about these animals and offering helpful suggestions. Daniel Stuntz straightened out the section on fungi and reviewed much of the material on lichens and other lower plants. Paul Illg patched up my account of termites, and Richard Norris gave advice with respect to a few botanical questions. Bastiaan Meeuse, after plowing through the entire manuscript, good-naturedly exposed my ignorance in several areas and persuaded me to mention some topics that will be of interest to many readers. My warmest thanks go to all of these friends for their expert counsel. I will be embarrassed by any mistakes that have survived, but I accept responsibility for them. I hope users of this book will not hesitate to point them out.

I am indebted to Elaine and James Butler for providing four color photographs, of the Trowbridge shrew, shrew-mole, coast mole, and Beechey ground squirrel; all other color photographs were taken by me. I must also thank C. Leo Hitchcock and Jeanne R. Janish for permission to use numerous drawings prepared by Mrs. Janish for the monumental *Vascular Plants of the Pacific Northwest.* A few other illustrations have been taken from sources either not copyrighted or presently in the public domain. Most notable of these are some excellent drawings of mammals made by Leon Pray for a publication of the Field Museum of Natural History.

It is hardly possible to acknowledge everyone who has aided me in my efforts to learn the fauna and flora of this region. Field trips taken with Francis Gilchrist, James Stauffer, and the late Benjamin Thaxter in the early stages of my career as teacher are remembered with appreciation. Hundreds of students, amateurs, and professional biologists have asked questions or given answers that have directly influenced the contents of this book. In recent months valued assistance, scientific and logistic, has come from Nina and Virgil Hicks, Louisa Norris, Estelle Johnson, Joyce Lewin, Eve Verhoeff, Grace Archambault, Roxie and Ronald Shimek, Nancy and Clayton Ham, Robert Fernald, Dennis Willows, Charles Eaton, and the staff of Woodland Park Zoo, Seattle.

Much of the manuscript was typed and retyped by my daughter, Rae. My wife, Anne, suggested clarifications and simplifications, read the proofs, and helped prepare the index. Another member of our family has been a tireless and patient ally in the field for nearly thirteen years. Her caprices contented by chasing sticks, racing through tall grass, and getting muddy, Rocket's companionship has made my work with camera and notebook supremely enjoyable.

EUGENE N. KOZLOFF

Friday Harbor, Washington
1976

Contents

Plants and Animals
of the Pacific Northwest

1

Introduction

A Little Geography

The Cascade Mountains separate a mild and relatively humid western sector from a drier interior that is cold in winter, hot in summer. From late autumn through much of the spring, moisture-laden winds from the Pacific Ocean bring heavy rains to the coastal strip and to the slopes of the Coast Ranges, Olympic Mountains, and Cascades. The lowland troughs running north and south between these ranges receive substantially less rainfall, but few people who live there would ask for any more. The summers are comparatively dry because the storm tracks shift farther north at this season.

The region covered by this book can be subdivided, for convenience, into three areas. Each of these is considerably diversified in topography, geological features, soil types, and climate. The physical conditions in a particular situation decide, to a large extent, which animals and plants will be present, and which will be especially successful. Certain species, or assemblages of species, may be limited to restricted portions of just one area, while others can be found nearly throughout the whole region. One is almost never very far from a Douglas fir or grand fir, and Garry oak and madrone show up here and there over a wide range. Yet the occurrence of Rocky Mountain juniper on Vancouver Island and on the islands of the San Juan Archipelago is truly remarkable, for this tree is found nowhere else west of the Cascades.

THE COASTAL STRIP, COAST RANGES, AND OLYMPIC MOUNTAINS

Along the coast, the average annual precipitation varies from about 150cm (60 inches) near Coos Bay to more than 250 cm (100 inches) on the Olympic Peninsula. At higher elevations in the Coast Ranges and Olympics, the precipitation may reach 300 cm (120 inches). The coastal strip and the mountains directly behind it thus constitute one of the wettest areas of North America.

The rather narrow coastal strip includes salt marshes, sand dunes, true bogs, grassy slopes, and dense forests. The forests may extend right to the edges of bluffs that look down on the beaches, especially where foothills of the Coast Ranges reach nearly to the shore. From about Coos Bay, Oregon, to fairly far north on Vancouver Island, the obvious features of the vegetation on the coastal strip are similar. The predominant forest trees are western hemlock, western red cedar, lodgepole pine, Douglas fir, grand fir, and Sitka spruce (which is not often found more than a few kilometers inland). Typical shrubs include the rhododendron (except on Vancouver Island), evergreen huckleberry, red huckleberry, salal, red elderberry, and salmonberry. There is a rather distinctive maritime flora on the sandy beaches and rocky cliffs. The bogs are characterized by *Sphagnum* moss, sundew, cranberry, Labrador tea, swamp laurel, cotton-grass, and a few other species restricted to this kind of situation.

South of Coos Bay some novelties occur. Most noticeable of the trees and shrubs found here but not farther north are Port Orford cedar, Oregon "myrtle," and western azalea. There are, of course, many other species unique to this area and to the contiguous section of California.

The Olympic Peninsula requires some special consideration here, in part because the narrow coastal strip soon gives way to a block of mountains that has peaks twice as high as any in the Coast Ranges to the south. The entire coastal area on the west side of the peninsula has an annual rainfall of more than 180 cm (72 inches), and as stated above, the slopes of the mountains may receive nearly twice that amount. On the east side of the peninsula, however, precipitation drops off sharply. At Port Angeles the annual average is around 80 cm (32 inches), and still farther east, at Sequim and Port Townsend, it is only about 60 cm (24 inches). This sector is said to be in a "rain shadow": the storms that approach the Olympics come principally from the southwest and drop most of their rain at the coast and on the mountains, so little is left for the area just beyond. The territory within the rain shadow is really a part of the Puget Trough and is discussed in that section below.

In any case, although the vegetation at lower elevations on the west and northwest aspects of the Olympic Peninsula is similar to that of the coastal strip in general, the higher ridges and peaks of the Olympic Mountains have a distinguished flora. Many of the obvious elements are likewise found at comparable altitudes in the Cascades; but there are some interesting endemic species that are restricted to the Olympics, or only rarely found anywhere else.

THE WILLAMETTE VALLEY

The Willamette Valley of Oregon lies between the Coast Ranges and Cascade Mountains. It extends from a few miles south of Eugene, where the Coast Ranges and Cascades run together, to Portland, where the Willamette River joins the Columbia. Although the floor of the valley is on the whole rather flat, and slopes only gently from south to north, it is interrupted here and there by substantial hills and scattered rocky buttes. The climate is mild. In January the average minimum temperature is a little above freezing, and in July the average maximum temperature is about 27° C (80° F). The annual rainfall is around 100 cm (40 inches).

The fauna and flora of the Willamette Valley are varied and interesting. Moving southward from Portland to Salem, Albany, and Eugene, one sees several distinctive vegetational assemblages. These may intergrade to some extent, and they show the influences of civilization. After all, the Willamette Valley has more than two-thirds of the population of the state of Oregon, and its resources have been intensively exploited.

The principal vegetational assemblages are coniferous forests, consisting mostly of Douglas fir; scattered stands of Garry oak; riverbank woods composed mostly of cottonwoods, alder, and ash; brushy areas with relatively few trees; and grasslands.

THE PUGET TROUGH

The Puget Trough may be viewed as a northward extension of the Willamette Valley. It includes the territory bordering Puget Sound and the Strait of Georgia, as well as the islands of the San Juan Archipelago. But it also includes the lowland areas between the Cascades and Coast Ranges in southern Washington. The cities of Centralia and Chehalis are therefore just as much in the Puget Trough as Olympia, Seattle, and Victoria. With some exceptions, the annual precipitation in the area ranges from about 80 cm (32 inches) to 120 cm (48 inches).

The principal vegetational types found in the Puget Trough include those noted in the Willamette Valley, but in the northern part of the region—as around Puget Sound proper, the Strait of Georgia, and in the San Juan Archipelago—there are some interesting additions. The following trees, for instance, are not regularly noted in the Willamette Valley or southern portion of the Puget Trough: lodgepole pine, western white pine, paper birch, quaking aspen, and Rocky Mountain juni-

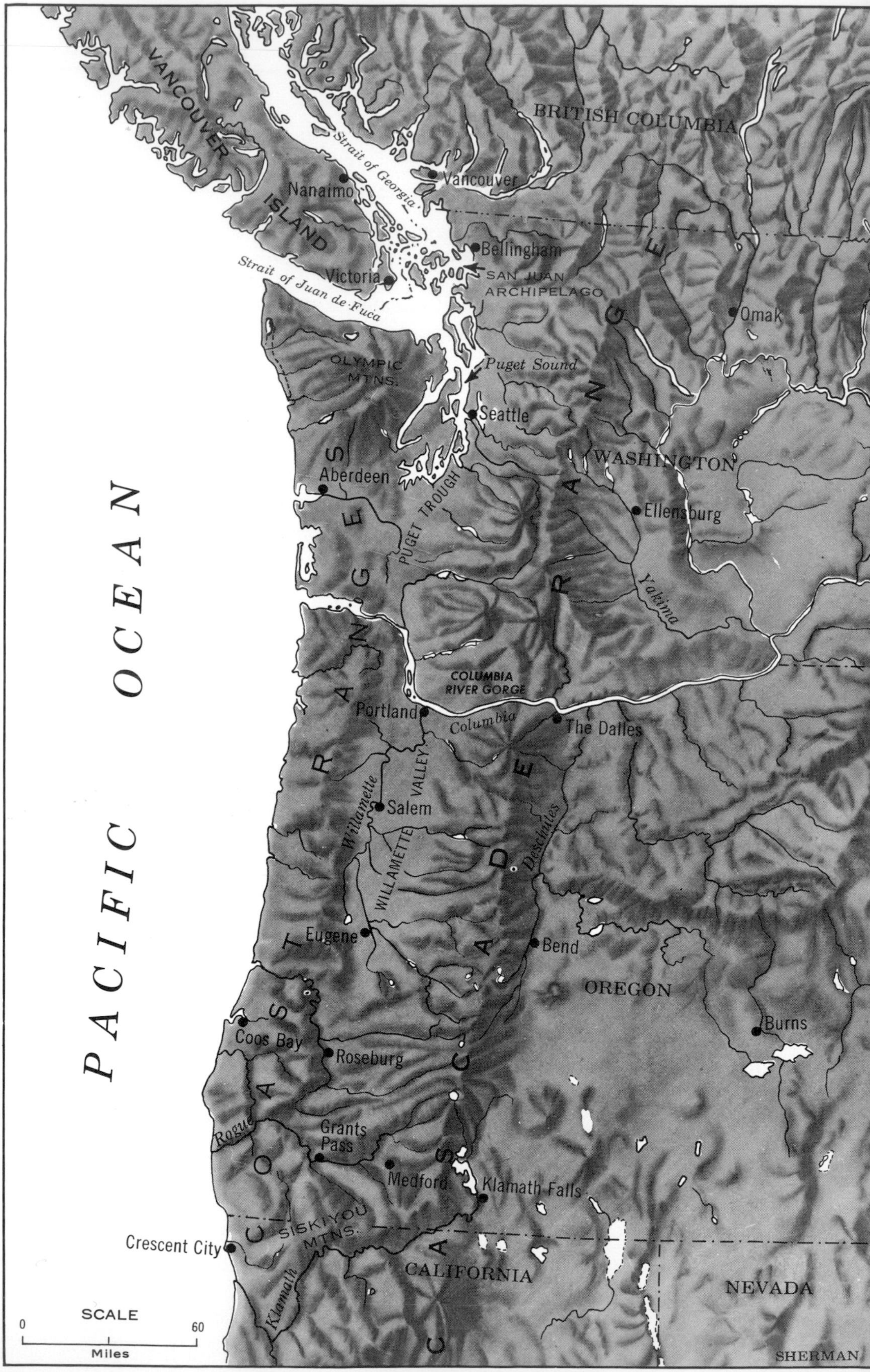
VANCOUVER
ISLAND
BRITISH COLUMBIA
Strait of Georgia
Vancouver
Nanaimo
Bellingham
SAN JUAN
ARCHIPELAGO
Strait of Juan de Fuca
Victoria
Omak
OLYMPIC
MTNS.
Puget Sound
Seattle
WASHINGTON
Aberdeen
PUGET TROUGH
Ellensburg
Yakima
PACIFIC OCEAN
COLUMBIA
RIVER GORGE
Portland
Columbia
The Dalles
WILLAMETTE VALLEY
Willamette
Salem
Deschutes
Eugene
Bend
OREGON
Burns
Coos Bay
Roseburg
Rogue
Grants
Pass
Medford
Klamath Falls
Crescent City
SISKIYOU
MTNS.
Klamath
CALIFORNIA
NEVADA
COAST RANGE
CASCADE RANGE
SCALE
0
60
Miles
SHERMAN

per. In some specific situations in the northern portion of the trough, however, one or another of these species may predominate, or at least be so abundant that its presence is decidedly noticeable. The northern part of the Puget Trough has sphagnum bogs quite comparable to those found along the open coast.

In the Puget Trough, as in the Willamette Valley, there is considerable intergradation of vegetation types. Grasslands, as those of the Tacoma Prairies, may have a good mix of Garry oak, Douglas fir, lodgepole pine, and even ponderosa pine, which is only rarely found west of the Cascades.

On the mainland north of Vancouver, the land rises rather steeply from the shore, so that the lowland area is just a narrow strip. The so-called Coast Mountains that overlook the Strait of Georgia are really a western division of the Cascades rather than a part of the Coast Ranges; in southern British Columbia the latter are represented only on Vancouver Island. Along the northern portion of the strait one may find, at elevations of less than 500 m (about 1600 feet), a few plants that are not often seen below about 1000 m in the Cascades, Olympic Mountains, and Coast Ranges of Oregon and Washington. Most notable of these is the yellow cedar.

Between Bellingham and Vancouver, the valleys of the Fraser and Nooksack rivers form a relatively flat plain, in which coniferous forests are comparatively scarce and deciduous trees predominate. The more abundant species are red alder, big-leaf maple, vine maple, cascara, and Pacific dogwood. Here and there, however, are large stands of paper birch and black cottonwood; quaking aspen may be locally abundant.

The driest portion of the Puget Trough—and of our entire region, for that matter—is the area that falls into the rain shadow of the Olympic Mountains. It includes the northeastern corner of the Olympic Peninsula, the southeastern corner of Vancouver Island, Whidbey Island, and the islands of the San Juan Archipelago. Much of the land within the rain shadow, being rocky, gravelly, or sandy is well drained.

The vegetation of this area is, in general, much like that in certain other portions of the Puget Trough and in the Willamette Valley, where Douglas fir and grand fir are intermixed, or alternate, with Garry oak and madrone. Lodgepole pine is abundant, however, and white pine is a conspicuous element of the vegetation in some places, especially in the region of Hood Canal. The appearance of Rocky Mountain juniper on the San Juan Islands and Vancouver Island comes as something of a surprise, for it is hardly to be expected anywhere west of the Cascades. The absence of poison oak, regularly associated with

Garry oak through much of the range of this tree, will bc cheered by hikers, puzzled over by botanists. In spots where the soil has sufficient moisture or is otherwise favorable for the growth of western hemlock, western red cedar, and Pacific yew, these trees do very nicely. Even Sitka spruce may be found in a few places. There are many other peculiarities in the vegetation of the region, with respect to what is present and how it is mixed together, as well as with respect to what is absent, even if it would seem to fit perfectly.

Scientific Names and Common Names

All of our birds have official common names, agreed upon and published by the American Ornithological Union, and zoologists concerned with amphibians, reptiles, and mammals have taken steps in the direction of fixing common names for these animals. Trees, shrubs, wildflowers, ferns, and well-known mushrooms generally have one or more vernacular names. In the case of mosses, lichens, slugs, millipedes, and other groups of lower animals or plants, however, it is unusual to find any that are sufficiently appreciated to merit more than a scientific name. In this guide, both the scientific name and a common name are given for most of the organisms covered; but where no accepted common name is available, only the scientific name is given.

Scientific names are Latinized words, and the roots from which they are compounded are usually drawn from Greek or Latin, or from the proper names of geographic regions or persons, real or mythical. For example, the scientific name of the California poppy, *Eschscholzia californica,* commemorates Johann Friedrich Eschscholtz, a naturalist on a Russian expedition to California in 1816, as well as the region where the flower was found. (The name was bestowed long before California was a state as we now know it.) Many names are designed to be somewhat descriptive: *Polytrichum juniperinum,* the scientific name of the haircap moss, refers to "many hairs" (found on the capsule in which the spores are produced) and also to certain junipers whose branchlets this moss resembles.

The first of the two Latin names given to an animal or plant is the genus name. It is always capitalized. The second name, for the species, is not capitalized. (Until a few years ago, botanists capitalized it if it was based on the name of a person or another genus.) A genus may include just one species or many. Frequently—and especially in the case of vertebrate animals and flowering plants whose variability over a wide geographic area has been intensively studied—a third Latin name is added to the genus and species. This indicates a subspecies (or variety, a term preferred by botanists), which may be somewhat isolated from other subspecies or may intergrade freely with them.

Scientific names are international and reasonably stable. Changes are made when new findings clarify differences between closely related species or when the priority and validity of the several names that may have been applied to a particular species are reinterpreted and revised. The changes are published in scientific journals, so that experts will be informed of them. In addition, there are rules that govern the uses of scientific names and spell out the procedure for instituting changes.

In this book, identifications are ordinarily carried to genus and species. Sometimes only the genus is given, mainly when it is judged impossible for a nonexpert to distinguish between two or more closely related species, or when the name of even a common and easily recognized species is in doubt. In a few instances, identification is carried all the way to the subspecies. This is appropriate when there is just one recognized subspecies in the region covered by this book, or when separate subspecies can be distinguished on the basis of reasonably simple characteristics or geographic distribution. For instance, although the western terrestrial garter snake, *Thamnophis elegans,* has a number of subspecies, only two of them are found in our region. *T. elegans elegans,* found in Oregon, generally can be separated from *T. elegans vagrans,* found in Washington and British Columbia.

A Word of Caution

Anyone who writes a book of this sort runs the risk of unintentionally deceiving a beginner who may not realize that something he holds in his hand is not quite the same as the nearest species he can find by flipping through the pages. There is only one lizard in our region with a cobalt blue tail and only one snake that has a red belly and a red ring around its neck. But there are some real look-alikes, especially among the lower animals and lower plants. Thus not every cup fungus that happens to be more nearly orange than brown need necessarily be *Aleuria aurantia.* There are more than two kinds of lichens whose upright stalks have red tips. So always be wary.

If your specimen agrees just about perfectly with the picture and description, you probably have arrived at the right answer. When the agreement is decidedly less than satisfying, it is the better part of valor to admit that the identification is tentative or just reasonably close. You would be surprised, if you visited an expert working with an especially numerous and difficult group of plants or animals, how many of the labels on specimens he has studied show that identification is uncertain. Perhaps some of the species have never been described and named; or the variability and intergradation of closely related species may be so great that he is unsure about the systematic status of particular individuals. The situation in certain groups, as birds and flowering plants, is far better than it is, for example, with fungi, lichens, and insects.

The Metric System

Throughout this book, measurements of tree heights, flower diameters, and body lengths are given in meters (m), centimeters (cm), and millimeters (mm). The metric system is destined eventually to replace our present system of weights and measures, and is already routinely used in specialized references to which one may turn for further information about plants and animals. If you are not experienced in dealing with metric measurements, it will be a good idea to learn right away that a meter (100 centimeters) is $39\frac{1}{3}$ inches, or a little more than a yard. A centimeter (10 millimeters) is about two-fifths of an inch, so 2.5 centimeters equal 1 inch, 5 centimeters equal 2 inches, and 25 centimeters equal 10 inches. A comparison of metric and English scales is given here.

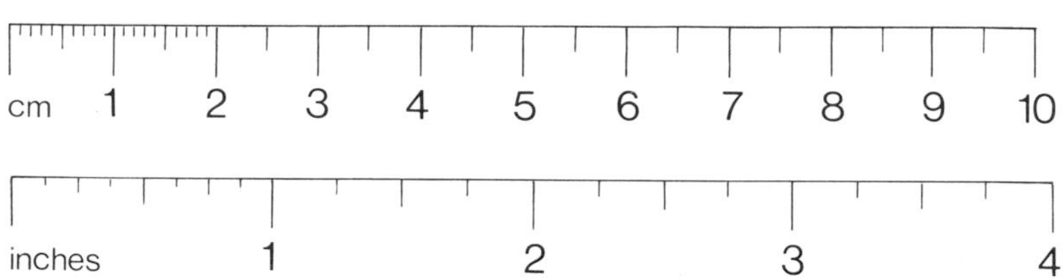

The use of the metric system in dealing with longer distances and for measuring weight and volume probably presents more formidable problems of conversion. Even a scientist who regularly thinks in metric units may be excused for buying milk in quarts, not liters, and for figuring the distance he drives to work in miles, not kilometers. Therefore, some measurements in this book are given in both metric and conventional units.

Conservation and Common Courtesy

As the population of a region increases, the area of undeveloped land generally decreases, so the pressure on what remains is continually intensified. Even large regional and national parks are not immune to adversity. More people means wider roads, larger parking lots, more misdirected beer cans, and more danger to wildlife. Areas that can be reached quickly or easily, and where picnicking and camping are permitted, are the ones that probably will be most heavily exploited.

In the Pacific Northwest, the destructive forces of industrial expansion and population growth are not so painfully apparent as they are in some other regions. Animal and plant life are still abundant, and there are natural areas near almost every city and small community. The climate is favorable for rapid restoration of forested lands from which timber has been harvested, and implementation of laws against pollution is helping to make our air, rivers, and estuaries cleaner. The protection of areas that are especially scenic or undefiled, or that are characterized by features of unusual scientific interest, is another step in the right direction. This is not to imply that everything in the Northwest is perfect. Much of the damage resulting from necessity, greed, and bad taste can never be undone. But let us try to improve our surroundings and definitely not let matters get any worse.

This book has been written not only to inform those who are already interested in the natural history but also to encourage others to explore a subject that may prove to be an engaging, lifelong hobby. With the pleasure of providing this kind of instruction comes the responsibility to teach that an enthusiasm for finding things and for studying them must be tempered by consideration for the animals and plants, for the habitat, and for others who will visit the same places later.

Some of the worst damage to natural areas is inflicted by rolling over logs, turning boulders, and ripping off bark and moss. While it is true that this is the only way you may be likely to see certain things, it must be done gently and in moderation. And when you put a log or rock back in place, be sure nothing underneath will be crushed. It will be better to move a snail, millipede, or salamander a little off to one side before trying to put the place it calls home back together.

Where picking of wildflowers, collecting animals, or turning rocks and logs is expressly forbidden, don't do it. The restriction is almost certainly based on the idea that the area is to be kept as close to a wild state as possible, or on the assumption that the number of people who visit will be large. Where collecting is not restricted, do not pick plants just to get a bouquet of flowers. If you are sufficiently interested to need a good-sized piece of a plant in order to identify it positively and to study it more thoroughly, that is certainly justifiable. If you have any reason to believe that the plant is rare or limited to a particular area, it will be best to leave it in peace.

Requiring students to turn in collections of plants or animals to meet the requirements of a course is a practice that probably should be abolished. The bigger a collection gets, the more chance there is that some rare or endangered species will end up glued to a sheet of paper or in a jar of rubbing alcohol. Besides, the size or completeness of a collection is not necessarily correlated with what the student has learned or how deeply he has been influenced by the course. Some better alternatives exist for assessing his intellectual involvement. In any case, if the object is to have him learn common animals or plants, this can be achieved without turning him and all of his classmates loose to collect on their own. What has just been said is not directed at the training of future professional biologists, whose field work is logically related to advanced study in universities, and whose collections will be added to those of the institutions with which they are affiliated. What we need are good reference and research collections, not thousands of accumulations that serve no purpose.

One thing will be perfectly clear to anyone who goes where roads are being built, where land is being cleared for farming, and where new real-estate subdivisions are being opened: one bulldozer will thoroughly and irreparably destroy many square meters of a natural habitat in just a few minutes. The moral of this is that collecting in places marked for destruction takes the pressure off areas that will hopefully be left in a wild state.

Many lovers of nature enjoy growing native plants in a wild garden of their own. In front of a bulldozer is the place to dig trees, shrubs, and flowers that may grow well if moved to appropriate situations elsewhere. Why not try to keep them going if you can provide the right conditions and if they would be destroyed if you did not save them? Growing plants from seed does little violence to the native flora. It is slow in the case of most perennial species, but it is often more successful than transplanting. Growing wild plants is not a hobby to which every backyard in the city can be adapted, but where woodland conditions already prevail, it is a pleasing way to learn more about natural history.

2

A Coniferous Forest

In the more humid portions of our region—as in the Coast Ranges and on the western slopes of the Cascades—a very old forest is generally dominated by western red cedar and western hemlock. But nearly all virgin stands of cedar and hemlock were cut down long ago. In most coniferous forests, Douglas fir routinely predominates, and grand fir is generally also abundant; hemlock and cedar are likely to be present, but they will probably be less numerous than the firs. Douglas fir is relatively intolerant to shading, and grand fir is only moderately tolerant. These trees therefore grow well on land that has been cleared or burned over, and they set the stage for the return of the shade-tolerant cedar and hemlock. If a young forest of firs were to remain unmolested, the climax vegetation of cedar and hemlock would undoubtedly return, but only after a long time.

What has just been said does not mean that forests of Douglas fir are a strictly modern phenomenon. Even before the Northwest was settled by white men, there were fires that forced the long process of succession to begin all over again. The Douglas fir is a pioneer that comes back quickly after an area is disturbed. It is also a long-lived tree, so an old second-growth stand may resemble a virgin forest. Besides, there are some areas whose general topography, geological characteristics, or soil are simply unfavorable for a climax growth of cedar or hemlock. Such areas, if they are forested by conifers, are usually characterized by Douglas fir and grand fir.

For a discussion of the common animals and plants of a coniferous forest, a climax growth of hemlock or cedar is not the best place to start. A woods of this type is hard to find, and it is not likely to have a rich variety of shrubs and smaller plants, or even of other trees. A forest dominated by older Douglas fir almost always has a diversified flora that includes most of the trees of the region, except those that can tolerate no shade and that are not normally associated with conifers. The type of forest serving as a framework for this chapter will be found close to, if not actually within, the boundary of every major city west of the Cascades.

Trees

Distinguishing a tree from a shrub generally presents no problems. If the plant has just one main trunk and grows to a height of about 4 or 5 m or more, it can definitely be called a tree. If, on the other hand, it has a number of main stems and is no taller than 3 or 4 m, it should probably be called a shrub. There are some woody plants that may not fit neatly into either category, but they will not really complicate matters.

Trees and shrubs, like all plants, are classified on the basis of characteristics that are thought to show evolutionary relationships. The structure of the flower and fruit, for instance, is more important than whether the leaves have marginal teeth or not. This is not a book about classification of plants, so the simplest possible approach to recognition of the trees and shrubs of our region will be followed. Three main categories will be set up, and the plants that fit into these will then be segregated according to superficial characteristics.

EVERGREEN TREES WITH NEEDLELIKE OR SCALELIKE LEAVES

This category consists of the conifers—the pines, firs, hemlocks, cedars, junipers, and yews. None of them produces flowers. The seeds in most are borne on the surface of woody scales that form cones. In junipers, however, the cones are somewhat berrylike, and in yews the seeds are borne singly in juicy cups. All trees in this category also have small, short-lived cones for the production of pollen.

Throughout our region nearly every coniferous forest, except some in the relatively dry area within the rain shadow of the Olympic Mountains, will have the following conifers:

Douglas fir	Western hemlock
Grand fir	Western red cedar
Pacific yew	

Learn to recognize these right away. You will then find it easy to fit in a few other conifers that contribute to the forests of certain areas. Chief among these are Sitka spruce, white pine, and lodgepole pine (shore pine). Altogether, there are not many conifers to deal with. Most of those not already mentioned have restricted distributions in our region, and one of them—the Rocky Mountain juniper—is not really characteristic of coniferous forests. It will be simplest, however, to consider all of the conifers in this chapter.

Conifers with Needlelike Leaves

Most of the trees in this subdivision produce their seeds in cones and belong to the pine family. The one exception is the Pacific yew, which bears its seed singly in little fleshy cups.

As a rule, the most common conifer is the Douglas fir, *Pseudotsuga menziesii* (pl. 1). This is the principal lumber tree west of the Cascades. In our region, nearly every plank, two-by-four, or piece of shiplap or plywood used in construction comes from the Douglas fir, which cannot be mistaken for any other tree. Its pendent cones, generally about 7 or 8 cm long, are distinctive in having little three-pronged bracts alternating with the larger scales that bear the seeds. The needles, usually about 2 cm long, typically stick out in all directions from the twigs, like bristles on a bottle brush. The profile of an uncrowded tree tends to be like that of a tall triangle, the branches nearest the ground being the longest. The bark of a large Douglas fir is thick and cracked into coarse furrows. The height of giant specimens is about 90 m.

The true firs belong to the genus *Abies,* and there are several species in the Northwest. The only one that is widely distributed in the lowlands is the grand fir, *Abies grandis* (pl. 1). Its needles, mostly 3 to 4 cm long, tend to form two opposing series. They are much broader than those of the Douglas fir and are notched at their tips. The upper surface of the needles is glossy green, and the lower surface has a pair of whitish bands separated by the green midrib. The cones, which grow up to about 10 cm long, are found only on the upper branches, pointing upward. They lack the three-pronged bracts characteristic of Douglas fir cones. Normally the cones of this and other true firs neither survive into the winter nor fall intact: they simply break apart when the seeds are ripe or they are dismembered by birds and rodents. The profile of the grand fir is often, but not always, somewhat cigar-shaped, as the longest branches are nearer the middle of the tree than its base. The bark is typically grayish, and even in larger trees it is not deeply cracked. The maximum height is about 90 m.

The lovely fir, *A. amabilis* (fig. 1), is most likely to be encountered at elevations of approximately 1000 m, but in parts of Vancouver Island, the northern portion of the Puget Trough, and the Olympic Peninsula it is sometimes found close to sea level. Its needles resemble those of the grand fir. They are rarely more than 2.5 cm long, however,

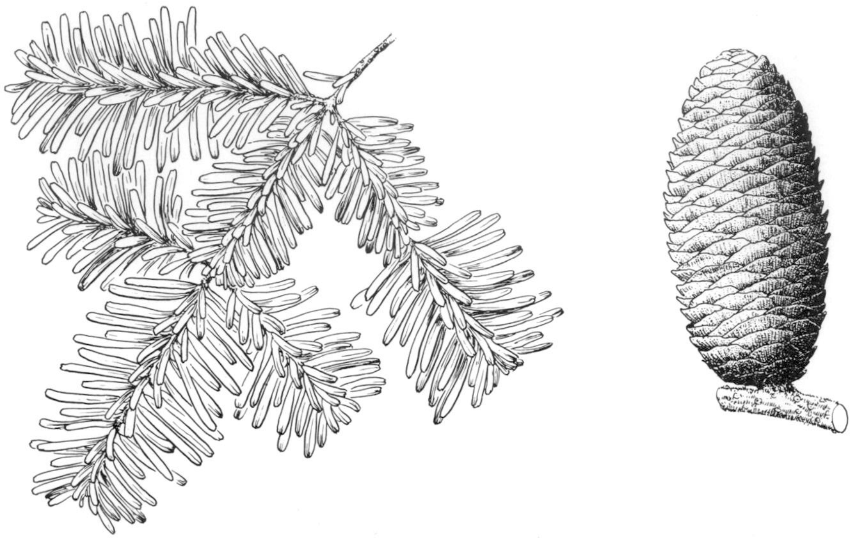

1. Lovely fir, *Abies amabilis*

and the ones that arise from the upper side of a twig tend to be directed toward the tip instead of laterally; the twig is thus nearly hidden. The cones, until they start to dry out, are purplish rather than green.

The noble fir, *A. procera,* and white fir, *A. concolor,* should perhaps also be mentioned here, although the occurrence of either in the lowlands is exceptional. The needles of these trees are not normally notched at the tip. In the noble fir, whose foliage is bluish green (often with a silvery cast), the needles are noticeably thickened along the midline. They are generally less than 3.5 cm long and typically turn upward. The noble fir is found in the Cascades and Coast Ranges of Oregon and Washington. It is most prominent at elevations of about 1200 to 1500 m, but in the Willapa Hills of western Washington there are some specimens at approximately 200 m.

The needles of the white fir are usually bluish green and not appreciably thickened along the midline. They spread outward in much the same way as the needles of the grand fir. Their length is regularly about 4 cm and may slightly exceed 6 cm. This tree occurs at elevations of around 1000 to 1500 m in the Cascades of Oregon; farther east its range extends from parts of Idaho and Wyoming to northern Mexico and California.

The western hemlock, *Tsuga heterophylla* (pl. 1), has a more delicate foliage than any of the several conifers that have just been described. The needles are flat, thin, dull green above and paler below, and nearly rounded at the tip. Typically, there are short needles intermixed with longer ones, which reach about 1.5 cm. (Hence the reason for the specific name, *heterophylla,* which means "varied-leaved.") A distinctive feature of the hemlock is the way the "leader" at the tip of the tree droops. Because of this, a hemlock can be recognized from a considerable distance. The cones are produced over most of the outer branches and hang down like those of the Douglas fir. They are, however, rarely more than 2 cm long, and there are no three-pronged bracts alternating with the seed-bearing scales. The longest branches are usually those nearest the base of the tree, and the bark is relatively smooth. The hemlock does not normally grow in dry situations, so it is excluded from many forests that support good stands of Douglas fir and grand fir.

The Sitka spruce, *Picea sitchensis* (pl. 1), is almost completely restricted to the humid belt close to the open coast. It does penetrate inland for 20 or 30 miles along the Columbia River and for somewhat shorter distances up other river valleys that reach the coast. It is decidedly uncommon in the general region of Puget Sound and the Strait of Georgia, but there are small stands on some of the islands of the San Juan Archipelago and elsewhere. This fine tree requires considerable moisture and does not grow well where the soil is too well drained or where there is insufficient rainfall.

The Sitka spruce may reach a height of 70 m, and where it is happy, it may constitute a large percentage of the trees in the forest. The bark is characteristically cracked into scales rather than furrows. The needles, like those of most spruces, are so stiff and so sharp-tipped that grabbing a twig too vigorously may prove a bit painful. The needles are on distinct little stalks that persist after the needles themselves fall away. This is another feature that helps distinguish spruces from other conifers of our region. The elongated cones reach about 10 cm in length and have almost paper-thin scales. They are still yellow-green even in late summer, but soon after that they turn brown.

Of the several species of pines occurring in the Northwest, only two are likely to be found in the lowlands of our area. These are the lodgepole pine and western white pine. The yellow pine turns up in a few places, though, so it will be mentioned also.

The needles of the lodgepole pine, *Pinus contorta* (pl. 1), are about 5 cm long and borne in pairs. The cones, often slightly lopsided, reach a length of 5 or 6 cm. This species, whose extensive distribution is largely outside our region, varies considerably in habit of growth. The "lodgepole" form, once useful to Indians of the Rocky Mountains for supporting teepees covered with hides of bison, is slender and straight and may reach a height of 35 m. Trees of this type belong to the variety *latifolia* and constitute almost pure stands in the Cascades, especially on the east side of the crest, at elevations of approximately 1200 to 1500 m. They have thin bark, and the needles are typically yellowish green.

Along the coast and in the lowlands of the northern half of the Puget Trough, *P. contorta* is represented by the variety *contorta.* This is usually called the beach pine or shore pine. Its needles are normally dark green, and its bark may be as much as 2 cm thick. At the coast this variety is rather bushy and often distorted by exposure to strong winds. In the area of Puget Sound, the Strait of Georgia, and the San Juan Archipelago it generally grows fairly tall and straight, but is still not quite like the lodgepole pines seen in the mountains.

The western white pine, *Pinus monticola* (pl. 1), is a five-needled species, found primarily on the western slopes of the Cascades, in the Coast Range, and in the Siskiyou Mountains, mostly at elevations of around 1300 m. It is abundant, however, in the lowland areas bordering Puget Sound and is found on Whidbey Island and occasionally elsewhere in this general region. It can be recognized even at a distance because of its relatively long needles (they are about 7 or 8 cm long) and the fact that these are less inclined to be directed upward —or at least toward the tips of the branches—than they are in the lodgepole pine. The cones reach a length of about 15 cm and are relatively slender. The white pine is a substantial tree, sometimes attaining a height of more than 50 m, and generally grows rather straight.

The yellow pine, *Pinus ponderosa* (pl. 1), is an important lumber tree east of the Cascades, where it is found at elevations of approximately 1000 m. It does occur on the western slopes of the Cascades in the southern part of Oregon and also in the Siskiyou Mountains. There are a few small, scattered stands—apparently native trees—in the Willamette Valley and Puget Trough, and there are also some plantations that have the look of being natural. The yellow pine is a large tree, reaching a height of more than 50 m and developing a trunk up to a meter thick. The bark is cracked into irregular plates. The needles—generally about 10 cm long—cannot be mistaken for those of any other pine found in the lowlands, for they are typically in bundles of three. The cones are regularly about 10 cm long and are less elongated than those of the white pine.

Although the Pacific yew, *Taxus brevifolia* (pl. 2), is widespread in our area, it is unobtrusive and often overlooked. It is not an imposing tree, for it tends to grow more like a large bush or a deciduous tree than like most conifers. Its trunk is not often straight, its system of branching is loose, and healthy-looking twigs are often sparse. Even the largest trees, which may exceed a height of 20 m, are usually in the shade of Douglas fir and other conifers.

The needles of the yew are about 2 cm long, flattened, sharp-tipped, green above and yellowish green below. They generally form two ranks pointing away from one another. More distinctive than the needles is the fleshy structure in which each seed is produced. Botanists call this waxy-looking red cup an aril. It is usually just under 1 cm long. The single large seed peeks out of the open end. The arils ripen in late summer and do not last long after birds begin to notice them. Although yews are conifers, in the broad sense of this term, their method of producing seeds is decidedly different from that of cone-bearing trees and they are sequestered in a family of their own.

Conifers with Scalelike Leaves

The trees in this group either have small cones or somewhat fleshy, berrylike counterparts of cones. As small seedlings, they have sharp needles, but this type of foliage normally does not persist; on mature growth the leaves are scalelike. These trees belong to the cypress family, but that does not prevent us from calling some of them cedars, even though the only true cedars—as the deodar cedar and cedar of Lebanon—are limited to the Old World. They have needles and fit into the same general group as pines, spruces, firs, and hemlocks.

The most abundant and widely distributed cypress of our region is the western red cedar, *Thuja plicata* (pl. 2). This is the tree the Indians of the Northwest use for totem poles and dugout canoes. Because its wood is so durable and so nearly straight-grained that it can be split neatly into sheets, it is the source of most of the shingles and shakes used in the United States and Canada.

The western red cedar grows to a height of more than 70 m, and the branches tend to droop. Its general coloration is lighter and somewhat more yellowish than that of firs and hemlocks. In larger specimens, the lower part of the trunk usually has a number of buttresses. The thin, reddish brown bark peels off in strips, which have been useful to Indians for making clothing and other articles. The scalelike leaves are arranged in such a way that they form two sets of alternating pairs. The cones, characterized by only a few scales arranged in a pattern of several opposites, are about 1.5 cm long. At first, while they are still yellowish, they point upward. After the scales separate to liberate the seeds, the empty cones hang downward.

The incense cedar, *Calocedrus decurrens* (pl. 2), is common in the

Cascades of southern Oregon and in the Siskiyou Mountains, but is rarely found in the range covered by this book. Because it is planted in the Willamette Valley and elsewhere, however, it would be helpful to point out how it differs from the western red cedar. First of all, its leaves are much longer than they are wide and the pairs have little tendency to alternate, so that there are four leaves encircling a branchlet at a particular level, and these are succeeded by another set of four. The foliage is usually a darker green than that of the western red cedar, and the flattish sprays are somewhat twisted. The foliage also has a slightly disagreeable, almost fetid odor. The cones are quite unusual in size and appearance. They are generally at least 2 cm long and are made up of six scales, two of which bear the seeds. When these begin to separate, the cones look much like duck bills. This tree grows to a height of about 40 m. Its wood has been much used in the manufacture of pencils.

The Port Orford cedar (or Lawson cypress), *Chamaecyparis lawsoniana* (pl. 2), is a specialty of the southwestern corner of Oregon and the adjacent part of northern California. It is primarily a coastal tree, and the Coos Bay area is at the northern limit of its range. It is widely planted in milder areas of the Northwest, however, both as a decorative tree and to form a windbreak, so it should be easy to locate a tree in order to check out its distinctive characteristics. The branches tend to grow almost directly outward from the trunk and to droop only near their tips. The foliage is often more nearly blue-green than green, and the pairs of leaves alternate as they do in the western red cedar. On the undersides of the branchlets, a white deposit that is concentrated in the valleys between leaves forms a pattern of repeating Xs. The seed-bearing cones are almost globular and have more scales than the cones of the western red cedar and incense cedar. The Port Orford cedar grows to a height of about 50 m. Its wood is fragrant, having an aroma a little like that of lemon rind.

The yellow cedar, *Chamaecyparis nootkatensis* (pl. 2), is rarely found below an altitude of about 1000 m; but on Vancouver Island and the mainland of British Columbia well north of Vancouver, it is sometimes seen below 500 m. This representative of the cypress family is a rather slender tree up to more than 30 m high, with a tip that tends to droop. The bark, like that of red cedar, peels off in strips, but is usually grayish brown externally instead of reddish brown. The branchlets are somewhat prickly because the leaves have sharp tips. When crushed, the foliage gives off a smell that many find disagreeable. The seed-bearing cones, about 1 cm in diameter, are almost round. The common name of this tree refers to the yellow color of its wood.

The junipers may as well be disposed of here, too, although our only species has a very limited distribution and will not normally be part of a forest that is at least moderately dense. The cones of junipers are somewhat fleshy, so they are often called "berries." They are highly resinous and when ripe are usually bluish, with a whitish "bloom." Most large junipers, like cypresses, have scalelike leaves rather than needles. Young seedlings, however, regularly have needles, and occasionally one finds mature specimens with needles on some or all of the branches.

In the Northwest the two species of junipers that form trees typically grow in hilly country east of the Cascades, mostly at elevations of approximately 700 to 900 m. The western juniper, *Juniperus occidentalis,* ranges from Idaho westward to the foothills of the Cascades. It is the one that is abundant near Bend and Ellensburg. A second species, the Rocky Mountain juniper, *J. scopulorum* (pl. 2), is found in the easternmost part of Oregon and a few localities in Washington, but it has a wide range that extends to Nebraska and the Dakotas. The two species are similar, although the Rocky Mountain juniper is the one more likely to have a pointed crown rather than a rounded top, and its twigs are slightly four-sided instead of cylindrical. In both there is a little gland on the exposed surface of most foliage scales, but in the western juniper this usually bears a drop of resin.

From what has just been said about the distribution of the two species in the Northwest, one might assume that if either species were to be found west of the Cascades, it would be the western juniper. The surprising fact is that on Vancouver Island and the islands of the San Juan Archipelago, the Rocky Mountain juniper is locally abundant, although in this area it is not inclined to form pure stands the way it does in the interior. It is usually found in relatively open areas, among a few Douglas firs, madrones, willows, and oaks.

TREES WITH BROAD LEAVES

All the trees in this category have leaves with wide blades. They also have flowers. These may be small and, if they are grouped into catkins, it may not be easy to appreciate that they are indeed flowers. The main requirement for being a flowering plant, put simply, is that the seeds must be formed within structures called pistils. A pistil, and sometimes considerable tissue adjacent to it, develops into a fruit. The seeds are thus completely enclosed until the fruit ripens and either cracks open, decays, or is eaten by some animal. (In the case of some one-seeded, dry fruits, such as those of maples and all representatives of the aster family, the fruit is tightly bound to the seed up to the time of germination.) Compare this situation with that in needle-leaved trees, in which the seeds are borne superficially on scales that form a cone, or borne in a little open cup. The production of pollen in a flowering plant is the responsibility of the anthers; these, together with the stalks that support them, constitute the stamens. The petals and sepals that we associate with most flowers are not directly involved in reproduction; but if they are present, the recognition of a flowering plant is certainly made easier.

In some flowering plants, pollen-producing anthers and one or more pistils are found in the same flower. In others, they are in separate flowers, and perhaps on separate plants.

A few of our broad-leaved trees are evergreen, for they do not drop their leaves all at once in autumn. Most do, however, and these are said to be deciduous. In summer, when all of our trees have their foliage, one may be unable to decide whether a particular species is evergreen or not. For this reason, the species likely to be found in a coniferous forest are here divided into two groups on the basis of their having leaves and branches that are alternate or opposite. Such characteristics can be determined as easily in winter as in summer because the branches are perfectly obvious at any season and leaf scars indicate the position of the leaves. In any case, if the leaves and branches originate in pairs on opposite sides of the stem, or in whorls of more than two, they are opposite. If they come off singly, they are alternate. When there is opposite branching, some buds fail to make the grade; but the pattern for the tree as a whole should be perfectly clear.

The broad-leaved trees likely to be found in almost any more or less typical coniferous forest in a reasonably humid area are:

Big-leaf maple — Pacific dogwood
Vine maple — Red alder
Cascara

These should be learned along with the five conifers that were singled out earlier. Two other broad-leaved trees will also be described here, but a discussion of species that typically dominate other habitats will be deferred until the next chapter.

Broad-leaved Trees with Opposite Leaves and Branches

This category includes three species of maples, with leaves deeply cut into several lobes, and the Pacific dogwood, in which the leaves are not divided. In the dogwood, moreover, the branches are not just opposite, but usually come off in fours.

glas fir, *Pseudotsuga menziesii*

Lodgepole pine, *Pinus contorta*

Western white pine, *Pinus monticola*

Yellow pine, *Pinus ponderosa*

Grand fir, *Abies grandis*

Western hemlock, *Tsuga heterophylla*

Sitka spruce, *Picea sitchensis*

PLATE 1

Pacific yew, *Taxus brevifolia*

Western red cedar, *Thuja plicata*

Port Orford cedar, *Chamaecyparis lawsoniana*

Yellow cedar, *Chamaecyparis no*
tensis (with pollen-producing co

Incense cedar, *Calocedrus decurrens*

Rocky Mountain juniper, *Juniperus scopulorur*

PLATE 2

Big-leaf maple, *Acer macrophyllum*

Vine maple, *Acer circinatum*

Dwarf maple, *Acer glabrum* variety *douglasii*

Red alder, *Alnus rubra*

Cascara, *Rhamnus purshiana*

Chokecherry, *Prunus emarginata*

Western crabapple, *Pyrus fusca*

Black hawthorn, *Crataegus douglasii* variety *douglasii*

Crataegus monogyna

PLATE 4

Garry oak, *Quercus garryana*

Galls on Garry oak induced by a wasp, *Cynips maculipennis*

Pacific dogwood, *Cornus nuttallii*

Black cottonwood, *Populus trichocarpa*

Quaking aspen, *Populus tremuloides*

Paper birch, *Betula papyrifera*

Madrone, *Arbutus menziesii*

Salal, *Gaultheria shallon*

Rhododendron, *Rhododendron macrophyllum*

Oregon myrtle (California laurel), *Umbellularia californica*

PLATE 6

Oregon grape, *Berberis aquifolium*

Long-leaved Oregon grape,
Berberis nervosa

Red huckleberry, *Vaccinium parvifolium*

Evergreen huckleberry, *Vaccinium ovatum*

Kinnikinnick, *Arctostaphylos uva-ursi*

PLATE 7

Western azalea, *Rhododendron occidentale*

False boxwood, *Pachistima myrsinites*

Devil's club, *Oplopanax horridum*

Mock-orange, *Philadelphus lewisii*

Creek dogwood, *Cornus stolonifera*

Red currant, *Ribes sanguineum*

PLATE 8

Osoberry, *Oemleria cerasiformis*

Hardhack, *Spiraea douglasii*

Nootka rose, *Rosa nutkana*

Baldhip rose, *Rosa gymnocarpa*

Ocean spray, *Holodiscus discolor*

Ninebark, *Physocarpus capitatus*

PLATE 9

Thimbleberry, *Rubus parviflorus*

Salmonberry, *Rubus spectabilis*

Blackcap, *Rubus leucodermis*

Serviceberry, *Amelanchier alnifolia*

Dewberry, *Rubus ursinus*

PLATE 10

Snowberry, *Symphoricarpos albus*

Pink honeysuckle, *Lonicera hispidula*

Orange honeysuckle, *Lonicera ciliosa*

Bush honeysuckle, *Lonicera involucrata*

PLATE 11

Red elderberry, *Sambucus racemosa* variety *arborescens*

Blue elderberry, *Sambucus cerulea*

Oval-leaved viburnum, *Viburnum ellipticum*

Redstem ceanothus, *Ceanoth sanguineus*

Soapberry (buffalo-berry), *Shepherdia canadensis*

Poison oak, *Toxicodendron diversiloba*

PLATE 12

Trillium ovatum

Sessile trillium, *Trillium sessile*

Fairy lanterns, *Disporum hookeri*

Wild lily-of-the-valley, *Maianthemum dilatatum*

Large smilacina, *Smilacina racemosa*

Small smilacina, *Smilacina stellata*

Beadlily, *Clintonia uniflora*

PLATE 13

Pink fawn-lily, *Erythronium revolutum*

White fawn-lily, *Erythronium oregonum*

Camas, *Camassia quamash*

Death camas, *Zigadenus venenosus*

Rice-root lily, *Fritillaria lanceo*

Columbia lily, *Lilium columbianum*

Hooker's onion, *Allium acuminatum*

PLATE 14

Harvest lily, *Brodiaea coronaria*

Brodiaea hyacinthina

Brodiaea congesta

Grass-widows, *Sisyrinchium douglasii*

Oregon iris, *Iris tenax*

Blue-eyed grass, *Sisyrinchium angustifolium*

PLATE 15

Rattlesnake plantain, *Goodyera oblongifolia*

Fairy-slipper, *Calypso bulbosa*

Striped coral-root,
Corallorhiza striata

Spotted coral-root, *Corallorhiza maculata*

Phantom orchid,
Eburophyton austiniae

Elegant rein-orchid, *Habenaria elegans*

Ladies-tresses, *Spiranthes romanzoffiana*

PLATE 16

Of the maples of our area, two kinds are so widespread that they can probably be learned on the very first trip into the woods. The big-leaf maple (or broad-leaf maple), *Acer macrophyllum* (pl. 3), forms a large tree whose height may exceed 25 m and whose trunk may be thicker than 1 m. In the autumn, most of the yellow foliage that one sees when looking at a coniferous forest from a distance belongs to this tree. The branches are opposite and the internodes between branches are long, especially in younger trees, because the annual growth in spring is so rapid. The blades of the leaves are regularly more than 20 cm across—sometimes more than 25 cm—and normally divided into five primary lobes. The upper surface of mature leaves is deep green, the under surface is paler. The greenish yellow flowers, in drooping clusters, generally appear as the tree is leafing out.

The one-seeded fruits, called samaras, are borne in pairs. They are full size (about 3 or 4 cm long) by midsummer. At first they are light green, but they turn brown as they dry and get ready to drop. They twist like propellers as they are carried by the winds of autumn. In spring, the two-leaved seedlings come up almost everywhere in the woods, but relatively few of them manage to survive. A certain percentage of the seedlings produced by some trees are albinos, unable to manufacture chlorophyll. The recessive gene for albinism, when not overshadowed by a normal gene favoring production of chlorophyll, is lethal; as soon as the little plants have used up the food that was stored in the seeds from which they sprouted, they must die.

The vine maple, *Acer circinatum* (pl. 3), does not grow into a large tree—it rarely exceeds a height of 6 or 7 m—but it has the distinction of providing most of the bright splashes of orange and red that characterize our forests in the autumn. Its bright green leaves are up to about 10 cm across and generally have seven or nine clear-cut lobes. These lobes are toothed along their margins, but are not deeply divided. The vine maple may have several principal trunks, and trees growing in very shady places often let their lower branches creep along the ground for some distance before they reach more light and turn upward. The trunks are rarely thicker than 15 cm, and even the larger of them remain green. The flowers are small and borne in clusters of only a few. The fruits, about 3 cm long, are paired, as in the big-leaf maple. Instead of forming a V-shaped configuration, however, they point away from one another. The vine maple is found mixed with conifers almost throughout our range but is rare in the San Juan Archipelago and some other areas where the woods tend to be dry and rocky.

The dwarf maple (or Douglas maple), *Acer glabrum* variety *douglasii* (pl. 3), is not widely distributed in our region, though its range east of the Cascades is extensive. In the San Juan Archipelago, it more or less takes the place of the vine maple. Elsewhere, however, it is rare or absent. Its leaves resemble those of the vine maple, but have only three or five main lobes. The two fruits in each pair form a V. In addition, the dwarf maple tends to produce a single main trunk and not to sprawl the way many vine maples do. In some areas the dwarf maple is really dwarf; but when it is found west of the Cascades, it may be a tree 10 m in height. In the autumn its foliage merely turns pale yellow, instead of orange and red.

The Pacific dogwood, *Cornus nuttallii* (pl. 5), is found almost throughout our range. It is especially abundant in coniferous forests that have a good mix of deciduous trees, such as big-leaf maple and vine maple. Its virtual absence from the islands of the San Juan Archipelago must be lamented. When in blossom, this is certainly our most distinguished tree, and those who chose it for the provincial flower of British Columbia knew what they were doing. But a little explanation of its "flowers" is in order. The four or six conspicuous white "petals" are not petals, and properly are not even part of the flower; rather, they are leaves that arise at the base of a buttonlike cluster of small flowers. Thus, they are fully comparable to the bright red leaves beneath the true flowers of a Christmas poinsettia.

The Pacific dogwood regularly blooms in April and May in the lowlands, and then in September at least a few trees flower again. The leaves turn pinkish red in the fall. The dogwood is second only to the vine maple in contributing reddish tones to the autumn scene. It would seem enough that it produces such beautiful "flowers" and leaves; but the dogwood's bright orange-red fruits, most conspicuous in August and September, are also attractive and sought out by some birds.

The Pacific dogwood regularly grows to a height of 10 m, but may be considerably larger. It ordinarily has a single trunk, unless the tree has been cut back at some time. Side branches generally originate in fours, but there is some variation on this point, partly because not all of the prospective branches materialize. In any case, this dogwood is easily distinguished from maples in which the branches normally arise in pairs. In addition, as dogwood branches grow outward, they also curve upward so that each successive year's growth on a branch viewed from the side will have an appreciable curvature. This feature, along with the fact that the branches generally arise in whorls of four, enable one to recognize the dogwood in winter. The leaves are mostly about 8 or 10 cm long and bright green on the top surface. The margin is not toothed, but it is usually wavy.

Broad-leaved Trees with Alternate Leaves and Branches

In almost any portion of our range, the red alder, *Alnus rubra* (pl. 3), is the most abundant deciduous tree. It forms dense stands, especially where there is plenty of moisture either in the form of fog and rain or of ground water. After a coniferous forest is cut down, it is the alder that soon takes over the land. The red alder regularly grows to a height of 20 m, and may be even taller. Its crown may be rounded and bushy or it may be slender, depending on the extent to which the tree is crowded. The bark is silvery brown; but if it has been heavily colonized by certain species of lichens, it may seem to be almost as white as that of a birch. The dark green leaves are generally about 6 to 12 cm long, with coarse teeth that are subdivided by smaller teeth. One odd feature of the alder is that it generally drops at least a few of its leaves in late summer, even before they have begun to turn brown. In late winter, when the catkins composed of pollen-bearing flowers are about 4 or 5 cm long, they almost suddenly stretch to a length of about 10 cm and liberate their bright yellow pollen. The seed-bearing catkins start out in little clusters that look like tiny pine cones and then grow to a length of about 1.5 cm. By autumn they have turned dark brown, but many of them remain on the trees throughout the winter. Alder is a prodigious seeder, and the seedlings grow so fast that a temporary road in the woods may almost disappear in a couple of seasons.

The success of alder in colonizing land that has been cleared or burned over may be due at least in part to the nitrogen-fixing bacteria on its roots. Nitrogen is an essential ingredient of all proteins, and most green plants get their supply of nitrogen in the form of nitrates or ammonia. Among the relatively few organisms capable of exploiting the nitrogen gas that makes up about four-fifths of the atmosphere are bacteria concentrated in nodules of root tissue of alder, members of the pea family, and certain other flowering plants. These bacteria incorporate nitrogen into compounds synthesized by their host plants and thus manufacture the building-blocks of proteins. Plants that are involved in symbiotic associations with nitrogen-fixing bacteria are less dependent on the availability, in the soil, of nitrates and ammonia.

Cascara, *Rhamnus purshiana* (pl. 4), is most commonly found in woods in which other deciduous trees, such as alder and maple, are mixed with conifers. Its height may reach 15 or 20 m, but trees taller than 10 m are not abundant. The harvesting of cascara bark, which contains a potent laxative used in compounding proprietary remedies, has contributed to the demise of large and medium-sized trees. The dark green leaves of cascara are usually about 6 to 10 cm long and have an almost elliptical outline. They are distinctive because the main veins on each side of the midrib are nearly straight and practically parallel to one another. The surface is almost like that of a washboard, because the veins are set in furrows. The margins are finely and evenly toothed. Although cascara is a deciduous tree, young saplings often retain their leaves through the winter. The flowers are small, greenish, and decidedly unspectacular. The black berries, however, which grow to about 6 mm in diameter, and ripen in late summer, are attractive. Birds help disseminate this tree because its seeds are tough enough to pass through the digestive tract unharmed.

The genus *Prunus* includes plums, cherries, and a good many other trees or shrubs cultivated for their fruits or flowers. We have two native species in our area, but only one, the chokecherry, is widespread. *Prunus emarginata* (pl. 4) is a tree up to about 10 m high. The oblong, blunt leaves are about 5 or 6 cm long and are finely toothed along the margins. In April the white flowers are borne in little side clusters, on twigs that have just leafed out. They are about 1 cm across and similar to those of plums. The bright red fruits ripen in late July and August and resemble miniature cherries. Unfortunately, what they look like and what they taste like are almost unbelievably different.

Shrubs and Vines

Shrubs and vines found in the lowlands of our region are broad-leaved flowering plants. Some are evergreen, others deciduous. As in the case of the trees, they will be sorted out into two groups: those with opposite leaves and those with alternate leaves. The following will almost routinely be found in coniferous woods, and a beginner will probably want to learn them first:

Snowberry	Red huckleberry
Hazelnut	Salmonberry
Red currant	Thimbleberry
Long-leaved Oregon grape	Dewberry
Salal	Osoberry

A few of the shrubs dealt with in this chapter are not truly typical of an evergreen forest. They are closely related, however, to some that are regularly found in this kind of situation, and they are very likely to be growing at the brushy edge of a forest. It seems best to include them for purposes of making comparisons. Similarly, the chapter that covers deciduous woods and brushy areas will deal with some shrubs and vines that may be seen in some coniferous woods.

SHRUBS WITH OPPOSITE LEAVES AND BRANCHES

The snowberry, *Symphoricarpos albus* (pl. 11), is a deciduous shrub that is common almost everywhere. It grows in rather dense woods as well as in brushy areas and along roadsides. It is absolutely unmistakable when carrying its white fruits, mostly about 1 cm in diameter, from late summer to the following spring. Snowberry grows to a height of about 2 m, and the stems of relatively recent growth are very slender. The leaves, borne in pairs, typically have more or less oval blades about 2 cm long. On young plants, and occasionally on mature plants, some of the blades will be larger and deeply lobed. The flowers are less than 1 cm across, and the five pink petals are united for much of their length to form a distinct tube, as in honeysuckles, which belong to the same family. The blooming season is long, extending from spring to late summer.

A relatively rare deciduous shrub—and something of a curiosity—is western wahoo, *Euonymus occidentalis* (fig. 2). It is generally 2 or 3 m tall and branches rather loosely. The bark of even the larger stems is smooth. The leaves, on short petioles, have thin blades about 5 to 7 cm long. These are usually drawn out to a point at the tip and are finely

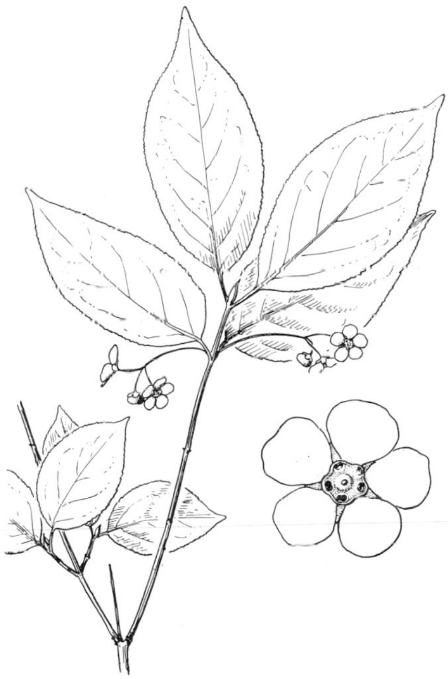

2. Western wahoo, *Euonymus occidentalis*

toothed all around the margin. The flowers, borne in little clusters of two or three, measure about 1 cm across. The petals are almost circular in outline and usually maroon, or sometimes a mixture of maroon and green. The ovoid fruit, approximately 1 cm in diameter, is three-lobed, and when it cracks open in late summer it reveals what is probably the most attractive feature of the plant: the seeds. There are one or two in each lobe, enclosed by bright orange-red husks. The northward distribution of this plant stops in southern Washington.

Pachistima myrsinites, the false boxwood (pl. 8), is an unobtrusive evergreen shrub, generally under 60 cm high, with opposite leaves that slightly resemble those of the cultivated boxwood. The leaves are somewhat leathery, weakly scalloped along the margins and up to about 2 cm long. The inconspicuous, greenish flowers are borne in small clusters. This plant is abundant in the mountains at elevations of around 1000 to 1300 m, but its distribution in the lowlands is spotty. It occurs here and there in the region of Puget Sound and on some of the islands of the San Juan Archipelago, as well as along the Strait of Georgia.

SHRUBS WITH ALTERNATE LEAVES AND BRANCHES

The hazelnut, *Corylus cornuta* (fig. 3), is one of our larger deciduous shrubs, regularly reaching a height of 3 or 4 m. Typically, it has a number of main stems and is very bushy. By late winter the yellowish

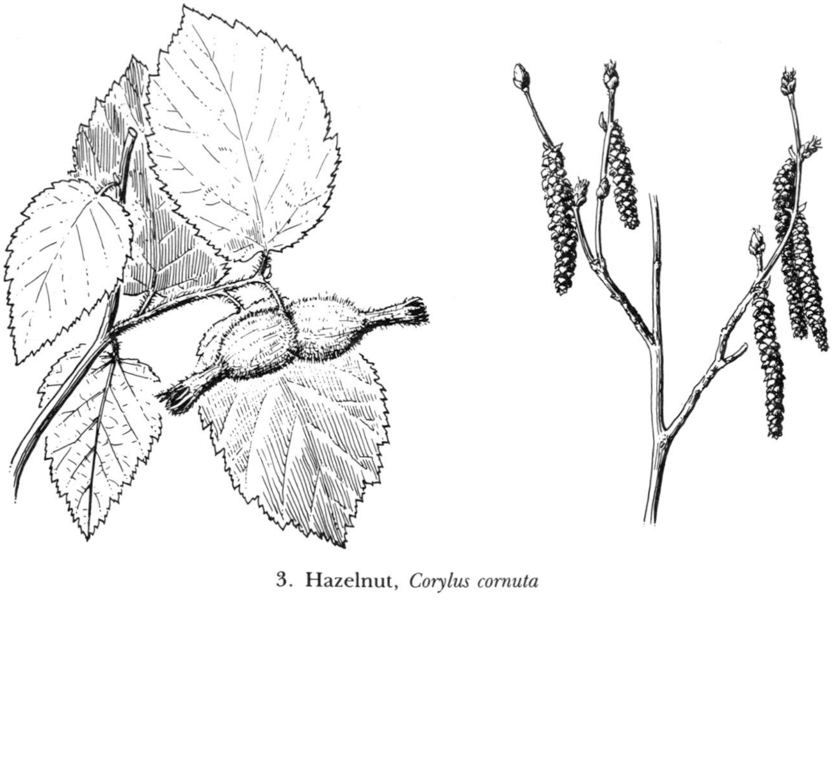

3. Hazelnut, *Corylus cornuta*

green, pollen-producing catkins, about 5 cm long, have reached the peak of their development. The small pistillate flowers that eventually produce the nuts are usually borne in pairs; they have neither petals nor sepals, but the tips of the pistils are bright red. Of the several pistils in each flower, only one develops into a nut. The leaves appear in spring and are rather strongly corrugated. They are more or less oval, about 5 or 6 cm long, and slightly asymmetrical at the base. Each nut is enclosed by two leaves that form a vaselike husk. The hazelnut is a wild relative of the garden filberts, many strains of which have been developed from a European species. The hard-shelled nuts of our wild species are about 1.5 cm across and are perfectly edible, but the meats are so small that they are not likely to become popular with the masses. Squirrels, mice, and some birds make good use of them.

The genus *Ribes,* which includes all shrubs called currants and gooseberries, has a large representation in the Northwest. Only three species, however, are common in lowland areas west of the Cascades. All of these are deciduous. The most distinguished is the red currant, *Ribes sanguineum* (pl. 8). It is found in brushy areas as well as in woods. When it flowers, in late March and April, its only rival is Oregon grape. Its value as an ornamental plant is recognized far beyond the region where it grows wild, and its beauty is matched by the ease with which it can be propagated from seeds and cuttings. To show its appreciation, it flowers with abandon in the greenest parks of London and in the Jardin des Tuileries in Paris.

Large currant bushes may be 3 m high and are usually thickly branched. The flowers range from very pale pink to deep rose pink. They are about 1 cm across and borne in rather dense, drooping clusters. The flowers are longer than wide, and the five sepals are united into a tube for much of their length. The leaves, which may appear with the flowers or a little later, are light to dark green, generally rough in texture, and shallowly divided into three or five lobes. The nearly spherical berries are less than 1 cm across and basically purplish black, but they have a whitish bloom that makes them appear much lighter. They are rather dry and taste a little too much of pine resin to be enjoyable.

The other common species of *Ribes* are gooseberries, characterized by spiny stems. In the straggly gooseberry, *R. divaricatum* (fig. 4), the twigs have scattered, stout spines; in the swamp gooseberry, *R. lacustre* (fig. 5), they are almost completely covered by a mixture of small and large spines. *Ribes divaricatum* tends to form tall bushes, sometimes more than 2 m high, in which the stems are arched. *Ribes lacustre* rarely reaches 2 m, and its stems are usually nearly straight. The leaves of

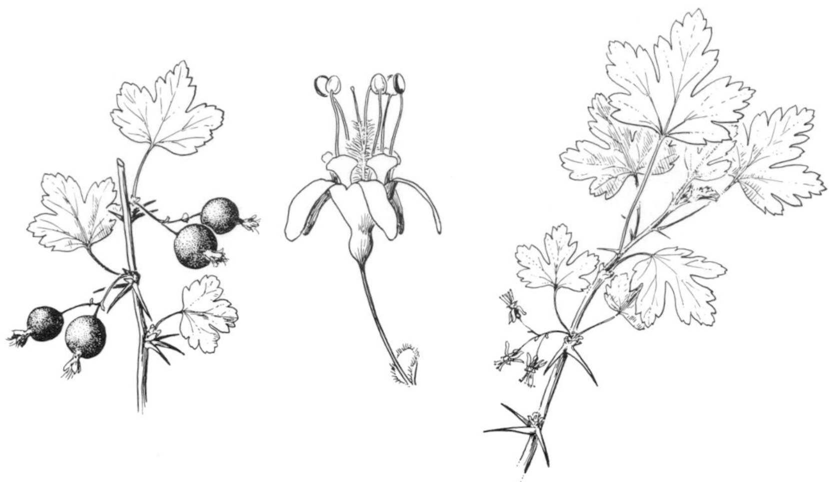

4. Straggly gooseberry, *Ribes divaricatum*

the two species are similar, being mostly about 4 or 5 cm across and cut deeply into lobes; there are generally three distinct lobes in *R. divaricatum,* five in *R. lacustre.* The flowers of the two species are very different. Those of *R. divaricatum* appear much longer than broad because the stamens stick out; the color of the petals ranges from nearly white to pale brown or reddish brown. In *R. lacustre* the flowers

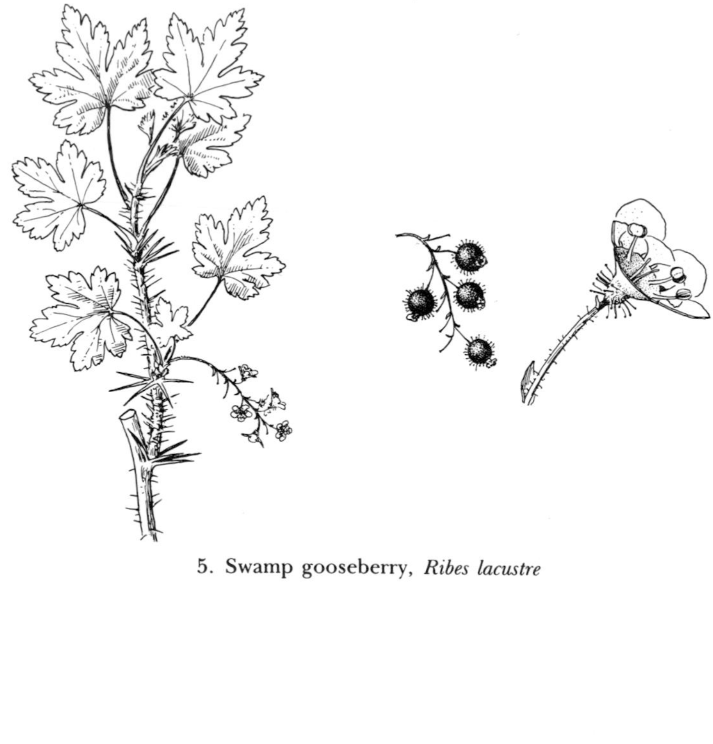

5. Swamp gooseberry, *Ribes lacustre*

appear broader than long, as the stamens are short; the petals are a muddy pink. *Ribes divaricatum* has smooth, purplish black berries about 1 cm in diameter; *R. lacustre* has slightly smaller berries in which the dark purple color is partly hidden by gland-tipped hairs. The berries of both are edible, but those of the former are the better.

Ribes divaricatum generally grows in rather open woods and brushy areas, and it is unusual to find it in really deep woods. *Ribes lacustre* also likes open woods and brushy situations, but prefers places where there is considerable moisture. The two species are often found together, however.

Devil's club, *Oplopanax horridum* (pl. 8), is a markedly distinctive deciduous shrub. It prefers moist woods, and where it is abundant, as on the Olympic Peninsula, in the Coast Ranges, and on the western slopes of the Cascades, it can be seen growing in profusion along roadsides. The common name is thoroughly appropriate for this terribly spiny shrub. The stiff, sharp spines are not limited to the stems, but are on the leaf petioles and even the leaf blades. Devil's club grows to a height of about 3 m. The leaves are large, usually about 20 or 25 cm across, and divided into several lobes with shallow marginal teeth. The greenish flowers are small, only about 5 mm across, and crowded into tight buttons capping short stalks that arise from the sides of the main stem of the inflorescence. The shiny, slightly flattened berries, up to about 8 mm long, are brilliant red.

The barberry family is represented in our region by four common plants, two of which are evergreen shrubs. *Berberis aquifolium* (pl. 7) is the state flower of Oregon and is regularly called the Oregon grape. *Berberis nervosa* (pl. 7) is usually called the long-leaved Oregon grape, or mountain Oregon grape. *Berberis aquifolium* is generally restricted to open places, whereas *B. nervosa* likes shady woods. The two species mix to some extent, however, and they may as well be compared right away.

Berberis aquifolium may grow to a height of 2 m, but plants growing in situations exposed to full sun are generally less than 1 m high. The leaflets on each compound leaf usually number five or seven. They are shiny, and the few marginal serrations, resembling those of English holly leaves, are tipped with needlelike points. In the late summer or fall some of the leaves or individual leaflets may turn red. In spring the bright yellow flowers, produced in tight clusters, are a characteristic feature of roadsides, brushy areas, and open woods. When the berries are ripe, in late summer, they are of a tempting purplish blue color, but their sourness is so intense that few animals feel the urge to make a meal of them.

The leaves of *Berberis nervosa* have many more leaflets than those of *B. aquifolium*—usually there are fifteen to nineteen. The leaflets are dull instead of shiny, and the serrations lack prickly points. Older plants, which are generally about 80 cm tall, grow something like palm trees, with the leaves of the last few seasons being concentrated in the upper portion and the rest of the stem being bare. The flowers, arising within the crown of leaves, are typically produced in several elongated spikes. They are greenish yellow and less attractive than those of Oregon grape. The berries of the two species are similar.

In most woods the salal, *Gaultheria shallon* (pl. 6), covers more ground than any other shrub. It normally forms a rather dense cover less than 1 m high, but in some places, especially near the coast, it forms thickets more than 2 m in height. The evergreen leaves, up to about 8 cm long, are oval, usually with a rather sharp apex, and have a stiff, leathery texture; the margins are finely serrated. The twigs and leaf stalks are often reddish. Where the climate is mild, the blossoms may appear at almost any time of the year; but the normal flowering season is late spring. The flowers are similar to those of some other members of the heath family, being shaped something like lanterns, with the open end a little smaller than the greatest diameter. The corolla is pale pink or white, and the calyx is both hairy and sticky, as is each peduncle on which a flower is borne. The fruits, up to about 1 cm in diameter, are blackish purple, with a little whitish bloom on them. They resemble huckleberries, but are less juicy and taste something like huckleberries marinated in a dilute extract of fir needles. They are perfectly edible, however, and are certainly important to some of our birds and mammals. It is perhaps wise not to eat too many salal berries at a time, for they seem to have a laxative effect.

"Salal" comes from an Indian word for the shrub. Indians made much use of its fruits; and when David Douglas arrived in Oregon in 1825, he was so impressed by salal that he later tried to promote cultivating it in England and Europe as a berry plant. But salal did not catch on, though it has become a useful foliage plant for gardens.

A number of species of huckleberries are native to the Northwest. A few of them are limited to moderate or higher elevations in the mountains, and it is the delicious berries of certain of these that attract berry pickers in late summer. The huckleberries in the lowlands produce fruits whose sweetness and flavor ranges from passable to pleasant or even good. Some of them are not likely to be encountered, and it will be best to concentrate on two species that have extensive ranges.

The red huckleberry, *Vaccinium parvifolium* (pl. 7), is an oddity because its berries are red instead of dark blue or black. This deciduous shrub grows about 1 or 2 m tall, sometimes larger. It is distinctive even when it has no leaves, flowers, or berries, for its stems are green and strongly angled. The leaves, mostly 1 to 2 cm long, are thin, oval, and bright green. (On young seedlings the leaves frequently persist through the winter and are smaller and more leathery in texture than those on larger plants.) The pendent, vase-shaped flowers are only about 6 mm long and are usually greenish, tinged with pink. The berries are about 8 mm in diameter. They have a nice flavor, but are too sour to become popular. The red huckleberry is almost routinely found in moist coniferous woods, where it often grows out of old stumps and rotting logs. It is scarce or absent in dry woods.

The evergreen huckleberry, *Vaccinium ovatum* (pl. 7), generally grows 1 or 2 m high and has crowded, rather thick leaves. Because of the durability of its evergreen foliage, it has been widely used in the florist trade for "greens." The flowers are pale pinkish bells about 8 mm long. The berries are produced generously and ripen in very late summer or early autumn. They are shiny black, small (only about 7 mm across), and a little sour, but are pleasant to eat.

Fool's huckleberry, *Menziesia ferruginea* (fig. 6), is aptly named. When it is in leaf and in flower, it looks so much like a huckleberry of some

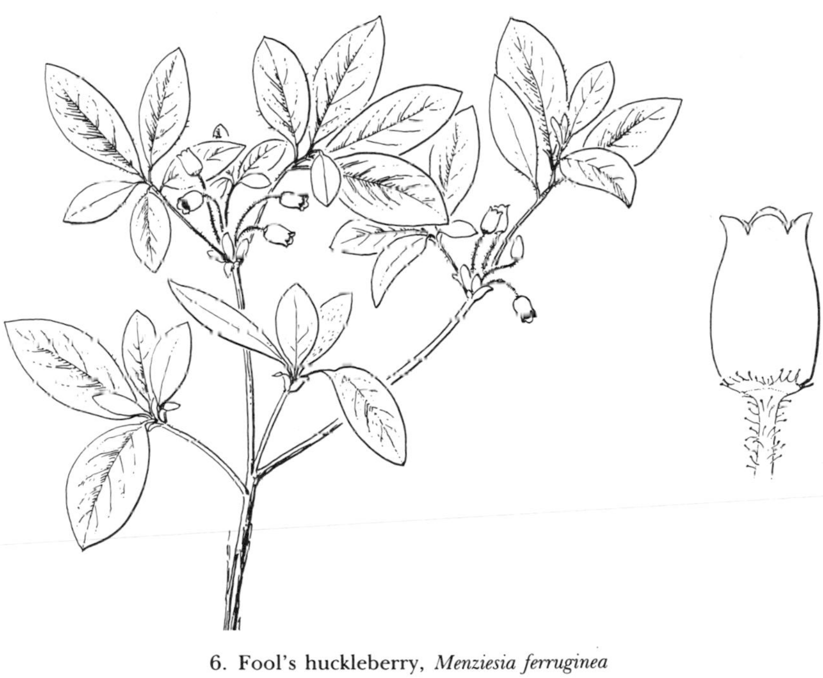

6. Fool's huckleberry, *Menziesia ferruginea*

sort that one is inclined to make a mental note to return in late summer with a big bucket. Unfortunately, the fruits of this shrub ripen into dry capsules. *Menziesia* grows to a height of 1 m or more and has thin, bright green leaves, usually with small brownish hairs on the upper surface (hence the name *ferruginea*—"rusty"). The petals form a little urn that is yellow or reddish and about 6 or 7 mm long. This shrub is common in coniferous woods at moderate elevations in the Cascades, in the Coast Ranges and Olympic Mountains, and right at the coast. It is missing from most lowland areas of our region.

The rhododendron, *Rhododendron macrophyllum* (pl. 6), is the state flower of Washington. Its range, however, extends from northern California to British Columbia. The distribution of the rhododendron in our region is not general. It may be expected on the western slopes of the Cascades at elevations of 1000 to 1500 m (about 3300 to 5000 feet), and it turns up again along the coast of Oregon and Washington. It is rare on Vancouver Island; most British Columbia populations of this shrub are found in the mountains. It is common on Whidbey Island and in a number of areas around Puget Sound and Hood Canal.

The rhododendron is evergreen and regularly grows up to 4 m high, although some plants do get larger. There are often a number of main stems growing up from the base, and the lower portions of these may be almost bare. The leaves range from light to dark green, depending on conditions, and are up to 20 cm long. Through much of the year the rhododendron is nothing special to look at, but when it flowers—from May to July—it puts on a spectacular show. The blossoms, 3 or 4 cm across, are pale to deep pink, usually with some reddish brown spots. The fruits are woody capsules and contribute to the half-dead look of many rhododendrons when they are neither flowering nor making new growth.

The Northwest is blessed with a generous variety of shrubs and vines classified as raspberries and blackberries. They are all members of one genus, *Rubus:* any whose ripe fruits come clean of the core when picked are raspberries; those whose fruits do not separate from the core are blackberries. It should be mentioned that in these plants the so-called berries are really tight clusters of individual fruits.

There are three common raspberries in our region: the thimbleberry, salmonberry, and blackcap. Then there is a native blackberry—the dewberry—and two common introduced species, the Himalayan blackberry and evergreen blackberry. The last two will be dealt with in chapter 3, because they are usually found in open places.

The thimbleberry, *Rubus parviflorus* (pl. 10), is a thornless shrub up to more than 2 m high. It often grows in nearly pure stands, especially at the edges of woods, where it gets ample sunlight. The leaves, up to 15 cm across, are very light green and shaped something like those of maples, but they are covered with a felt of short hairs. The five-petaled flowers are almost pure white and about 2.5 cm across. (The species name, meaning "small-flowered," is not very apt.) The hemispherical berries turn bright red, and they are still tart even after they have passed their prime. (For some people, thimbleberries seem not to have a prime: they are either underripe or overripe.)

The salmonberry, *R. spectabilis* (pl. 10), forms a high shrub, sometimes up to 3 m tall. The lower stems may be somewhat prickly, but new growth is not. The leaves are completely divided into three dark green leaflets. The attractive flowers are unusual for a raspberry in being light purple or magenta. They are about 2 cm across. The berries are longer than wide and, when ripe, are commonly yellow-orange, though the color varies from pale yellow to nearly red. The fruits are juicy and have a nice consistency, but they are not very sweet. The salmonberry is partial to damp situations, and its occurrence in coniferous forests is generally limited to stream banks, ravines, and other wet places. It also grows happily in exposed areas, if it gets plenty of moisture, as at the border of a marsh or lake.

The blackcap, *R. leucodermis* (pl. 10), resembles certain cultivated raspberries. The stems are prickly and have a whitish purple "bloom." Some of them fall down and sprawl like vines, so the shrub is often poorly defined. The flowers are inconspicuous and often overlooked, for the white petals are small and widely spaced. The berries are neat domes about 1 cm across. They turn blackish purple as they ripen and are delicious, even if rather seedy. Blackcap grows in sun or shade, but seems to be most common in open woods and brushy areas.

Our only native blackberry in the lowlands is *R. ursinus,* the dewberry (pl. 10). Although its fruit is small, only about 1 cm in diameter, this plant has figured in the parentage of some important varieties, including the loganberry and boysenberry. It creeps over the ground, in shade or sun, but is generally most abundant in drier situations dominated by shrubs and small trees. The thin but tough stems are armed with small prickles that break off easily and bring misery to gardeners in suburban and rural areas where the dewberry behaves as a weed. The flowers that produce only pollen and those that produce fruits are on separate plants; the pollen-bearing flowers have appreciably longer petals, up to about 1.5 cm long. The berries change from red to black as they ripen.

The osoberry, *Oemleria cerasiformis (Osmaronia cerasiformis)* (pl. 9), begins to flower in February and early March, before spring officially opens. As a rule, the first blossoms are ahead of the leaves. The bushes grow to a height of about 4 m and almost qualify as small trees, but the form is more nearly shrublike in the sense that there are a number of more or less equal main trunks. The flowers, borne in elongated clusters, are about 1 cm across and have greenish white petals. Those destined to produce fruits have slightly larger petals than those which produce pollen; the two types of flowers are on separate plants. The leaves of the oso berry are of a beautiful pale green color. They are fairly narrow, up to about 10 cm long, and have smooth margins. The attractive bright orange fruits ripen between June and August. These are about 1 cm long and have a large pit. The bushes are so generous with their fruits that it is a pity these have to be so bitter. Osoberry is common almost throughout our area, growing in thickets as well as in coniferous forests. It does seem to require a fair amount of light, so it is excluded from very deep woods. It also needs more moisture than some of our shrubs, and in relatively dry areas it will probably be found only in ravines or at the edges of wet places.

Most of us have no trouble thinking of plums, apples, raspberries, blackberries, and some other cultivated or wild plants as belonging to the rose family. But this group is highly diversified and includes many species with small flowers, dry fruits, and some other characteristics we may not readily associate with what we know to be "roses." A good example is ocean spray, *Holodiscus discolor* (pl. 9), a common shrub in our region. It usually grows about 2 or 3 m high and has at least several main trunks. The leaves are generally 3 or 4 cm long, oval (but widest slightly below the middle), dull green, and coarsely toothed. In winter, when the plants are leafless, they are so uninteresting that one can scarcely believe how beautiful they become in June or early July. The individual flowers, cream-white in color, are only about 5 mm in diameter, but they are produced in dense, branching clusters. After the petals fall off, the plants lose most of the appeal they had for a few weeks; however the reddish tints that appear in the leaves in the fall are attractive. Ocean spray is abundant in almost any coniferous woods that is not especially dense or dark; it is a particularly conspicuous element of the vegetation in open woods and in brushy situations.

Wildflowers

In a book such as this, only a few of the hundreds of herbaceous flowering plants that occur in our region can be discussed in satisfying detail. The species included in this and subsequent chapters are those that are almost universally present in the habitats under which they are listed. No pretense will be made at classifying them according to details of flower structure. It will be both useful and convenient, however, to group the wildflowers according to the families to which they belong.

LILY FAMILY

In plants of the lily family, the flowers almost always have three equal petals and three equal sepals, but usually all six look like petals. There are six stamens, and the tip of the pistil, where pollen sticks, is divided into three lobes. All of our species are perennials that come up each spring from a bulb or underground rhizome.

The trillium, *Trillium ovatum* (pl. 13), is perhaps our best-known wildflower. It is found in coniferous woods almost throughout the region, although it does not occur on most of the islands of the San Juan Archipelago and some other places. It comes up every spring from a perennial underground rhizome. The stem is usually about 40 cm high and has a whorl of three broad leaves beneath the single flower. As previously mentioned, the petals and sepals are alike in many members of the lily family; but in the trillium the three petals are unwilling to share their whiteness. Occasionally, however, plants showing deviations from the typical number of petals are found. The flowers last a long time and as they age, the petals turn pink, then a dirty rose color. By late summer the fat fruits, with winglike ridges, crack open and expose their seeds, glued together in a sticky mass that usually falls to the ground. The seeds of trilliums have a little appendage that is rich in oil and attractive to ants. Most ants that carry away the seeds consume only the oily material, so the seed proper is spared and may germinate far from the plant that produced it. This is an effective mechanism for dispersal.

A question that is regularly asked of a naturalist who is supposed to know about such things is: "If I pick a trillium, will it really take it seven years to bloom again?" Well, if you break off the stem, the plant can no longer make food for itself and has nothing to store up in its rhizome for the succeeding year. It will probably survive, however, and send up a puny shoot the next spring. If left alone, the plant will, over a period of several years (not necessarily seven), regain enough strength to bloom again. If only the flower is picked off above the leaves, the plant itself will not suffer; only its seed-producing capacity will be ruined. What has just been said will fit most plants that die down in autumn and depend on food stored in underground parts to make good growth and flower the next year. Anyway, why pick trilliums? The short time that they last in a bowl on the dining room table (if they are lucky enough to get that far) will give much less pleasure than the same plants could if they were seen in their natural habitat.

The sessile trillium, *T. sessile* (pl. 13), is uncommon in our region, but it does occur in somewhat open woods in the Willamette Valley. It is on the whole smaller than the white trillium, and its leaves are mottled with a mixture of dark green and grayish green. The flower has no peduncle, but is set on the stem directly above the leaf bases. The narrow petals are usually greenish white. This species, occurring in both eastern and western North America, has many variants, some with petals that are chocolate or nearly blood-red.

Fairy lanterns, *Disporum hookeri* (pl. 13), is abundant in humid woods through much of our range. It commonly grows up to 50 cm high, and a large plant usually branches several times. The oval, bright green leaves, about 5 to 7 cm long, tightly clasp the stems. The flowers, with cream-white petals and sepals about 1.5 cm long, are borne in groups of two to five and hang down; the stamens stick out beyond the petals and sepals. The ovoid berries, ripening in late summer, are 1 cm long and bright orange.

Disporum smithii is similar, but its flowers are slightly larger and more nearly pure white, and the stamens do not stick out. This species is found in the Coast Ranges and at low to moderate elevations in the Cascades.

Considerably less common than fairy lanterns, but not really rare, is twisted-stalk, *Streptopus amplexifolius* (fig. 7). The common name alludes to the zigzag course of the stems and the twisting and looping of the delicate peduncles. The leaves of this plant are dull green, whitish below, and clasping. The almost bell-like flowers, arising singly or in pairs from the leaf axils, are greenish white and about 1.5 cm across. The tips of the petals and sepals turn upward. The berries, ripening in late summer or in autumn, are close to 1 cm in diameter and deep red.

The genus *Smilacina* includes two of our more common liliaceous plants. They are often called false Solomon's seals because they slightly resemble the true Solomon's seals of the genus *Polygonatum,* found in eastern North America and in the Old World. Perhaps it is just simpler to call ours smilacinas. Both species form colonies with many arching stems. The large smilacina, *S. racemosa* (pl. 13), grows up to 1 m tall. Its slightly shiny leaves are narrowly oval and mostly about 10 cm long; they have no petioles, but do not clasp the stem so strongly as those of fairy lanterns or twisted stalk. The small flowers, about 5 mm across, are produced in dense inflorescences. The round

7. Twisted-stalk, *Streptopus amplexifolius*

fruits are a little more than 5 mm in diameter. As they ripen they first are mottled red and green, then turn deep red all over.

The small smilacina, or star-flowered smilacina, *S. stellata* (pl. 13), is generally not more than about 40 cm high and has leaves that are about 6 cm long. The inflorescences are loose and have only a few flowers, but these are nearly 1 cm across and are individually more attractive than those of *S. racemosa.* The berries, slightly under 1 cm in diameter, are at first light green with bluish streaks, but become red or dark blue when fully ripe.

The so-called wild lily-of-the-valley (or mayflower), *Maianthemum dilatatum* (pl. 13), hardly resembles the garden plant for which it is named. Its white flowers are more nearly starlike than bell-shaped, and its leaves are dark green and heart-shaped rather than light green and oval. But it does creep along by an underground rhizome and is about the same size as the lily-of-the-valley—about 15 or 20 cm tall. The flowers are succeeded by spherical, bright red berries, not quite 1 cm in diameter. Inland, this nice groundcover grows in shady places, especially where there is plenty of moisture, as at the bottom of a wooded ravine. Close to the coast, where there is considerably more rainfall, it is often seen in the open, particularly if it has survived the clearing of a forest.

Erythronium revolutum, the pink fawn-lily (pl. 14), is almost strictly limited to the coastal strip of our region, where it is found in woods and grassy areas. It does turn up in a few places in the northern part of the Puget Trough, but its occurrence there must be regarded as exceptional. The leaves of this species are more faintly mottled than those of the inland *E. oregonum* (see chap. 3). The flowers range from very pale pink to deep rose, and the petals and sepals are marked with white and also some yellow on the inside, near the base. The anthers are bright yellow, and the whole ensemble is one of exceptional beauty and charm.

The beadlily, *Clintonia uniflora* (pl. 13), is a creeper that likes humus-rich soil and grows especially well where the top dressing of conifer needles is thick and corky. The flowers, borne singly, are about 2 cm across, and the pure white sepals and petals are all alike. A large bed of the beadlily in full bloom is a marvelous sight. When it grows with the bunchberry, the beauty of both seems to be heightened. The attractive leaves of *Clintonia,* up to 10 cm long, come up in groups of two to five, and typically their margins are beset with delicate hairs. The flowers are succeeded by dark blue berries, which are dusted with a whitish bloom and do indeed resemble beads. The beadlily is not likely to be found in the lowlands except near the coast. It is abundant, however, at moderate elevations in the Cascades, Coast Ranges, and Olympic Mountains.

ORCHID FAMILY

Plants of the orchid family are perennials, but only one of our species, the rattlesnake plantain, is evergreen. The flowers of orchids, with three sepals and three petals, are irregular, and the lowermost petal is generally greatly enlarged. There is usually just one stamen, sometimes two.

It is probably fair to say that the fairy-slipper, *Calypso bulbosa* (pl. 16), is our most delightful orchid. It usually grows out of a thick deposit of decaying fir or hemlock needles, or out of a bed of moss. In the spring a single dark green leaf unrolls. This is oval, slightly serrated along the margin, and about 4 cm long. The flower, on a stalk 6 or 8 cm high, opens up in April or May in the lowlands, in May or June at moderate elevations in the mountains. It is pinkish purple, trimmed with yellow and pink, and has a fragrance similar to that of the cultivated lily-of-the-valley. The fairy-slipper, common as it is in some places, is extremely vulnerable. Its tuber ("bulb") is close to the surface and subject to attacks by rodents and slugs. Its seed production will be low if it is not successfully pollinated, and there are only a few insects that can do this. In addition, its survival beyond the seedling stage depends on its establishing a permanent relationship with the right kind of fungus, without which it cannot live. The fungus spreads through the woodsy soil and absorbs and modifies nutrients which are necessary to both the orchid and fungus. Transplanting *Calypso*, even to an obviously favorable habitat, is not likely to be successful. Picking the flowers should be discouraged not only because it reduces the seed crop but because pulling on the flower stems may disturb the shallowly planted bulbs enough to kill the plants. No matter how tempting the flowers are, this jewel of our woods needs all the protection it can get.

The rattlesnake plantain, *Goodyera oblongifolia* (pl. 16), is an orchid that produces a spike of undistinguished, greenish white flowers. The evergreen leaves of the plant, however, crowded into a basal group, are strikingly marked with a network of white lines, and sometimes with white blotches or streaks. As a rule, rattlesnake plantain grows out of beds of moss. It can tolerate rather dry conditions and thus is found in rocky, well-drained woods, as well as in situations where there is considerable moisture near the surface throughout the summer.

The coral-root orchids of the genus *Corallorhiza* are essentially leafless and lack chlorophyll. Being unable to make their own food from inorganic compounds, as green plants are able to do, they depend on organic substances that are released into the soil when leaves and other plant and animal materials decay. The uptake of nutrients by corallorhizas is accomplished with the help of fungi associated with their roots. The roots of the orchids themselves are short and knobby, but the fungi plugged into them spread out for some distance into the soil and thereby bring in food from a considerable area. Not only are the orchids dependent on the fungi but the fungi are in some way also dependent on the orchids. Thus these associations are cases of mutualistic symbiosis.

Our corallorhizas generally produce flowering stalks from 20 to 30 cm high. There are three species, and they are easy to tell apart. The striped coral-root, *C. striata* (pl. 16), is the most robust and has the largest flowers, with petals and sepals regularly about 1.5 cm long. These are brownish pink with dark reddish brown or purplish brown streaks. The spotted coral-root, *C. maculata* (pl. 16), has smaller flowers, with petals and sepals not more than 1 cm long. The three petals usually have distinct spots of a deep reddish brown color; the spots are especially conspicuous on the large lower petal ("lip"), which is normally white. This species is variable, however, and some plants have unspotted petals; others are largely yellowish green, lacking any trace of the brownish tints that characterize the stalks and flowers of most specimens. *Corallorhiza maculata* generally starts to bloom just a little later than *C. striata,* but the flowering period of the two species —April and May in the lowlands—is substantially the same. Mertens' coral-root, *C. mertensiana,* flowers later, in June and early July. The stalks are slender, and almost the whole plant is a rich purplish red color. The flowers are about the same size as those of *C. maculata;* the lip, which is usually slightly lighter than the rest of the flower, has two dark streaks running lengthwise near the midline. *Corallorhiza mertensiana* is likely to be found only in very dense coniferous woods, especially those consisting of crowded small trees.

The phantom-orchid, *Eburophyton austiniae* (pl. 16), grows much like a coral-root orchid, but is totally white except for a little yellow that tints the lower lip of its flowers. It normally grows only in dense, dark woods into which little sunlight penetrates. This species does not range as far northward as British Columbia.

VIOLET FAMILY

The only common violets in shady, moist woods are two yellow-flowered species. Both start to bloom in March, sometimes earlier if the winter has been mild. They are easily distinguished. In the evergreen violet, *Viola sempervirens* (fig. 8), the leaves persist throughout the

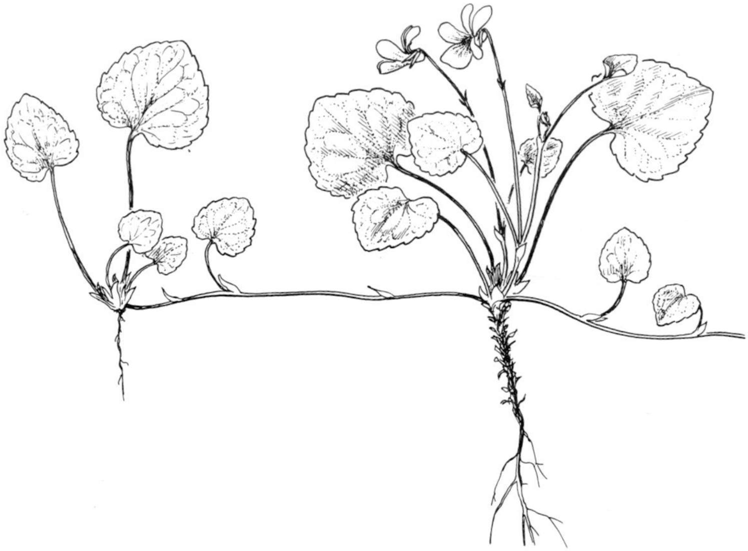

8. Evergreen violet, *Viola sempervirens*

year. This is a creeper that hugs the ground and spreads by slender runners, often forming large mats. Neither the leaves nor the flowers are apt to be more than 5 or 6 cm from the ground. The dull green leaf blades are heart-shaped, about 2 or 3 cm across, toothed along the margins, and rather firm. The flowers originate from close to the base of the plant. They are about 1 cm across, and the three lower petals are strongly marked with purplish lines.

The smooth violet, *V. glabella* (pl. 19), is a perennial, but its leaves die down in autumn. It does not have the slender runners characteristic of *V. sempervirens,* although it does spread to some extent by thick stems close to the surface of the ground in much the same way as the common blue violet grown in gardens. It forms rather bushy growths 10 to 20 cm high, and the flowers, a little more than 1 cm across, are produced from near the top of leafy, branching stems. As in those of the evergreen violet, the lower three petals have purplish lines. Larger leaves of the smooth violet may have blades more than 5 cm across, and these are dark green and generally look shiny above, even if they have a coating of fine hairs. This is one of our more obvious early spring flowers and one of several plants called "johnny jump-up."

PURSLANE FAMILY

Miner's lettuce, *Montia perfoliata* (pl. 17), is a perfectly good salad plant, but it is peppery enough that few will want a lot of it at one sitting. From the base, where some long-petioled leaves originate, it sends up several juicy stems. These terminate in a cluster of small white flowers set above a pair of leaves that are typically joined to form an oblong or disklike contraption around the stems. The plants are generally under 25 cm tall, and where the soil is relatively dry, most of them will be much smaller. Where miner's lettuce does grow, it is usually abundant, and it may form a nearly continuous cover. It is an annual that comes up each year from seed.

The candyflower, *Montia sibirica* (pl. 17), is a close relative of miner's lettuce, and the basal leaves of the two plants are rather similar. Candyflower grows taller (up to about 30 to 40 cm high) and its upper leaf-pairs are not joined by their bases. Its flowers are about 1 or 1.5 cm across, and the petals range from white to deep pink. If white or almost white, they frequently have dark pink lines.

BARBERRY FAMILY

Vanilla leaf, *Achlys triphylla* (pl. 17), spreads by creeping stems and may form extensive beds. At close intervals it sends up a single leaf about 20 or 30 cm high, which is divided at its apex into three wedge-shaped leaflets that are held almost horizontally. The leaflets have no luster but they are very bright green. Most of the larger leaves are accompanied by a slightly taller stalk bearing a terminal spike of small white flowers. The dried leaves of this plant have the fragrance of vanilla, and this accounts for the common name. After the leaves die, the lacy networks formed by the veins persist through much of the autumn and winter.

The inside-out flower, *Vancouveria hexandra* (pl. 17), is sometimes mistaken for a fern when its leaves first appear in spring. Each leaf has a number of nearly six-sided leaflets, which are attached to the several delicate branches of the leaf stalk. Late in the spring *Vancouveria* sends up a panicle of white flowers in which the white sepals—there are no petals—are turned back. The stamens thus appear especially long. The diameter of the flowers is about 5 mm, and the inflorescence as a whole, which normally is much taller than any of the leaves, may be up to about 50 cm high.

BUTTERCUP FAMILY

Buttercups proper are primarily plants of wet, sunny places. The only common species in coniferous woods is *Ranunculus uncinatus,* the little buttercup. In spite of the fact that it grows to a height of 30 cm or more, its flowers are small and inconspicuous. The petals are pale yellow, only about 3 or 4 mm long, and usually one or two of the five does not develop completely. A rather distinctive feature of this plant is its fairly thick, hollow stem. The lower leaves are divided into three lobes, each of which is further divided as well as coarsely toothed.

The three-leaved windflower, *Anemone deltoidea* (pl. 18), is abundant in shady woods in the southern part of our range, but unfortunately it drops out just south of Seattle. It has such pretty white flowers that its absence farther north is regretted. By its creeping underground stems the windflower forms large beds—often nearly pure stands—that die back in winter. The plants are usually about 10 or 15 cm high and have three leaves forming a foil beneath the single flowers. The flowers are about 2.5 cm across.

The handsome blue-flowered anemone found in woods at moderate elevations in the Cascades is *A. oregana.* Occasionally it has flowers that are pink or white, but it can always be distinguished from *A. deltoidea* by the fact that each of its leaves has a distinct petiole and each is deeply divided into three lobes. In dry woods in the San Juan Archipelago and some other places in this general area, there is an anemone with white or pink flowers only about 1 cm across and with much-divided, almost fernlike, leaves. This is *A. lyallii,* otherwise found only at higher elevations.

The baneberry, *Actaea rubra* (pl. 18), is a large plant, sometimes up to 1 m high, that prefers shade. Its small white flowers are arranged in a raceme that reaches well above the much-divided leaves. The plant as a whole, in spite of its size, is undistinguished until July or August, when the fruits ripen. These are so red and so shiny that they resemble the artificial berries that once were used to decorate ladies' hats and dresses. After the fruits begin to shrivel, the shininess disappears. Appetizing as they look, they are, unfortunately, quite poisonous.

9. Western meadowrue, *Thalictrum occidentale*

The meadowrues, species of *Thalictrum,* have much-divided, slightly grayish leaves that look much like those of columbines. Their flowers lack petals and individually they are not showy. The western meadowrue, *T. occidentale* (fig. 9), is widespread in our region, though it is partial to moist situations. Its flowers, borne in a loose spike at the top of a stem that may be nearly 1 m tall, have sepals ranging in color from almost white to purplish. There are numerous stamens and several pistils. The latter become seed capsules that are elongated, slightly flattened, and marked by three lengthwise ridges on each side. The stigma persists as a long beak. As they start to ripen, the capsules spread out into a rosette.

Thalictrum polycarpum, which is found in western Oregon, resembles *T. occidentale* in habit of growth. Its seed capsules, however, are decidedly different. They are strongly flattened and not much longer than wide, and the ridges on the surface branch.

BIRTHWORT FAMILY

Wild ginger, *Asarum caudatum* (fig. 10), can be recognized by its

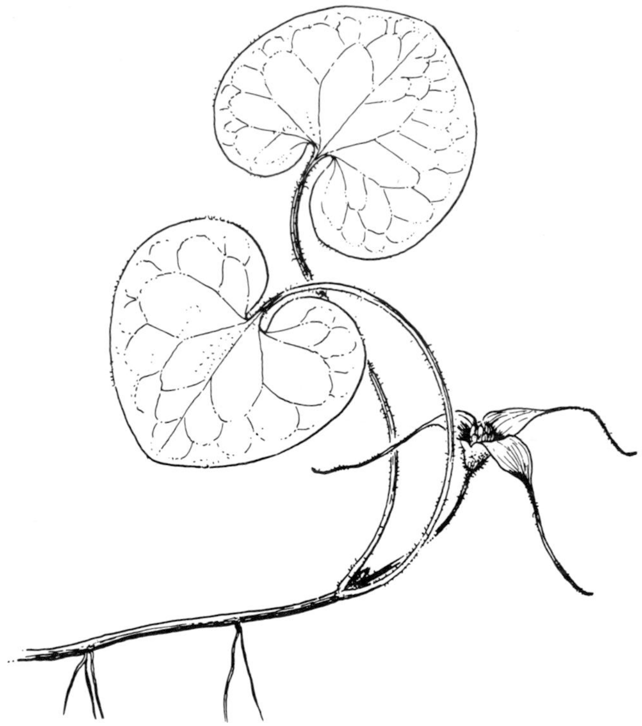

10. Wild ginger, *Asarum caudatum*

shiny, heart-shaped leaf blades. These are mostly 5 to 7 cm long, and the long petioles come off a stem that creeps along at the surface. The flowers, attractive in an odd way, are usually hidden by the leaves. There are no petals, but the three sepals, united basally to form a cup in which the stamens and pistil are situated, are large and drawn out into long, filamentous tips. Altogether, the sepals are about 4 cm long. They are usually purplish brown, but the coloration may be pale. In any case, it is an unusual color for any flower. Sometimes the sepals are yellow or greenish. If the plant is bruised, an odor much like that of tropical ginger (no relation) is noted. The rhizome is especially fragrant. Wild ginger is widespread in our region, but is limited to fairly moist coniferous woods. It is not likely to be found where the ground is so well drained that it dries out in summer.

PINK FAMILY

Arenaria macrophylla (fig. 11) is one of the sandworts, but this particular species, like others found in the northwest, does not grow in really sandy situations. It is common in coniferous woods, where it creeps along unobtrusively. The more or less upright stems, about 10 or 15 cm tall, have opposite leaves without any petioles. The flowers, with white petals, are produced in loose clusters of two to several, and are less than 1 cm across.

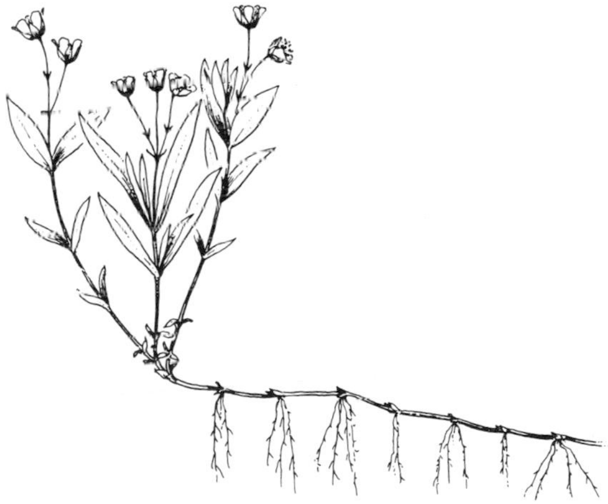

11. Sandwort, *Arenaria macrophylla*

SAXIFRAGE FAMILY

Fringecup, *Tellima grandiflora* (fig. 12), is very common in any coniferous woods where the soil holds moisture fairly well. It produces a compact mass of many basal leaves with long, hairy petioles; the broadly heart-shaped blades, about 5 to 7 cm long, have toothed margins and are cut into a number of shallow lobes. The almost leafless flower stalk may be more than 50 cm tall, and there are usually twenty or thirty flowers strung out along its upper portion. The sepals are fused to form a cup not quite 1 cm long; the small petals, at first greenish, then red, are deeply cut into several almost hairlike lobes.

Youth-on-age, or piggy-back plant, *Tolmiea menziesii* (fig. 13), is an oddity among our native plants because it forms buds near the bases of its leaf blades. The buds grow into little plants that eventually strike root and become independent of the mother. Otherwise, this species is not particularly impressive. It grows something like fringecup. Most of its leaves are basal; and the heart-shaped blades, on hairy petioles, are shallowly divided into several lobes, each with a few coarse teeth. The flowers, borne in a spikelike group at the top of a stem that may be over 50 cm tall, have hairlike petals of a pinkish brown or nearly chocolate color.

The leafy mitrewort, or bishop's-cap, *Mitella caulescens* (fig. 14), is sometimes common in moist woods. It is usually about 30 cm tall, and its habit of growth is similar to that of fringecup and youth-on-age. The flowers, slightly less than 1 cm across, are reminiscent of snowflakes. Each of the five greenish petals is divided into a number of hairlike lateral lobes. *Mitella pentandra,* found in woods near the coast, resembles *M. caulescens,* but its stamens are situated at the bases of the petals, instead of alternating with them.

The false mitrewort, *Tiarella trifoliata,* likes woods that are decidedly moist. Most of its leaves are basal, with blades about 5 or 6 cm across. In the variety *trifoliata* (pl. 17) the blades consist of three completely separate lobes, each of which is toothed; one or two of the lobes may be rather deeply divided again. In the variety *unifoliata* the blades are only slightly three-lobed. The flower stalks are generally 20 to 30 cm tall and bear a number of small flowers with narrow white petals. The slender fruits poke out quickly after the flowers start to wither and reach a length of about 1 cm when they are ready to discharge their seeds. *T. trifoliata* is widely distributed almost throughout our region, but in the lowlands the variety *trifoliata* prevails. On Vancouver Island and some islands of the San Juan Archipelago, there is still another variety, *laciniata.* In this plant, as its name suggests, the three primary leaflets are again divided for more than half their length.

12. Fringecup, *Tellima grandiflora*

13. Youth-on-age, *Tolmiea menziesii*

14. Leafy mitrewort, *Mitella caulescens*

ROSE FAMILY

The genus *Geum* has provided gardeners with a few colorful plants, most of which seem to have been selected for their freakiness. Our only common wild species, the large avens, *Geum macrophyllum* (pl. 19), may not be spectacular, but it is plentiful and its yellow flowers brighten up shady woods. Avens sometimes grows up to nearly 1 m tall, though most specimens are about half this size. The basal leaves are elongated and compound, with the terminal leaflet being much larger than the lateral ones. The leaves along the flower stalk are small and are usually divided partially or completely into three lobes. The flowers, up to about 1.5 cm across, look much like those of buttercups. The petals are not shiny, however; and as the numerous pistils start to ripen as little dry fruits, their long and hairy styles are distinctly unlike those found in any buttercups.

Goatsbeard, *Aruncus sylvester* (pl. 18), closely resembles the astilbes grown in gardens. It is much taller, however, regularly reaching a height of 1 or 2 m or more. Its size may make one think of it as a shrub, but it is not at all woody. Although it is a perennial, it dies back to an underground stem in the autumn. Goatsbeard is a striking plant when it blossoms in late spring and summer. Its cream-colored flowers are tiny, hardly more than 2 mm across, but there are hundreds of them concentrated on each caterpillarlike side shoot of the inflorescence. The large compound leaves, usually divided into secondary and sometimes tertiary leaflets, are bright yellowish green. The individual leaflets, mostly 5 to 10 cm long, are toothed and drawn out to a point at the tip. A well-established plant usually branches several times. Goatsbeard is abundant at moderate and lower elevations on the western slopes of the Cascades, Coast Ranges, and Olympics. Elsewhere its distribution is spotty. In general, it prefers shady situations, but there are places around Puget Sound and near the coast where it grows out in the open.

Strawberries also belong to the rose family. The species most likely to be found in moist woods is *Fragaria vesca; F. virginiana* is partial to relatively dry, open situations. Both are described in chapter 3.

EVENING-PRIMROSE FAMILY

Enchanter's nightshade, *Circaea alpina* (fig. 15), is an unobtrusive perennial that propagates itself by rhizomes just below the surface and typically forms extensive beds. It is usually 15 or 20 cm tall and has opposite leaves. The blades of the larger leaves are about 4 cm long and have a nearly heart-shaped outline; there are widely spaced teeth

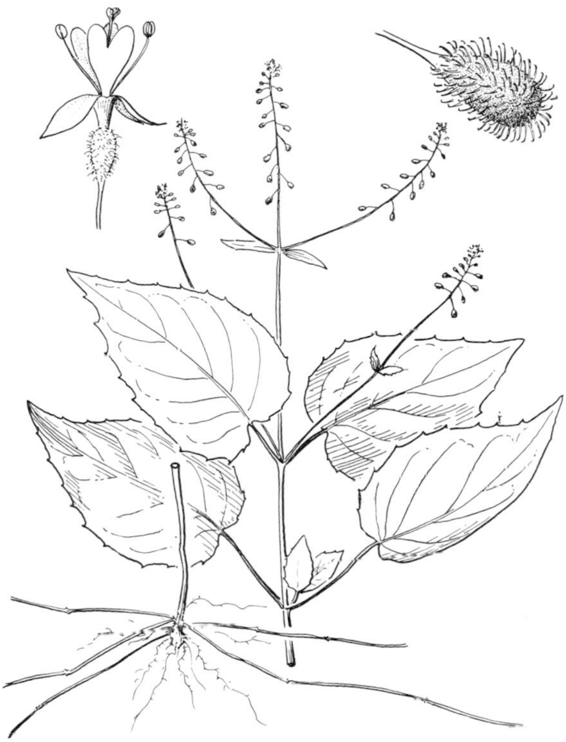

15. Enchanter's nightshade, *Circaea alpina*

along the margins. The white flowers, less than 4 mm across, are arranged in one or more slender racemes arising from upper parts of the plant. There are only two petals (most members of the evening-primrose family have four), and these are deeply divided into two lobes; there are also two sepals. The fruit, which produces a single seed, is a small capsule with little hooks.

PARSLEY FAMILY

Most representatives of this group grow in sunny situations, or in places that are wet much of the year. There are, however, a few species characteristic of coniferous woods. Sweet-cicely, *Osmorhiza chilensis* (fig. 16), is probably the most common of these. It is a perennial, sprouting up each year from a taproot, and grows to a height of 50 cm or more. It is usually slightly hairy, especially on the stems and leaf petioles. Most of the lower leaves are divided into three main portions, each cut again into three toothed leaflets that may be further subdivided. The leaves on upper parts of the plant are reduced. The tiny white

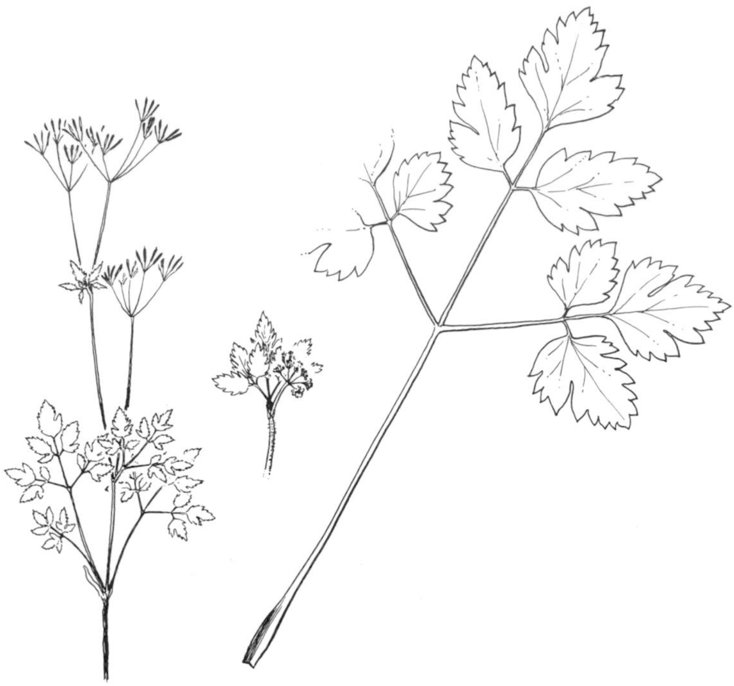

16. Sweet-cicely, *Osmorhiza chilensis*

flowers are organized into several clusters that form a nearly flat-topped inflorescence. The fruits are slender, angled, and up to about 2 cm long. They are typically bristly on the angles and below the middle.

The Pacific sanicula, *Sanicula crassicaulis* (fig. 17), is partial to comparatively dry woods. It is a perennial with attractive basal leaves. The blades of these, dark green and up to more than 10 cm across, are deeply divided into three to five main lobes. The teeth along the margins of the lobes are usually sharp-tipped. The upright shoots, 30 to 50 cm tall, have only a few small leaves, and end in inflorescences consisting of a number of globular clusters of small yellow flowers. The ovoid fruits, 4 or 5 mm long, are distinctive in being almost completely covered with hooked bristles. In the Puget Trough and Willamette Valley, there is a variety *(tripartitum)* with leaves that are decidedly longer than broad, and in which the flowers are purplish.

FUMITORY FAMILY

The Pacific bleedingheart, *Dicentra formosa* (pl. 19), is a creeping, deciduous perennial that prefers very moist woods and is most com-

17. Pacific sanicula, *Sanicula crassicaulis*

mon near the coast and in the foothills of our mountains. It does occur at some places in the lowlands, especially in the northern part of the Puget Trough. Although it is a close relative of the cultivated bleedingheart, its odd flowers, in which the outer two petals have a deep, saclike spur, are uniformly colored, ranging from pale to deep pink. The flowers are produced in clusters on stalks about 30 or 40 cm high. The juicy, dull green leaves resemble those of ferns in being much divided. When a bit of the plant is crushed, it smells much like a poppy. This is not surprising, for although poppies and bleeding hearts are in separate families, the two groups are rather closely related.

The black seeds of bleedingheart deserve special attention. If you examine one with a hand lens, you will see a little white appendage attached to it. This contains oil that attracts certain ants. When they carry off the seeds with a view to using the oily material for food, the ants act as agents of dispersal.

MUSTARD FAMILY

The mustard family is large and well represented in the Northwest by many genera. Most of them are plants of open places.

The slender toothwort, *Cardamine pulcherrima* (pl. 17), flowers early in the lowlands, usually beginning in March. It is a perennial that comes up from a fleshy, underground stem and does not often grow taller than 15 cm. The blades of the basal leaves, about 2 or 3 cm in diameter, would be heart-shaped or nearly circular if it were not for the fact that they are coarsely toothed. Generally, they are purplish or reddish underneath. The upper leaves, on the stems that bear the flowers, are typically divided completely into three leaflets. The flowers, about 1.5 cm across, are most commonly very pale pink, but sometimes are of a deeper shade. As in all members of the mustard family, there are six stamens, two shorter than the other four. The fruits are slender pods up to about 3 or 4 cm long. The toothwort is common throughout much of our region and is not strictly limited to coniferous woods. It is rare or lacking, however, on most islands of the San Juan Archipelago. At moderate elevations there is a variant in which the basal leaves are deeply lobed. In *C. integrifolia,* found close to the coast, the underground stem that persists through the winter is swollen into a potatolike tuber.

WOOD-SORREL FAMILY

In wet woods of the Olympic Peninsula, Coast Ranges, and Cascades of Oregon and Washington, a native species of wood-sorrel, *Oxalis oregana* (pl. 19), often forms extensive beds. This plant is a perennial that spreads by creeping rhizomes. Its leaves, which have hairy petioles about 10 or 15 cm long, are divided into three leaflets, after the fashion of a clover. The leaflets are a light but intense green and approximately heart-shaped, with the narrow end attached to the petiole. They fold at night and when the soil becomes dry, and if they are touched or rained upon they will slowly respond in the same way. The five-petaled flowers, on peduncles about as long as the petioles, are basically white or pale pink and have delicate red veins. When the flowers are fully open, they are about 1.5 or 2 cm across. The fruits are ovoid capsules a little less than 1 cm long.

Oxalis suksdorfii is a yellow-flowered species abundant in woods and clearings west of the Cascades in Oregon and southern Washington. Although its flowers are about the size of those of *O. oregana,* the leaves and plants as a whole are less robust. *Oxalis suksdorfii* must not be confused with *O. corniculata* and *O. stricta,* which are pests in gardens.

Both of these weeds have relatively small flowers, mostly under 1 cm in diameter, and the leaves of plants growing in sunny situations often turn bronze.

DOGWOOD FAMILY

The bunchberry, *Cornus canadensis* (pl. 19), is one of our most delightful and choice ground covers. It loves a corky deposit of humus under conifers and when happy it will form extensive beds, often mingling with the beadlily. The upright stems of new growth, about 10 or 15 cm high, arise from the creeping stems in spring or early summer, depending on the altitude. The upper leaves are borne in a symmetrical pattern of four or six. Above them is the "flower," which more properly should be called an inflorescence, for it consists of what are essentially four pure white leaves and a convex, buttonlike cluster of inconspicuous flowers. It looks like a miniature dogwood tree. The flowers are succeeded by bright orange fruits.

Bunchberry has a wide distribution in cooler portions of North America. In the Northwest, it occurs in coniferous woods near the coast and also at the borders of coastal bogs. Then it is common in the mountains at elevations of around 1000 m (about 3300 feet) or a little higher. Its absence from the lowlands of most of our region is to be regretted, for it is a plant whose simple beauty no one can resist.

HEATH FAMILY

The shinleaf, *Pyrola asarifolia* (fig. 18), may be expected in deep, moist woods at moderate elevations in the mountains as well as in the lowlands. It is not found, however, in every place where conditions may seem right for it. Creeping along by runners just below the surface of the ground, it forms extensive beds. The leaves are basal, with rather long petioles and heart-shaped blades about 5 cm long (there is a variety of this plant in which the leaves are simply oval); the blades are very shiny above and sometimes tinged with a purplish color below. The flowers are about 1 cm across, deep pink or purplish pink, and borne in a spikelike cluster raised well above the leaves. The stigma of the pistil turns down, then out, so that it reminds one of an elephant's trunk. The fruits are little capsules that eventually dry out.

Several other species of *Pyrola* occur in our region, although these are not often encountered in the lowlands. The most striking is *P. picta,* which has white-veined leaves. A real oddity is the so-called "*P. aphylla*": this is not a species, but a practically leafless, reddish or nearly colorless form of some other species, generally either *P. picta* or *P.*

asarifolia. It is a saprophyte, unable to make its own food. These and other pyrolas are similar in flower structure and the spikelike nature of the inflorescence. If you encounter them, you can identify them to species with the help of one of the comprehensive guides to the flowering plants of the region.

The pipsissewa, or prince's pine, *Chimaphila umbellata* (fig. 19), is in general more common at moderate elevations in the mountains than in the lowlands. It is abundant, however, in the northern portion of the Puget Trough, including the islands of the San Juan Archipelago.

18. Shinleaf, *Pyrola asarifolia*

19. Pipsissewa, *Chimaphila umbellata*

It is an attractive groundcover, mostly about 20 cm high. The leaves are arranged in whorls of about six or seven; the blades are about 5 cm long, rather narrow, and toothed at the margins. The several nodding flowers, lifted clear of the uppermost leaves, are produced in loose clusters; they are about 1 cm across and have five pink petals. The fruits are capsules that dry and split open on ripening.

A smaller species, *C. menziesii,* may also occasionally be encountered in the lowlands. It is usually only about 10 cm high, and its leaves are only about twice as long as wide. There are no more than three flowers in each cluster.

In some coniferous woods the trees are so crowded that little sunlight reaches the forest floor. Consequently, there are few ferns, shrubs, or other green plants. The layer of humus may be very deep, however, and in such a situation one may expect to find Indian pipe, *Monotropa uniflora* (pl. 20). Its waxy, almost translucent stems often grow in clusters, but each stem bears only one flower. Delicate fungi associated with the root system of Indian pipe provide the plant with nourishment drawn from the humus and in turn obtain some benefit from their host. The mutualistic symbiosis makes it possible for Indian pipe to survive without chlorophyll.

PRIMROSE FAMILY

The starflower, *Trientalis latifolia* (pl. 19), is one of the more numerous woodland wildflowers of our area. It does not look much like a garden primrose, but belongs to the same family. It is sometimes called "Indian potato" because of its little tuber just 1 or 2 cm below the surface of the ground. The slender stem, generally 10 or 15 cm high, is topped by a crowded cluster of oval leaves and a few flowers on almost hairlike peduncles. The flowers are light to deep pink, usually around 1.5 to 2 cm across, and a bit odd because the number of petals is not consistent. Generally, there are six or seven, but sometimes as few as five or as many as nine.

WATERLEAF FAMILY

Waterleaf, *Hydrophyllum tenuipes* (pl. 17), is such a lush component of moist woods that it has to be mentioned, even if its flowers have little appeal to the average person. It is a hairy perennial mostly around 30 or 40 cm tall, coming up in spring from a shallow rhizome that has a peppery smell when broken. The leaves are large, with deeply divided blades about 10 or 15 cm long. The flowers, about 1 cm across, are borne in groups of several, lifted above the leaves by a stalk 10 or 15 cm long. The five petals are united by their bases, and the stamens are joined to them, so when one petal is pulled, the whole ensemble comes with it. The petals are regularly greenish or greenish white, but the purplish blue filaments of the stamens contrast effectively with them. In a few places on the Olympic Peninsula there are populations with nearly blue flowers.

FIGWORT (SNAPDRAGON) FAMILY

Synthyris reniformis (fig. 20) is found in coniferous woods as well as in rocky situations in which the Garry oak and madrone are conspicuous. It is common in the Willamette Valley and in the foothills of the Coast Ranges and Cascades bordering it, and it also grows in the Columbia River Gorge and the extreme southern part of the Puget Trough. Unfortunately, it is absent from the more northern part of our region. *Synthyris*—snow-queen is a name sometimes given to it—forms a nice clump with a number of basal leaves. These have long petioles and heart-shaped blades shallowly divided into several lobes and bluntly toothed along the margin. The blades are mostly about 4 or 5 cm long and are generally purplish beneath; the dark green color of the upper surface may also be tinged with purple or bronze. The flowers, produced in little clusters held just above the leaves, are only about 5 mm across, and the blue or purplish blue color of the corolla contrasts nicely with the reddish anthers. The flowers in this species are essentially regular, the free portions of all five petals being about the same size. This regularity is unusual for a member of the figwort family. In a mild winter, *Synthyris* may start blooming in December or January; and even after its normal flowering period in spring has

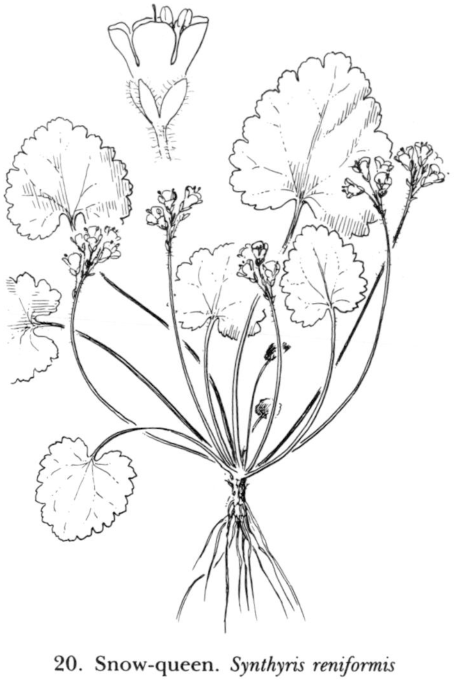

20. Snow-queen. *Synthyris reniformis*

ended, it may occasionally put up a few flowers during the summer, especially if there have been significant rains. The leaves persist throughout the year.

MADDER FAMILY

The genus *Galium* consists of weak-stemmed herbs that trail on the ground, wander over logs and other plants, and climb up into shrubbery. None of them is impressive, but all are interesting if looked at closely, and they belong to the same family as the plants that give us coffee beans, gardenias, and quinine. Some of the species in our area are native, others are introduced. Any delicate trailer with square stems (and usually also downward-directed hooks on the corners) and with leaves arranged in whorls will almost certainly be a *Galium*. If you pull the plant across your clothing or across your hand you will notice that the hooks make it cling. The white flowers are usually less than 5 mm across and are produced in loose clusters at the ends of terminal branches or side branches. Most galiums have four petals, united at the base. The two lobes of the ripening fruits are so distinctly set apart that they nearly look as if they have originated from separate flowers. The fruits of most species are covered with tiny hooks that undoubtedly help to disseminate the seeds. This is not the place to go into our species in detail. Most of the native kinds are rather similar, and one will just have to turn to a good manual on the flora to straighten them out. The species illustrated is *Galium aparine* (fig. 21), and it is thoroughly representative. The common names "bedstraw" and "cleavers" are applied to these plants.

HONEYSUCKLE FAMILY

The twinflower, *Linnaea borealis* (pl. 20), is an evergreen creeper whose delicate beauty, once appreciated, cannot be forgotten. It is found through much of the northern part of Europe as well as America, and was a favorite of Linnaeus, the eighteenth-century Swedish botanist and zoologist remembered for his contributions to the development of logical systems of classification. As the common name suggests, the flowers are paired. They are vase-shaped, about 1 cm long, and hang down. The color is white, tinged gently with pink. The bright to dark green leaves almost hug the ground and are so shiny, especially when young, that they appear to have been shellacked. The twinflower is happy in dry woods as well as in moist woods. A large carpet of it, in full bloom in May or June, is a touching sight.

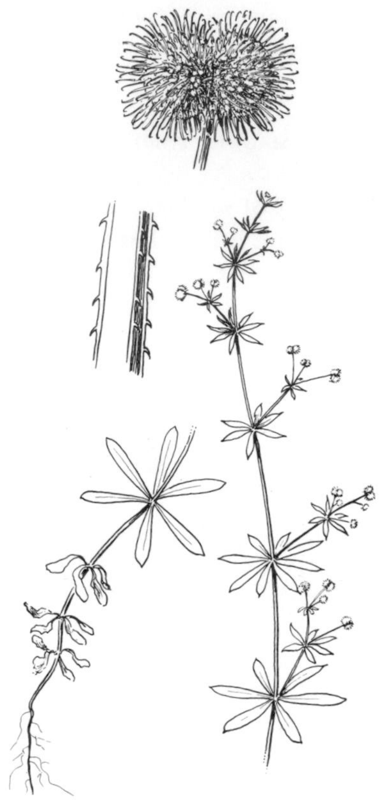

21. *Galium aparine,* one of the bedstraws

HAREBELL FAMILY

Campanula scouleri (pl. 23) is a tiny member of the genus that includes the cultivated Canterbury bell. This particular species is especially common in coniferous woods that are somewhat dry. It is not often more than about 10 cm high, and its flowers, no more than 1 cm across, are very pale blue. There are just a few of them, held up on a thin stem above the leafy shoots, and they usually appear in June and July, when other plants in the same habitat have finished flowering. The leaves are variable. Some of them, especially near the base, have nearly round blades; but in most of the leaves, the blades are oval or elongate, around 2 or 3 cm long, and toothed at the margins.

ASTER (SUNFLOWER) FAMILY

Trail plant, *Adenocaulon bicolor* (pl. 24), is recognizable from the time its leaves first unfold in spring. The blades are nearly triangular or somewhat heart-shaped and usually have rather coarse, indistinct teeth along the margins. The undersides of the blades are so white and woolly that the leaves have probably been used more than once for marking a trail in an unfamiliar area. Most of the leaves arise near the base of the stem, and typically their petioles are both long and broad. The whitish flower heads are on branches coming off the upper part of the stem. Individually, they are relatively inconspicuous, being less than 5 mm across and lacking ray flowers.

Ferns and Fern Allies

Ferns are less advanced than conifers and flowering plants, for they do not produce seeds. The perennial plants that almost anyone can recognize as ferns reproduce by spores formed in little sacs clustered on the undersides of the regular leaves or concentrated on one or more leaves specialized for this purpose. The spores that land in a suitably moist situation germinate into delicate little plants that are not at all fernlike, but look more like certain liverworts. They represent the sexual generation, which produces microscopic eggs and sperm, the latter having to reach the eggs by swimming to them in a film of water. After they are fertilized, the eggs develop into new fern plants. The sexual generation lives on only briefly, just long enough to get the young ferns started. This life cycle shows that although ferns are rather successful as land plants, their reproduction depends on availability of moisture at certain seasons.

The several groups of plants collectively called "fern allies" have the same general life history as ferns, but they are not necessarily closely related to ferns or to one another. Of the fern allies represented in our region, only a few are woodland plants. The rest are largely aquatic or prefer rocky situations or open fields, so they will be dealt with elsewhere.

EVERGREEN FERNS

The most conspicuous fern of reasonably humid woods is the swordfern, *Polystichum munitum* (pl. 28). It is generally rooted in soil, but sometimes becomes successfully established in rotten logs. Its leaves, regularly 70 or 80 cm long and occasionally larger, form a crown. The leaflets are serrated, and most of them have a nearly triangular projection directed toward the apex of the leaf. The petioles—especially the portions below the lowermost leaflets—are beset with chaffy, brown scales. The spore-bearing sacs are arranged in dense clusters (sori) on the undersides of the larger leaflets. Each cluster is covered by an umbrellalike shield called the indusium. Each spring, when new leaves unroll, the ones produced the preceding year are pushed closer to the soil; they generally survive for another year.

The deer-fern, *Blechnum spicant* (pl. 28), is vaguely similar to the sword-fern in habit of growth, and its leaves may be just as long. The leaflets, however, are attached by their full width, and below the point where the leaflets are longest, they gradually become smaller again. The petioles are much darker than those of the sword-fern. Still more important is the fact that the deer-fern has two entirely different types of leaves. A few arising near the center of the crown are the only ones that produce spores. These leaves have very slender leaflets and dry out before autumn, by which time they have accomplished their task. The deer-fern requires considerable moisture and thus may not be found in every coniferous forest. Near the coast, where rainfall is high, it is abundant, sometimes in the open; inland, it is most likely to be found near a marsh or the bottom of a ravine where there is running or standing water.

In the licorice-fern, or common polypody, *Polypodium vulgare* (pl. 28), the leaves arise from a creeping stem and thus do not form a neat crown, even though they may be crowded together. The individual leaves are relatively small, rarely exceeding a length of 30 cm. The leaflets may be narrow or broad, but they are attached by their entire width. The clusters of spore-bearing sacs are generally larger than those of the sword-fern and they are not covered by an indusium. The faint licorice taste of the stem of this species accounts for one of its common names. The licorice-fern does not often grow directly in soil, but is partial to mossy tree trunks and fallen logs, and also to rocks coated by moss. It is essentially evergreen, though it may wither in dry summer weather. New leaves are characteristically added in late autumn, when there is plenty of moisture, so the licorice-fern is at its best during the colder months.

In the common wood-fern, *Dryopteris austriaca (D. dilatata)* (pl. 28), a crown-forming species in which the leaves reach a length of 50 cm, the outline of the blade is triangular. Almost all parts of the blade are divided at least twice, and the portions nearest the base are divided three times; the ultimate leaflets are therefore small. The leaves survive the winter, though they may be badly battered and bruised by snow and harsh winds. The wood fern is typically restricted to shady places and almost invariably grows out of a well-rotted log or the remains of one. In spring and summer it could be confused with the lady-fern, a deciduous species. Its foliage is darker green, however, and in the lady-fern the leaf blade is not triangular and none of it is divided more than twice.

DECIDUOUS FERNS

The lady-fern, *Athyrium filix-femina* (pl. 28), usually grows in soil or muck. In wet places, as in a creek bottom or marsh, it is especially luxuriant and tolerates full sun. Its light green leaves may be more than 1 m long; the blades, divided only twice, are widest near the middle and become narrower again toward the base. The petioles are conspicuously chaffy, as in the sword-fern and wood-fern.

The bracken, *Pteridium aquilinum* (pl. 29), is our tallest species, sometimes attaining a height of 1.5 m. Its leaves arise singly from a creeping, underground stem. The blade has an approximately triangular outline, and some portions of it are divided as much as three times. The spore-bearing sacs are concentrated near the edges of the undersides of the leaflets and are partially covered by the inrolled margins. There is also a delicate membrane at the margins, but it is scarcely noticeable even when in its prime.

The maidenhair fern, *Adiantum pedatum* (pl. 29), is easy to recognize. It has a creeping stem, but the leaves arise so close together that the plant forms dense clumps. The shiny, blackish brown petioles divide into two subsidiary branches, which then send off the small branches on which the leaflets are borne. The dull green color of the leaflets is rather different from that of any other ferns of our region. The spore-bearing sacs are concentrated in almost rectangular units under the inrolled margins. This is a fern that loves shade and plenty of moisture. Large plants are about 50 cm high.

FERN ALLIES

A fern ally that is sometimes common in the mountains and near the coast is the clubmoss, or running pine, *Lycopodium clavatum* (pl. 30). It is basically a trailing plant, sparsely rooted, with stems up to 1 m long. The diameter of a branch, including the leaves, is about 1 cm. The leaves themselves, which taper to a hairlike tip, are up to about 7 mm long, but they tend to be incurved or held close to the stem. Some of the creeping stems give rise to short, upright branches that produce distinctly different shoots; these have scalelike leaves and terminate in elongate cones. The cones consist of leaves specialized for the production of spores. This species of *Lycopodium* may grow in the open or in shade and is often conspicuous on the banks of road cuts. It is evergreen, but the reproductive shoots are produced only in summer.

Mosses and Liverworts

Mosses and liverworts are more primitive than ferns and fern allies, and in general they are even more dependent on moisture. At this point, a little botany is essential to explain where mosses and liverworts fit into the general scheme of plant classification, and to make the descriptions of them more easily understood.

A leafy moss plant represents the sexual generation, and it therefore corresponds to the temporary sexual stage in the life cycle of a fern. As in the case of ferns, water must be present if the microscopic sperm of a moss are to swim to the eggs. Now remember that in the fern life history, the sexual stage dies soon after it has gotten a little fern plant started. In a moss, the sexual generation is perennial and keeps on growing and reproducing. But the spore-forming generation, derived from a fertilized egg, is temporary. It consists of a stalk and a capsule in which the spores are actually produced. A little dunce cap, called the calyptra, that partially or completely covers the capsule originates on the sexual phase but is lifted off when the stalk and capsule start to enlarge. In any case, the stalk and capsule constitute what is called the sporophyte, as distinct from the gametophyte that produced it and that contributes to its support. The sporophyte is comparable to an entire fern plant: it has the same function, which is production of spores, and it has the same origin, coming from a fertilized egg. The sporophytes on a moss plant have chlorophyll and can make some of their own food, but they are at least partially dependent; after their spore-producing function has been fulfilled, they wither.

The "leaves" of mosses, belonging as they do to the sexual generation, cannot be comparable to the leaves of a fern—or of flowering plants and conifers, either—which are part of the spore-forming generation. If you grasp this idea, you understand the major distinction between mosses and higher plants. Of course, there are other differences, too. The structure of mosses, for instance, is much simpler than that of ferns and more advanced types.

And now a few words about liverworts. These basically have the same life history as mosses, that is, they have a permanent gametophyte generation and a temporary sporophyte. The sporophytes are normally short-lived and, with few exceptions, they have no chlorophyll. They are thus more like fungi than like moss sporophytes. Some liverworts are leafy and grow much like mosses. Others, called thalloid liverworts, form flat, lobed growths that are plastered against soil or decaying wood, or that wander over beds of mosses.

Almost any moist coniferous woods in our region will have a wide variety of mosses and liverworts. About forty or fifty species are not too many to expect if one really works at the job of sorting them out carefully. Obviously, it will be necessary to concentrate here on just a few that are especially common or otherwise noteworthy. For convenience, the mosses will be segregated into two groups: those in which the sporophytes originate at the tips of essentially erect branches, and those in which they arise at almost any point along creeping stems. The liverworts will be divided into leafy and thalloid types.

MOSSES PRODUCING SPOROPHYTES AT OR NEAR THE TIPS OF UPRIGHT BRANCHES

Dicranum scoparium (pl. 32) is a plushy moss that generally prefers decaying logs, but it also grows at the bases of tree trunks and on shaded rocks. Its mats may be more than 10 cm thick, but usually only the upper 1 or 2 cm of the shoots are green. The slender, sickle-shaped leaves, almost all pointing in the same direction, are bright yellow-green, about 1 cm long, and crinkled when dry. The stems are reddish. The sporophytes originate at the tips of the shoots, but at least 1 cm of new growth is likely to be formed before the sporophytes mature. The stalks are up to 3 cm long, and the capsule, about 6 mm long, is distinctly curved.

Dicranum fuscescens is similar and about equally common, but its leaves are glossy and are not markedly crinkled when dry. It is a smaller plant than *D. scoparium,* and its mats are rarely more than 5 cm thick.

Any mosses that grow in moist, shady woods and that have broad, dark green leaves will almost certainly be in the genus *Mnium,* or in the closely related genera *Plagiomnium* and *Rhizomnium.* There are several species of this group in our area, and they may be found growing on soil or out of rotting wood. The leaves of these mosses (pl. 33) are generally about 5 mm long by 2.5 mm wide, but sometimes they are considerably larger. They are very thin and quickly shrivel when the woods begin to dry out. It is characteristic of mniums to form nearly pure stands. Male plants are easily recognized by the rather broad cups, formed of several leaves, at the tips of the shoots, in which the sperm-producing organs are concentrated. Female plants have comparable cups, but they are smaller. The sporophytes arise from within them after fertilization has been achieved during a period of abundant moisture. Usually there are two to several sporophytes growing from the tip of each female shoot. When the stalks of old sporophytes survive long after they have outlived their usefulness, the addition of new growth at the tips of the female shoots may make it appear that the origin of the sporophytes is lateral rather than terminal.

Leucolepis menziesii (pl. 33) is closely related to the mniums. It is a distinctive species that forms nearly pure patches in which almost all of the plants are about the same height. They look a little like palm trees because the leafy branches are concentrated near the top of a dark stem that is bare except for scattered, whitish leaves. The plants may be up to 5 cm tall, but generally are a bit smaller. The green branches are about 1 or 1.5 cm long and have overlapping leaves about 2 mm long. As in mniums, the sperm-producing organs of male plants are situated in a terminal cup formed of several leaves. In female plants the egg-producing structures are concentrated in a rather tall cup of slender leaves. Two to several sporophytes eventually grow out of this cup. They are about 3 or 4 cm tall, and their nodding capsules are about 6 mm long. *Leucolepis* is generally found in wetter portions of woods, growing either on the ground or on a decaying log. If there is a seepage area or small stream, it is more likely to be found close to this than in drier sites.

Orthotrichum lyellii (pl. 31) is common on the bark and branches of red alder and big-leaf maple, as well as on Garry oak (chap. 3). It usually forms loose tufts in which the stems are up to about 5 cm long. The older portions of the stems are often blackish when wet. The leaves, generally 4 or 5 mm long and 1 mm wide at the base, taper to a slender tip. The sporophyte has a stalk that is usually about 2 mm long and an upright capsule up to nearly 4 mm long. The calyptra persists for some time; it covers about half of the capsule and is fibrous. There are other species of *Orthotrichum* on deciduous trees, as well as on exposed rocks. In some of them the stalk of the sporophyte is much longer than it is in *O. lyellii.* Any similar moss with the same sort of capsule and a fibrous calyptra is likely to be an *Orthotrichum,* however.

Aulacomnium androgynum (pl. 32) is a tiny and unpretentious moss, but an especially interesting one. Its favored habitat is a rotting log from which the bark has long since disappeared. It grows in tufts generally less than 2 cm high, and the leaves are only 1 or 2 mm long. The color of the plants as a whole is bright green, but the lower portions of individual shoots, hidden away in the tufts, are brown with leaves that have died but have not fallen off. Many of the tufts—in spring and early summer, at least—bear what superficially look like sporophytes with minute, globular capsules. These are extensions of the gametophyte shoots, and the swellings at the tip consist of bits of tissue that correspond to gemmae of liverworts. Like gemmae, the little buds of *Aulacomnium* fall away and give rise to new gametophyte plants. This moss is capable of sexual reproduction and of forming true sporophytes; these have hairlike red stalks up to 1 or 2 cm tall and elongate capsules about 2 mm long. Sporophytes are much less commonly observed, however, than the stalks that bear gemmae.

MOSSES PRODUCING SPOROPHYTES ALONG CREEPING STEMS

Of mosses in this category, *Hylocomium splendens* (pl. 30) is perhaps the easiest for a beginner to recognize with absolute confidence. Because of its pattern of branching and large size, this species almost resembles a fern. It grows on the ground, on decaying logs, and on rocks that have a coating of soil or some other moss, and may spread over a large area, often forming pure stands. Each spring it produces an arching stem of new growth. For a time this is held above the old growth, but eventually it sinks down. The stems are reddish, with tiny hairlike scales. The leaves are relatively small—only about 3 mm long. Sporophytes are almost never observed. When they do appear, they are about 1 or 1.5 cm tall, and the capsules, about 3 mm long, stick out nearly at right angles to the stalks.

Rhytidiadelphus triquetrus (pl. 31) is a coarse, yellow-green moss that also spreads aggressively over the ground and clambers over logs and rocks. It seems, in general, to be more common in relatively dry, somewhat open woods than in those that are dark or especially moist. The stems are reddish, and the thin, chaffy leaves are usually about 6 by 3 mm. The sporophytes are not conspicuous, partly because they are short (only about 2 cm high) and partly because they may be scarce. The capsule nods and is about 3 by 1 mm.

Rhytidiadelphus loreus (pl. 31), although it has reddish stems, does not otherwise closely resemble *R. triquetrus.* Its leaves are smaller (up to about 4 by 1.5 mm), and its yellow-green shoots have a glossy appearance. The sporophytes are generally about 3 cm tall, and the capsules are not often more than 1.5 mm long. This species is most common on logs and tree trunks, but may occasionally be found growing on the ground.

Plagiothecium undulatum (pl. 31) is a pale, whitish green moss forming thin mats that tightly hug the surface of well-rotted logs. The leaves, about 3 mm long, have a wavy texture. The capsules of the sporophytes, on stalks about 3 cm high, are distinctly grooved when dry. *Plagiothecium denticulatum* is a close relative that is more nearly green than whitish green. Its leaves are not wavy, and the capsules of its sporophytes are less likely to become grooved when dry than those of *P. undulatum.*

Now the going gets tougher. There is a large complex of common mosses that creep over bark, logs, rocks, and sometimes soil, and that branch in a nearly regular, featherlike pattern. *Eurhynchium oreganum* (pl. 31) is perhaps the most easily recognized, because the lower portions of the stalks of its sporophytes are decidedly roughened. A strong hand lens will be needed to see this feature. *Eurhynchium stokesii* also has a rough sporophyte stalk, but this species differs from *E. oreganum* because its side shoots branch again. In *Claopodium crispifolium* the sporophyte stalks are slightly roughened, but the leaves of this moss are unlike those of the two preceding species because the narrow terminal portions are curled strongly to one side.

Of the featherlike mosses with smooth sporophyte stalks, *Hypnum, Hygrohypnum, Brachythecium,* and *Isothecium* are probably the ones most likely to be found in lowland forests. You will need a moss book to get them straightened out. *Hypnum subimponens* (pl. 31) can usually be recognized positively, however, because its capsules are nearly upright, three or four times as long as wide, and have a prominent white calyptra. In addition, its leaves are sickle-shaped. *Hypnum circinale* and *Hygrohypnum luridum* also have sickle-shaped leaves, but their sporophyte capsules are stubby. Species of *Brachythecium* and *Isothecium* have straight leaves.

In the "rain forest" of the Olympic Peninsula, as well as in other especially wet coastal woods, the moss growths that hang from tree branches consist largely of *Isothecium stoloniferum* (fig. 22; pl. 31). This is an exceedingly variable species, however, and in other situations it grows very differently. The stringy form that festoons branches is also found on tree trunks; in less humid situations away from the coast it

22. Festoons of moss (mostly *Isothecium stoloniferum*) in a humid coastal forest

is substantially restricted to this habitat. The growths are almost hair-like and may be more than 20 cm long. The narrow leaves, about 1 mm long, are widest near the base and have tiny teeth along the margins, but only above the middle. (The teeth are so small that they cannot usually be seen with a hand lens.) The sporophyte, usually 1 to 1.5 cm tall, has a twisted stalk when dry; the capsule, about 3 mm by 1 mm, nods slightly, and the calyptra falls away early.

More robust forms of *I. stoloniferum* look so different from the one just described that it is hard to believe they are of the same species. The sporophytes are identical, however, and the leaves, even if larger and of a different shape, are nevertheless toothed along the margins of the half nearest the tip. A form that grows in shady places—on tree trunks, rotting logs, and rocks—has side branches that reach a length of approximately 1.5 cm, and its leaves are about 3 mm long by 1 mm wide. A still more compact form, sometimes almost yellow in color, grows in rocky places that are exposed to considerable sun. Its branches are crowded and only about 1.5 cm long. The leaves are proportionately broader than those of other forms, and generally 2 mm long by 1 mm wide.

THALLOID LIVERWORTS

Conocephalum conicum (pl. 33) is a large and distinctive species with lobes up to about 1.5 cm wide. It is likely to be found only in wet places. It may grow on soil or on decaying wood, and is usually associated with one or more species of moss. The thallus has an almost leathery appearance and is characterized by conspicuous pores. Like most liverworts of the same general type, it branches dichotomously. The little buttons noted on some plants are umbrella-shaped upgrowths of the thallus, on the undersides of which the microscopic eggs are produced. The eggs, after being fertilized by sperm formed in wartlike protuberances on the thallus, develop into small, almost globular sporophytes. When the spores are ripe and ready to be shed, the umbrellas are raised up on slender stalks, and soon afterward they wither. The spores that germinate successfully produce new thalli.

The hornwort, *Anthoceros* (pl. 33), is not, strictly speaking, a liverwort. This is partly because its sporophyte—a slender, upright rod that splits lengthwise to liberate its spores—has chlorophyll and is therefore as green as the thalloid gametophyte. It is easier to deal with it here, however, than to make a separate heading just for it. We have only a few species. The gametophytes are generally in the neighborhood of 1 cm across. The sporophytes, mostly 2 to 4 cm tall, stick up like stiff little grass seedlings; as they split open progressively from the tip, they turn black. *Anthoceros* is more likely to be found in somewhat open places rather than in woods. It is sometimes common, however, in woodland situations where the ground has been disturbed.

LEAFY LIVERWORTS

Porella (pl. 33) is a particularly common and easily recognized genus that grows on branches and tree trunks, and sometimes on shaded rocks. Because it has "leaves," it superficially resembles certain mosses. The leaves are broad, about 2 mm long, and glossy when moist. They have smooth margins and are arranged in two rows, partially overlapping one another. If you look at the underside of a branch of *Porella,* you will see that each leaf has a secondary lobe tucked away under it and that there is also a series of small leaves running along the stem. The color is usually dark olive green. The sporophytes are plump and have blackish brown capsules that crack open when ripe. *Porella* is less likely to be noticed when dry than when wet, but just one prolonged rain is enough to revive it.

Several other genera—some with leaves as large or larger than those of *Porella,* others with very small leaves—are regularly found in our region, especially on bark of tree trunks or branches and on decaying logs. Certain of the tiny species, with leaves less than 1 mm long, produce sporophytes that may reach a height of more than 1 cm. In most species, when the sporophyte is nearly ready to discharge its spores, the delicate, watery stalk takes just a few hours to reach its full length, and the blackish capsule splits, usually into four divergent units that form a little cross.

ALGAE

Except for a few species that make feltlike mats on moist soil, the algae found in terrestrial environments are strictly microscopic types. Their presence will ordinarily not be noted unless they form recognizable coatings (pl. 40) on bark, old wood, and rock. The one-celled green algae that regularly do this belong to the genera *Apatococcus* and *Desmococcus,* which can only be separated on the basis of their cell structure. These algae, better known under the name "protococcus," multiply by division and are scattered by wind and water. The coatings resemble films of dull green paint and are most impressive on walls of old barns and on relatively smooth-barked trees growing where there is at least a moderate amount of light and moisture. Although it is often said that protococcus grows best on the north sides of trees, this is not necessarily the case.

Coatings that are bright yellow or decidedly grayish green, or that are especially thick and chalky when dry, are lichens in which one-celled green algae are mixed with fungi. Unless reproductive structures are elaborated by the fungal component, lichenologists are reluctant to apply names to such combinations.

FUNGI

The classification of fungi is an involved subject and requires an understanding of microscopic details of the reproductive cycle. In any case, some closely related fungi may be superficially dissimilar, and vice versa. The molds, for example, do not constitute a single unified group, and certain of them are related to larger fungi that some people might loosely call mushrooms. This is not the place to go into complexities. It will be best simply to point out that most fungi with real "substance"—something you can pick up or tear off without having first to scratch it off with a fingernail—belong to the Ascomycetes and Basidiomycetes.

ASCOMYCETES

The Ascomycetes include some yeasts and molds—including the one from which penicillin is derived—as well as the so-called cup fungi and morels. The unity of the group as a whole is based to a large extent on the fact that after two sex cells unite, there is formed a type of cell called an ascus, whose contents divide into spores (usually four or eight). In cup fungi the many asci are crowded on the inside face of a fleshy cup. In the morels and their allies there is a structure comparable to a cup, but it is turned inside out, usually convoluted, and mounted on a stalk, as the cap of a mushroom is.

Probably our most common and conspicuous cup fungus is *Aleuria aurantia* (pl. 34). In autumn, after the rainy season has set in, it can usually be found in areas where land has been cleared or new roads have been made. Its cups, each rather firmly attached to the soil, are thin, bright orange, and generally about 2 to 4 cm in diameter. They are neatest when they are young, intact, and unsullied by splashing mud; as they age, they crack at the edges, and the intensity of the orange color diminishes.

Aleuria is just one of many cup fungi in our region. There are types with deeper cups, and some in which the cups are scarcely concave. They come in many colors—white, yellow, orange, brown, red, and even purple. But *Aleuria* is probably the most ostentatious of the more common larger species.

Morels are more likely to be found in brushy places or deciduous woods than in a coniferous forest, but they may as well be discussed here with the cup fungi. They generally show up in spring, in situations where leaves that fell in autumn and have become compacted are just beginning to dry out. *Morchella esculenta* (fig. 23) is one of several fairly common species prized by mushroom hunters.

23. Morel, *Morchella esculenta*

In species of *Helvella* and *Gyromitra* the cap is usually shaped something like a saddle, although it may be thrown into complicated convolutions. *Gyromitra infula* (pl. 34) is one of several fairly common species in this region. It reaches a height of about 10 cm, and the cap is generally dark reddish brown. The slightly yellowish stalk is usually smooth, or just slightly porous. In another common species, *Helvella lacunosa,* the color of the cap varies from nearly white to dark gray; the stalk is ridged and has many oblong pits. A large plant may be 20 cm tall.

BASIDIOMYCETES

The true mushrooms, bracket fungi, bird-nest fungi, puffballs, and a few other diverse types belong in the Basidiomycetes. They are unified by the fact that after sexual fusion of the two nuclei in certain cells occurs, a club-shaped or elongate body, called the basidium, is formed. At the tip of each basidium four spores emerge, and these are shed when they are ripe. In mushrooms the basidia are concentrated either on radially arranged gills or on vertical tubes that open by pores on the underside of the cap. Bracket fungi also usually have pores. In other types, the basidia may be situated all over the surface, at the tips of branches, in the center of a globular mass, on toothlike downgrowths, or elsewhere. Mushrooms are intentionally omitted from this book because of the availability of authoritative references on the common species found in the Northwest. A few distinctive fungi, however, that might not be appreciated as Basidiomycetes will be mentioned.

Bracket fungi, or shelf fungi, are woody or leathery relatives of mushrooms. They have no stalk, except perhaps when young; the cap is simply attached by one side to a tree trunk, exposed root, or fallen log. It is only fair to say that the natural group (Polyporaceae) to which bracket fungi belong also includes some stalked types. But whether bracketlike or stalked, the underside of the cup is generally porous, as in mushrooms of the type called boletes, or clod-fungi.

Several genera and many species of bracket fungi are found in our region, but most of them cannot be identified except by experts. *Polyporus oregonensis (Ganoderma oregonensis)* (pl. 34) is easily recognized, especially in the case of a reasonably fresh growth, because of its shiny, dark brown upper surface. The porous lower surface is nearly flat and almost white. This species, which may reach a diameter of about 20 cm, grows out of the bark of Douglas fir and other conifers, and may be found on living trees as well as on stumps and fallen logs. Younger specimens may be distinctly stalked, but the stalk is usually soon obliterated.

Dryad's saddle, *Polyporus applanatus (Ganoderma applanatum)* (pl. 34), is typically rather flat and light brown above, pure white below. The whiteness is so superficial that the lightest touch of a finger will wipe it away and expose the darker tissue beneath. Dryad's saddle lives for several years and may reach a width of more than 50 cm. It is found on living or dead conifers and deciduous trees.

Another general type of *Polyporus* (pl. 34) forms rather thin shelves in which the upper surface is velvety and marked by narrow, nearly concentric bands that range from white to brown, reddish, and greenish, and sometimes even to bluish or blackish. The shelves become hard and generally curl at the margins when they are dry, but they soften and perk up after a good rain.

In a puffball (fig. 24) the portion of the plant that is above ground forms a globular or ovoid mass, and within the upper part of this is a multitude of tiny cavities in which spores are produced. Eventually, the puffball cracks open at the top and the spores can escape. We have a number of species, but anyone who needs to know what they are had better find an expert. Earth-stars (fig. 25) are similar to puffballs, but they have an inner, thin-walled capsule that remains intact for a time after the outer coat splits apart into several radial segments. The spores are formed within this capsule and released through an opening at its tip. Pressing just lightly on the capsule may force some spores out in what looks like a puff of smoke. Our more common kinds reach a diameter of about 3 cm before they crack open.

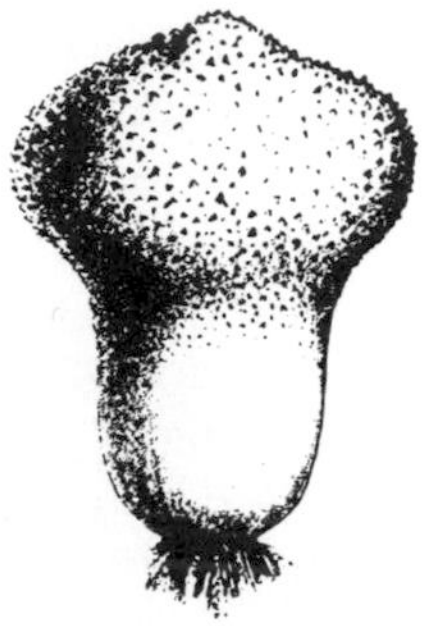

24. A puffball

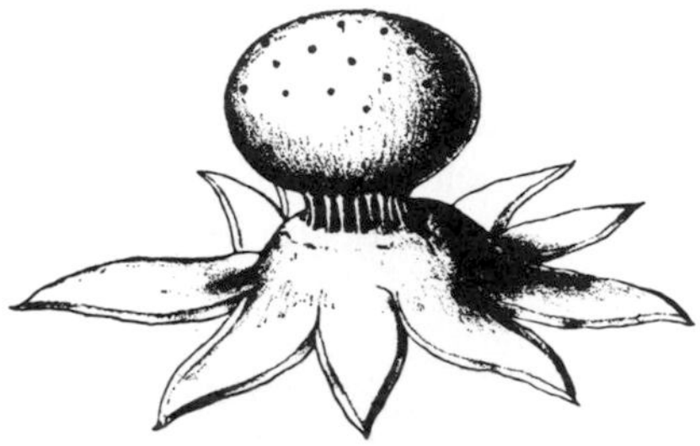

25. An earthstar

Bird-nest fungi form cup-shaped growths that open up at the top to expose several little masses that resemble eggs. These contain the basidia on which the spores are borne, and they must eventually crack open. In at least certain species, the "eggs" can be knocked out by raindrops, or perhaps be dislodged and even carried away by insects. The most prevalent bird-nest fungus in our region seems to be *Crucibulum vulgare* (pl. 34). Its cup reaches a diameter of slightly less than 1 cm, and the inside of its rim is usually white. It grows almost exclusively on small twigs that are partially embedded in soil or leaf litter.

Witches' butter, *Dacrymyces palmatus* (pl. 34), is an unusual basidiomycete that decorates dead branches and stumps, especially those in which decay has scarcely begun. It is gelatinous in texture, usually lumpy or convoluted, and bright orange-yellow, looking much like a big jelly bean that has been partly melted. The spore-producing tissue is at the surface. When this fungus dries out, there is almost nothing left of it. The common name comes from the fanciful idea that witches leave dabs of butter for elves and pixies carrying on in the woods at night.

LICHENS

A lichen is a double plant consisting of a fungus and an alga. The former is almost always one of the cup fungi, or Ascomycetes, and this is often superficially apparent in the shape of the fruiting body. The alga is usually one of the green algae of the same general type as those that form powdery green coatings on tree trunks. There are lichens, however, that contain a blue-green alga, or that have both a green and a blue-green alga.

The symbiotic associations between the algae and fungi that constitute lichens have fascinated biologists for a long time. The subject has become more and more involved as the physiological interrelationships have been investigated. Only the algal component can make food from inorganic substances by photosynthesis; the fungus must therefore depend on it and on soluble organic materials available in the environment. In any case, the combination of alga and fungus is a durable one, as will be perfectly evident to anyone who has seen patches of lichen growing on otherwise bare rock in the deserts or at high altitudes. Curiously, some species tough enough to grow happily for centuries on stone walls and church steeples in cities are dying out because of air pollution.

The body of a lichen is called the thallus. On the basis of the way their thalli are superficially organized, lichens can be arranged in four general categories: crustose lichens are those that form compact crusts on rock or bark; foliose types have decidedly leaflike elaborations; squamulose species are those in which the thallus appears to consist of crowded scales; and fruticose lichens are bushy. Not all lichens fit perfectly into one or another of these categories, but the terms are helpful.

Most lichens have cup-shaped or disk-shaped fruiting bodies, called apothecia, and spores may actually be produced in microscopic sacs within these. It is not clear to what extent the spores function in yielding a fungus that then is joined by the appropriate kind of alga. It is definite, however, that minute outgrowths that develop on the surface of many lichens may start new plants after they break away. These outgrowths, called soredia or isidia, depending on the way they originate, contain cells of both the alga and the fungus.

Lichens are given Latin names and are pigeonholed into groups in much the same way as other plants. The classification is based in part on form and microscopic structure, and in part on chemical tests. Some lichen "species" (remember that they consist of at least two separate species) are impossible to identify positively without testing them chemically to get a color reaction or to determine the presence or absence of particular substances, especially organic acids peculiar to some lichens. The descriptions and illustrations provided in this guide will help you recognize a number of common, widespread, and distinctive species. But there are many other kinds of lichens in our region, and some of them look much like the species that are dealt with in this and subsequent chapters. So do not push your luck too far. If you want to be able to distinguish the look-alikes, find one or more of the helpful references listed in the bibliography, get a microscope, a razor blade, and the essential chemical solutions, and prepare to enjoy yourself. Our lichen flora is fairly well known, but as progress has been made in understanding certain genera and species, their names may have been changed. Some useful older references employ names that must be reconciled with those in more recent works.

Shady woods generally have relatively few species of lichens, and most of these will be found growing on trunks and branches of trees and shrubs. The number of species growing on soil, rocks, and fallen logs is usually greater in open woods, at the edges of woods, and in clearings. Some of the species that will be described here are really more common in these somewhat exposed situations.

FRUTICOSE LICHENS

The extensively branched lichens that form grayish, beardlike growths, especially on branches of deciduous shrubs, are members of the genus *Usnea.* There are several species in our region, and it is unwise to try to separate these on the basis of superficial characteristics. The predominant species is *Usnea hirta,* old man's beard (pl. 35). This species branches repeatedly, and even in a large plant—one that hangs down for 6 or 7 cm—the main stalk may be no more than 1 mm thick. Although closely related usneas are difficult to distinguish, there is one feature that is decidedly characteristic of the group as a whole: when a branch is pulled until it breaks, it shows a central white core, a layer external to this, and another layer on the outside. Thus it resembles an insulated wire. Old man's beard and most other usneas do not often show fruiting bodies. When these do develop they are disklike and up to 5 or 6 mm in diameter. The little bumps regularly found on these lichens are simply bits of the plant that may break away and start new growths.

Two look-alikes often found with *Usnea* are *Ramalina farinacea* (pl. 35) and *Evernia prunastri* (pl. 35). Although both usually become pendent after they reach a certain size, they are not as extensively branched as *Usnea,* and the lobes of their thalli are decidedly flattened; the width of the larger lobes is generally between 1 and 3 mm. The color ranges from yellowish or cream to pale gray or olive gray, and soredia are plentiful. Now what is the easiest way to tell them apart? In *R. farinacea* the thallus-lobes are the same color on both surfaces; in *E. prunastri* one side is usually lighter than the other, especially in plants that are decidedly grayish. Even more conclusive is the appearance of a thallus lobe where it has been broken. In *E. prunastri* the core is so cottony that some of the fibers are pulled out beyond the edge; in *R. farinacea* the core is white and slightly fibrous, but not really like cotton. If both species are found growing together, or if they have been kept for a time at the same humidity, *E. prunastri* will probably be more flexible than *R. farinacea.* Neither of these lichens regularly produces fruiting bodies. Those of *R. farinacea* are so small and inconspicuous that they are not easily noted even when present. Those of *E. prunastri* have concave, dark brown disks that may be more than 4 mm in diameter.

Ramalina digitata (pl. 35) is similar in form and color to the two lichens that have just been compared, but it freely produces cup-shaped fruiting bodies near the tips of its lobes. The color of the cups does not differ appreciably from that of the thallus as a whole. This species is less inclined than either *R. farinacea* or *E. prunastri* to become pendent, and its thallus lobes do not become very long.

Sphaerophorus globosus (pl. 35) looks like a bad case of hardened arteries. When dry, it is a very brittle lichen. Each of the main stems, arising from the base, sends out a number of side branches that form little bushy growths. The plant as a whole may be nearly globular, and a large specimen is about 3 cm high. The surface is rather smooth, sometimes almost polished. The color is usually gray, but a reddish or brownish tinge is apparent on some plants. Fruiting bodies are not often noted. They are nearly globular, up to about 2 mm in diameter, and situated at the tips of some of the ultimate branches. When they break open, the concentration of spores within them is blackish and conspicuous. In our area this lichen prefers the bark of Douglas fir, but it is uncommon in the lowlands, except in ravines of larger streams rushing down from the mountains. At elevations of about 500 to 1000 m, however, it may be extremely abundant.

FOLIOSE LICHENS

Hypogymnia physodes (pl. 36) is abundant on bark of deciduous trees as well as conifers. Although the thallus branches extensively, the patches of this lichen tend to be rather compact and tightly bound to the bark, except at the edge of the colony, where the somewhat swollen tips of the ultimate lobes usually are pulled slightly away. If you slice a lobe with a razor blade, you will see that it is hollow. The diameter of a large growth may exceed 10 cm. Fruiting bodies are almost never found on this lichen.

Hypogymnia enteromorpha (pl. 36) is characteristically found on bare lower branches of conifers, especially Douglas fir, grand fir, and hemlock. It is easily recognized because the thallus, most of which is free of the bark, has somewhat inflated, tubular lobes branched in a staghornlike pattern.The upper surface is grayish green when moist, and the undersurface is blackish. This species freely produces fruiting bodies. The size of these varies, but they are not often as large as 1 cm in diameter; the color of the inside surface of the cups is generally reddish brown. *Hypogymnia vittata* (pl. 36) is similar, but the tips of its thallus lobes are pointed instead of rounded as in *H. enteromorpha.*

The genus *Parmelia* is closely related to *Hypogymnia,* and it has many variable and confusing species that must have driven more than one lichenologist to drink. The thallus lobes of parmelias are not inflated or hollow. *Parmelia sulcata* (pl. 36) is especially common in our region. It is light gray above, blackish below, and sticks almost like wallpaper to bark, especially of deciduous trees, to fence posts, and sometimes to rock. Close inspection will show that the upper surface has a network of delicate ridges. This species rarely produces fruiting cups, but does usually have tiny reproductive pustules along the ridges or at the margins.

Platismatia glauca (pl. 36) is abundant on branches, especially of various deciduous trees and shrubs, and on the denuded lower branches of conifers. The way it grows is reminiscent of a loose head of crinkly-leaved lettuce. The lobes of the thallus, about 1 cm wide, are often torn. *Platismatia glauca* is grayish above, dark brown or blackish below, and does not form fruiting bodies. *Platismatia stenophylla* (pl. 36) and *P. herrei* have narrow, branching lobes, generally pale olive, greenish gray, or yellowish. The former freely produces fruiting cups. *Platismatia herrei* almost never has them, and may also be distinguished by the fact that the margins of its thallus lobes are fringed by minute outgrowths capable of starting new plants.

The genus *Peltigera* consists of coarse foliose lichens found on soil or in beds of moss, and sometimes on mossy tree trunks. They will be most common in somewhat open woods. *Peltigera canina* (pl. 37) forms extensive growths in which the individual lobes are regularly at least 1 cm wide. Its color above is usually brown or greenish brown when wet, gray when dry; the underside is whitish, with distinct veins and hairlike downgrowths. The fruiting bodies, arising from the margins of the lobes, are brown or reddish brown. When they are well developed, they remind one of long fingernails. The algal symbiont in *P. canina* is *Nostoc,* one of the blue-green algae.

Peltigera aphthosa (pl. 37) is somewhat similar to *P. canina* in size and habit of growth, but its upper surface is bright green and dotted with little dark brown tubercles. These are interesting because they contain

Nostoc, while elsewhere in the thallus a green alga, *Coccomyxa,* is present. The fruiting bodies, formed at the margins of the lobes, resemble those of *P. canina.*

The lungwort, *Lobaria pulmonaria* (pl. 37), is one of the coarser lichens of our region. It is loosely attached to trunks and branches of trees, both coniferous and deciduous species, especially where there is considerable rainfall. It is so easily torn off by wind that it is often found strewn about on the ground. The thallus, which branches irregularly into broad, flat lobes, may be more than 20 cm across. The upper surface, bright green when moist, has ridges that run together to form a networklike pattern. Certain of the ridges may break up into little raised pustules. The underside is usually white with brown markings. The common name of this lichen goes back several centuries, to the time when diseases were often treated by using plants that resembled whichever part of the body seemed to need attention. The upper surface of *L. pulmonaria* does somewhat resemble the inner surface of a lung. *Lobaria oregana* is a similar species, but it lacks the little pustules characteristic of *L. pulmonaria,* and the lobes of its thallus are usually much broader.

CRUSTOSE LICHENS

Mycoblastus sanguinarius (pl. 38) is especially noticeable on the light-colored bark of alders and willows, but it is found on other deciduous trees, as well as on conifers. It forms a thin, gray coating dotted with convex, black fruiting bodies up to about 2 mm in diameter. If a fruiting body is sectioned, the tissue under it is bright red. This accounts for its specific name, as well as for the fact that it is sometimes called the clot lichen.

Ochrolechia pallescens (pl. 38) is another small species, but one that is fairly easy to recognize. Its encrustations, particularly easy to see on smooth bark of alders and willows, are gray or whitish gray and very thin. The disklike fruiting bodies, up to nearly 2 mm in diameter, are flat or slightly concave; they are mostly yellowish, but have white rims.

Lecidea cinnabarina (pl. 38) is fairly abundant, especially on portions of conifer branches that no longer have live twigs. In spite of its attractive fruiting bodies, which are about 2 mm in diameter and of an almost vermilion color, it is apt to be missed unless one looks closely at the bark. The thallus forms a thin, grayish coating.

Species of *Pertusaria* produce light-colored encrustations—usually whitish or grayish—on tree trunks and branches. *Pertusaria amara* (pl. 38) can be positively identified if the white, powdery soredial heaps that erupt from low warts on the thallus taste bitter, like quinine. (A little of *P. amara* will keep reminding you of it for a long time!) *Pertusaria multipuncta* has similar soredial heaps, but lacks a noticeably bitter taste. In addition, it often produces a few disklike fruiting bodies, less than 1 mm in diameter, which range from nearly white to black. *Pertusaria ambigens* (pl. 38) does not have soredial heaps, but it regularly has fruiting bodies about 1 mm across; as these age, their margins usually become cracked.

An odd lichen found on bark, especially of alder and other deciduous trees, is *Graphis scripta* (pl. 38). The plant actually pervades the bark, but the fruiting bodies erupt into blackish markings that suggest some ancient form of writing.

A Few Invertebrate Animals

SNAILS AND SLUGS

The humid woods of the Pacific Northwest have an interesting and varied fauna of land molluscs. Some of the common species will probably not be seen unless they are looked for under logs, but others crawl fearlessly in the open, at least at certain times of the year. Most of our native snails and slugs feed on fungi, decaying fruits, and dung; but a few consume foliage of herbaceous plants, and certain types are carnivorous. They all have a spongy lung, which air enters and leaves by a pore on the right side of the body.

As slugs are snails that have lost their shells in the course of their evolution, it seems fitting to discuss snails first. Our most striking species is *Monadenia fidelis* (pl. 41). Its shell, whose diameter may exceed 3.5 cm, is typically chestnut brown, with one or more darker bands, or with both darker and lighter bands. Shells that have yellow bands are especially pretty. The body of the animal is usually reddish and smells of garlic. *Monadenia* is most likely to be found crawling in the open during late spring.

Haplotrema sportella (fig. 26; pl. 41) and *H. vancouverense* (fig. 26) are also attractive snails, especially if examined closely. Their shells have a flattened spire and are greenish yellow; the animals are pearly white. The two species can be separated on the basis of the extent to which the upper lip of the aperture dips down. The dip is pronounced in specimens of *H. sportella* that are at least 2 cm in diameter, but in *H. vancouverense* it never becomes conspicuous, and only begins to show up about the time the shell reaches a diameter of about 2 cm.

Another common species in some areas is *Vespericola columbiana* (pl. 41). The shell is brown and beset with fine hairs, although these do not persist long after the snail dies. The animal itself is pale brown.

The diameter of the shell, up to about 1.5 cm, is slightly greater than the height. The aperture has a thickened lip.

Allogona townsendiana (pl. 41) is a close relative of *Vespericola* and shows the same sort of thickening at the lip. It is a much larger snail, however, with a shell diameter that may reach 2.5 cm. The shell is not hairy, but the whorls are sculptured by rather prominent lines. In most specimens the polished brown outer covering is at least partially eroded away, so the whitish, limy substance of the shell shows through. The living animal is very light brown. *Allogona* is generally common in humid forests near the coast, but in inland situations it tends to be limited to ravines and to woods that are not far from a stream or marsh. It is most active in late spring.

26. *Haplotrema sportella* (above) and *H. vancouverense* (below)

The banana slug, *Ariolimax columbianus* (pl. 42), is the largest land mollusc in our region. Its length frequently reaches 15 cm, and the opening to the lung, on the right side of the mantle hump, is obvious. The upper surface of that part of the foot behind the hump is strongly keeled. The color varies from individual to individual and from population to population. Most specimens are olive or brownish olive, with or without black blotches and spots. In some localities almost all individuals are so dark as to be nearly black. Very rarely, albinistic specimens are reported. These are ghostly, and their appearance reminds one of white candlewax.

The banana slug is a woodland species, but it gets into suburban yards. It eats a variety of foods and is not a serious garden pest, although it is capable of damaging cultivated plants. The presence of banana slugs in your garden is a pleasant reminder that you are close to nature, and they are interesting enough to tolerate even if they nip off a little new growth once in a while. Unfortunately, this species is attracted to commercial slug baits designed for the really destructive introduced kinds, so its visits may end in disaster even if you do not intentionally persecute it.

Prophysaon andersoni (pl. 42) is another common species that may occasionally turn up in suburban gardens. It reaches a length of about 6 cm and can be identified positively by the following combination of characters: the lung opening, on the right side, is near the middle of the mantle hump; there is usually a dark lateral band on each side of the mantle, and these do not extend backward to the foot; the upper surface of the foot is marked in a diamond-mesh pattern. The general coloration of *P. andersoni* varies from nearly lemon yellow to reddish brown, and the slime varies from yellow to orange. The only species with which this slug might be confused are *Arion circumscriptus* and *A. hortensis,* which are pests in gardens. In these, however, the dark bands on the mantle are continued, after a slight interruption, on the dorsal surface of the foot.

If you find a slug with a thin, partly exposed horny plate—actually a much-reduced shell—near the back of the mantle hump, it will be one species or another of *Hemphillia.* The slugs of this genus, which are found under logs, can twitch so violently that they may almost leap out of one's hand. Not all of the specimens that have been reported from widely scattered localities have been studied with sufficient care to make certain that they fit into the few described species. It is probably safe to say, however, that any *Hemphillia* found in the Cascades near Portland is likely to be *H. malonei* (pl. 42). It has been taken at elevations of up to about 1300 m (4250 feet), but it is also found in the lower reaches of ravines running down to the Columbia River Gorge. Large specimens are about 4 cm long. The coloration is typically brown, with darker mottlings. The horny plate is yellowish and translucent. That portion of the foot behind the mantle is decidedly lower than the hump and does not have a strong dorsal keel. *Hemphillia glandulosa,* which has a warty mantle hump and a sharp dorsal keel on the foot, is largely limited to the coastal strip. Some other species of *Hemphillia* have been described from the Olympic Peninsula.

SOWBUGS

The sowbugs, or woodlice, belong to a group of crustaceans called isopods. Most isopods are marine, but there are some in fresh water and in damp situations on land. Of the several terrestrial species found in our region, the majority are introductions from the Old World, and these generally stick close to human habitations. In the woods the only native isopod that is at all common is *Ligidium gracile* (fig. 27). When a log under which it is living is lifted, it moves quickly to hide in the loose soil. It has the fragile, moist look of an animal that cannot survive dryness. This species is about 7 mm long and is proportionately more slender than the introduced sowbugs. The color is basically grayish brown, and the body is usually mottled on both sides of a solid median streak.

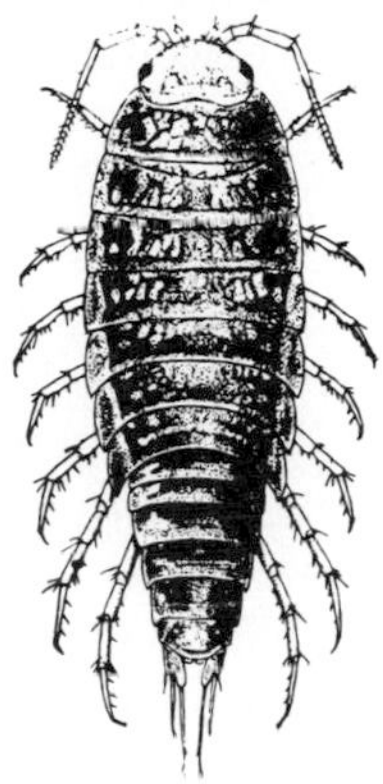

27. *Ligidium gracile*

CENTIPEDES AND MILLIPEDES

The centipedes and millipedes are fairly closely related and superficially look somewhat alike, being elongated and having numerous legs. It is easy enough to tell them apart, however. Just take a good look at the arrangement of the legs. If there is never more than one pair per segment, the animal is a centipede. If there are two pairs of legs on most segments, it is a millipede.

Centipedes live under logs and rocks, under bark, and in soil and leaf litter. They shun the light, and when exposed they immediately start searching for a place to hide. On the segment that follows the head they have a pair of substantial claws, backed up by venom glands, used for capturing prey. Their food includes insects and slugs, so any centipedes found in gardens should be left alone. Some of the larger species in the tropics have a convincing bite, but ours are not dangerous.

There are probably at least twenty species of centipedes in this region, and some of these are less than 1 cm long. Identification of even the more common kinds requires one to become almost a specialist. The most regularly encountered large centipede is *Scolopocryptops sexspinosus.* It reaches a length of about 8 cm and a width of about 5 mm, and has twenty-three pairs of legs. The color is uniformly reddish brown. *Scolopocryptops nigridia* also has twenty-three pairs of legs and is almost as large as *S. sexspinosus,* but it is a little more slender. The head and first and last segments behind the head are reddish brown; the rest of the body is greenish.

Most millipedes are a little more firm-bodied and crunchy than centipedes because their external skeletons are impregnated with salts of calcium. Like centipedes, they are animals of dark places. Their locomotion, however, is slower. Sometime watch the movements of the legs of a millipede. As each successively more anterior pair of legs is put forward, a wave moves up the body toward the head. But of course each pair of legs is then thrust backward again, so it is not long before another wave begins to move forward. Millipedes do not have poison claws, and they are primarily vegetarians and scavengers. Many kinds secrete substances that have pungent, protective odors. Certain species coil up almost like watchsprings, and this habit is probably helpful for self-defense, too.

Most of our millipedes are small and too insignificant to discuss here. The noteworthy types fall into two categories: those that are appreciably flattened and those that are almost cylindrical. The most striking species in the first group is *Harpaphe haydeniana* (pl. 43). It reaches a length of about 4 cm and is black except for the bright yellow patches on the lateral portions of almost all segments. Immature specimens are lighter, and the yellowness of the contrasting patches is less clear. When handled, this species exudes a fluid that has an odor much like that of a commercial extract of almonds. *Kepolydesmus pungo* (pl. 43) is smaller than *H. haydeniana* and proportionately more slender. It reaches a length of about 3 cm and is usually pinkish brown with yellowish patches on the lateral portions of the segments. Its characteristic odor resembles that of vinegar.

The nearly cylindrical millipedes are represented by a number of slender types, mostly less than 3 cm long, whose identification had best be left to experts. The one illustrated (pl. 43) is typical. *Californibolus uncigerus* is a fairly common large species found in Oregon. It is up to 8 cm long and 6 mm wide, and is leaden or silvery black.

3

Oak Woods, Rocky Slopes, and Brushy Areas

THIS chapter deals with some habitats that are abundantly represented in the Willamette Valley and in the Puget Trough, including the San Juan Archipelago and the southern part of Vancouver Island. In general, these situations are characterized by rocky or gravelly soils and are relatively well drained. The pattern of drainage in a particular area, however, may be such that the water moving downhill tends to be concentrated in certain places, and these, as a result, may become soggy in winter and early spring. Water may also saturate pockets of soil that fill depressions in bedrock.

Two of our trees, the Garry oak and madrone, normally grow only in well-drained soils. Where either or both of those trees are prevalent, the landscape will almost invariably include brushy areas, rocky knolls, and grassy slopes. Between March and July the knolls and hillsides produce a marvelous assortment of wildflowers. But in winter and very early spring the licorice-fern and mosses that carpet rocky outcrops are at their greenest and provide a background against which many lichens and the grayish green colonies of the broadleaf stonecrop stand out brightly. The various habitats intergrade, and some of the plants that will be described here are rather versatile. Besides, woods dominated by oaks and madrones are often bordered by coniferous woods or interdigitate freely with them. In certain areas, mossy knolls and grassy hillsides occupy open spaces between stands of conifers, particularly Douglas fir, grand fir, and lodgepole pine. These woods are usually somewhat drier than most coniferous forests. In the San Juan Archipelago and southern part of Vancouver Island, the conifers are regularly diluted by the madrone and Scouler willow, and the Rocky Mountain juniper is locally abundant in clearings. At the same time, many of the plants found in mainland coniferous forests are lacking.

The Garry Oak and Madrone, and Some of Their Associates

A dominant tree on many rocky soils is the Garry oak, *Quercus garryana* (pl. 5), which barely gets into the extreme southern part of the Willamette Valley. It is the only true oak in our region. It is a deciduous species, but the silhouettes of large trees, which may reach a height of 20 m, are handsome at any season.

Sometimes the Garry oak forms almost pure stands, and an area in which most of the specimens are large and well spaced may have the appearance of a park. In 1826, when David Douglas visited the northern part of the Willamette Valley, he described the countryside as "undulating, . . . with beautiful solitary oak and pine [Douglas fir] interspersed through it." Today, however, most groves of Garry oak consist of trees that are close enough together that their crowns form a canopy. These stands have almost certainly developed after savannas of the type Douglas saw were burned over by Indians and early settlers. Indians had long been burning woods, apparently to make it easier to collect honey, grasshoppers, and other foods, and to cause the deer to seek cover in unburned areas, where they could be more easily hunted. Very large trees, with trunks more than 1 m in diameter, are at least three hundred years old and are relicts of the old savannas.

In the Willamette Valley, but not often as far north as Oregon City, the Garry oak is commonly parasitized by the American mistletoe, *Phoradendron flavescens* (fig. 28). Mistletoe is a flowering plant, but it has no true root. The branched structure that penetrates into a limb and that steals water and nutrients from the host comes closest to being a modified stem. The little white "berries" of the mistletoe, traditionally used for decorations at the Christmas season, are so sticky inside that they may make a bird's beak uncomfortable. In rubbing its beak against a branch to get rid of the sticky stuff, a bird may press the seed into a situation where it can germinate. The first leaves do not appear until the second year, after the connection between the young mistletoe and its host is well established. Mistletoe has chlorophyll and is thus equipped to make at least some of its own food, so it is only a partial parasite. The species found on the Garry oak has fleshy, opposite leaves 2 or 3 cm long and clusters of small greenish flowers.

Another oddity associated with the Garry oak is a little green or yellowish ball, usually marked with red, attached to the upper side of some of the leaves (pl. 5). The ball may be up to 3 cm in diameter. This is an abnormal growth—a gall—formed by the oak around a clutch of wormlike larvae belonging to a tiny wasp. The gall-wasp lays its eggs on a bud before the leaves unroll, and as the gall develops,

Vanilla leaf, *Achlys triphylla*

Candyflower, *Montia sibirica*

Miner's lettuce, *Montia perfoliata*

Waterleaf, *Hydrophyllum tenuipes*

nder toothwort, *Cardamine pulcherrima*

Inside-out flower, *Vancouveria hexandra*

False mitrewort, *Tiarella trifoliata*

PLATE 17

Creeping buttercup, *Ranunculus repens*

Western buttercup, *Ranunculus occidentalis*

Three-leaved windflower, *Anemone deltoidea*

Red columbine, *Aquilegia formosa*

Klamath weed, *Hypericum perforatum*

Wild larkspur, *Delphinium menziesii*

Baneberry, *Actaea rubra*

Goatsbeard, *Aruncus sylves*

PLATE 18

Wood-sorrel, *Oxalis oregana*

Bunchberry, *Cornus canadensis*

Large avens, *Geum macrophyllum*

Starflower, *Trientalis latifolia*

Smooth violet, *Viola glabella*

Pacific bleedingheart, *Dicentra formosa*

PLATE 19

Blue violet, *Viola adunca*

California poppy, *Eschscholzia californica*

Indian pipe, *Monotropa uniflora*

Shooting star, *Dodecatheon hendersonii*

Ground cone,
Boschniakia hookeri

Orobanche uniflora, one of the broomrapes

Twinflower, *Linnaea borealis*

PLATE 20

Chickweed, *Cerastium arvense*

Ragged starflower, *Lithophragma parviflora*

Common vetch, *Vicia sativa*

Red clover, *Trifolium pratense*

Buck-bean, *Thermopsis montana*

Centaury, *Centaurium umbellatum*

Red-maids, *Calandrinia ciliata*,
with the moss *Rhacomitrium canescens*

Fiddleneck, *Amsinckia menziesii*

Monkeyflower, *Mimulus guttatus*

Mimulus alsinoides

Skunkweed, *Navarretia squarrosa*

Indian paintbrush,
Castilleja hispida

Blue-eyed Mary,
Collinsia parviflora

Parentucellia viscosa

Foxglove, *Digitalis purpurea*

Mullein, *Verbascum thapsu*

PLATE 22

Spring gold, *Lomatium utriculatum*

Yerba buena, *Satureja douglasii*

Self-heal, *Prunella vulgaris*

Hedge-nettle, *Stachys cooleyae*

Corn-salad, *Plectritis congesta*

Broad-leaved stonecrop,
Sedum spathulifolium

Bigroot, *Marah oreganus*

Campanula scouleri

PLATE 23

Oregon sunshine, *Eriophyllum lanatum*

Trail plant, *Adenocaulon bicolor*

Coltsfoot, *Petasites frigidus*

Gum plant, *Grindelia integrifolia*

Goldenrod, *Solidago canadensis*

Aster subspicatus

Fireweed, *Epilobium angustifo*

PLATE 24

Yarrow, *Achillea millefolium*

Pearly everlasting, *Anaphalis margaritacea*

Canada thistle, *Cirsium arvense*

Bull thistle, *Cirsium vulgare*

Cat's-ear, *Hypochaeris radicata*

Chicory, *Cichorium intybus*

Cat-tail, *Typha latifolia*

Skunk-cabbage, *Lysichitum americanum*

Yellow pond lily, *Nuphar polysepalum*

PLATE 26

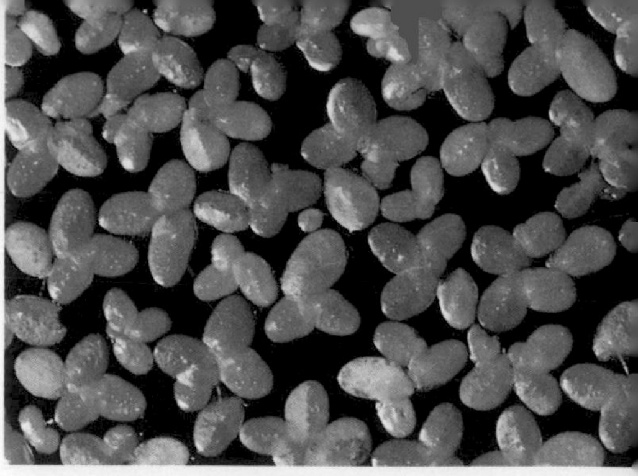

Duckweed, *Lemna minor*

Water-fern, *Azolla mexicana*

Riccia fluitans

Ricciocarpus natans

Sphagnum

Swamp laurel, *Kalmia occidentalis*

Labrador tea, *Ledum groenlandicum*

Cotton-sedge, *Eriophorum chamissonis*

Pacific cinquefoil, *Potentilla pacifica*

Trientalis arctica

PLATE 27

Sword-fern, *Polystichum munitum*

Deer-fern, *Blechnum spicant*

Licorice-fern, *Polypodium vulgare*

Common wood-fern, *Dryopteris austriaca*

Lady-fern, *Athyrium filix-femina*

Bracken, *Pteridium aquilinum*

Coastal shield-fern, *Dryopteris arguta*

Maidenhair spleenwort, *Asplenium trichomanes*

Maidenhair fern, *Adiantum pedatum*

Selaginella wallacei

Selaginella oregana

PLATE 29

Common horsetail, *Equisetum arvense*

Giant horsetail, *Equisetum tel*

Common scouring-rush,
Equisetum hyemale

Clubmoss, *Lycopodium clavatum*

Hair-cap moss,
Polytrichum juniperinum

Pogonatum contortum

Hylocomium splendens

Rhytidiadelphus triquetrus

Rhytidiadelphus loreus

Rhytidiadelphus squarrosus

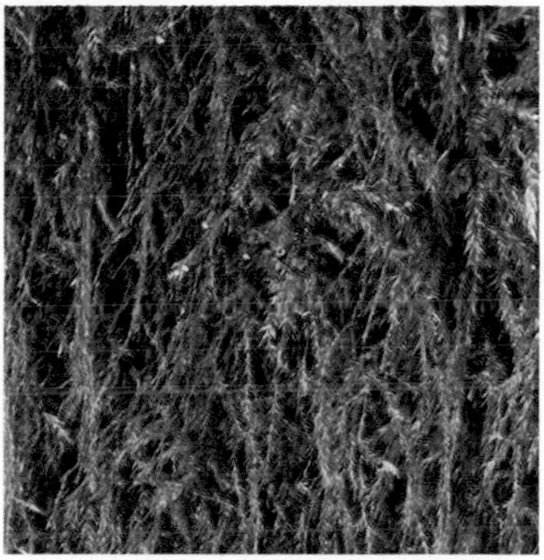

Isothecium stoloniferum

Hypnum subimponens

Eurhynchium oreganum

Orthotrichum lyellii

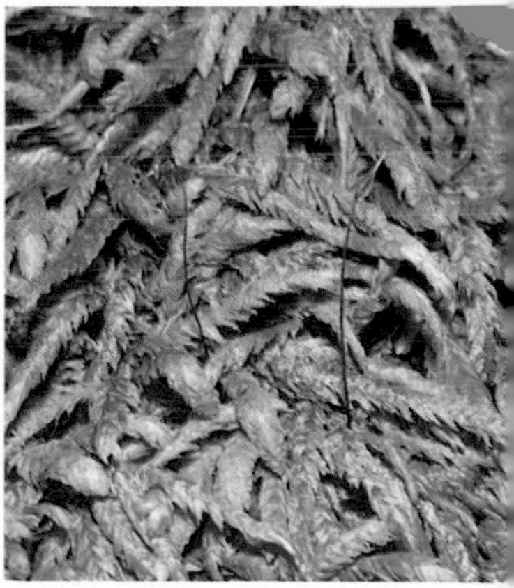

Plagiothecium undulatum

PLATE 31

Tortula muralis

Tortula princeps

Bryum capillare

Funaria hygrometrica

Dicranum scoparium

Aulacomnium androgynum

Dicranoweisia cirrata

Rhacomitrium canescens

PLATE 32

28. American mistletoe, *Phoradendron flavescens*

it encloses the larvae in a chamber suspended in the center by many radiating fibers. In time, the adult wasps emerge. Some galls contain additional species of wasps, which may be viewed as guests. Galls may also be invaded by insects that parasitize the one or more species of wasps that happen to be present. *Cynips maculipennis* is the principal gall-inducing wasp on Garry oak in our region.

In many places where oaks are abundant, they are mixed with other trees. Chief among these are the madrone, the big-leaf maple, cascara, Pacific dogwood, Douglas fir, and grand fir. All of these require at least a little more soil moisture than the Garry oak, and all except the madrone have already been described in connection with coniferous forests.

Arbutus menziesii, the madrone (or arbutus, as many Canadians in British Columbia prefer to call it) (pl. 6), is perhaps our most remarkable tree. Particularly obvious features are its evergreen leaves and the way its reddish brown bark cracks away from the trunk and branches. The leaf blades are broadly oval, shiny and dark green above, much lighter below, and up to about 12 cm long. The flowers, borne in dense clusters in May and June, resemble those of salal and some of its other close relatives in the heath family. The berries, about 7 mm in diameter, are bright orange-red and roughened with tiny tubercles. They ripen in autumn and may still be on the trees at Christmas. Gardeners will note the resemblance of these berries to the decidedly larger fruits of the strawberry tree, *A. unedo,* indigenous to the Mediterranean region. The berries of the madrone are eaten by birds, so the seeds are scattered widely.

The madrone, like the Garry oak, is almost completely restricted to areas where the soil is rocky and well drained, and where it is not completely shaded by other trees. It grows vigorously in some places around Puget Sound (as along Hood Canal), and also in the San Juan Archipelago and on both sides of the Strait of Georgia in British Columbia. It is not limited to situations close to salt water, for it is abundant in portions of the Willamette Valley, especially in the general vicinity of Lake Oswego and Oregon City. The admirable Archibald Menzies, botanist on Vancouver's expedition to the Northwest, received the supreme honor of having been commemorated in the scientific names of both the madrone and the Douglas fir.

The complex of shrubs, vines, wildflowers, grasses, and ferns forming the understory in oak woods varies according to physical features of the site. The extent to which the land slopes, the direction that the slope faces, and the characteristics of the soil influence, among other things, the availability of moisture. Thus some of the shrubs regularly found in coniferous forests—snowberry, hazelnut, osoberry, ocean spray, and thimbleberry—may not be abundant in more moist sites, but are rare or absent in exceedingly dry situations. There is one shrub, however, that is almost routinely associated with Garry oak: poison oak. It is proportionately more abundant among oaks growing in dry situations.

Poison oak, *Toxicodendron diversiloba (Rhus diversiloba)* (pl. 12), is not limited to oak woods, for it grows in many brushy places and sometimes in coniferous woods, especially if the soil is rocky. It is prevalent in the Willamette Valley and the Columbia River Gorge, and its range extends up the Puget Trough to the southern portion of Puget Sound. Fortunately, it does not occur in the San Juan Archipelago or on Vancouver Island, where there are many situations, with and without oaks, that would seem to be just right for it.

This plant can bring absolute misery to any who are seriously affected by an oil found in the leaves, stems, and roots. The usual symptoms—itching and the formation of watery blisters—usually do not appear until a day or two after contact. It is wise to wash oneself and one's clothing thoroughly with soap and water as soon as possible after touching any part of a poison oak bush. The average person is not likely to have a violent reaction, but it is best not to take chances.

Poison oak is sometimes called poison ivy, but this name is generally restricted to certain species of *Toxicodendron* whose range does not quite extend into our region. The sumac family (Anacardiaceae), to which *Toxicodendron* belongs, also includes the mango, the so-called pepper trees cultivated in southern California, and many other plants of horticultural importance. Poison oak is variable in its habit of growth. Generally it is a shrub just 1 or 2 m high, but sometimes, especially in shady woods, it will climb up into trees for 10 m or more. Positive identification is a matter of much concern to those who love the outdoors but do not want to start itching after they come home. It is easily recognized when it is in leaf, from late spring to fall. The leaves have three leaflets, which are oval, dark green, and very shiny. The leaflets are usually 3 or 4 cm long, sometimes slightly pointed, sometimes blunt; the two lower ones may have a small side lobe. The flowers, in rather dense clusters, are small and greenish. In the autumn most of the leaves turn pale yellow before they fall, but some turn red. The globular fruits, white and about 5 mm in diameter, persist into the winter. Even if there are no fruits, poison oak can be identified by its habit of branching. The branches are alternate and tend to be fairly short and thick; those originating near the bases of the main stems are often not markedly longer than those higher up.

Few of the common or conspicuous wildflowers found in oak woods are strictly limited to this habitat. Most of them are species that live in other places where the soil is well drained and there is light shade. Because many oak woods intergrade with brushy areas and with open, grassy situations, it seems best to treat the wildflowers of all these habitats as a unit. This will be done later on in this chapter. A few species that occur regularly—if not exclusively—with the Garry oak should be mentioned, however. These are the Columbia lily (pl. 14), fawn-lily (pl. 14), rice-root lily (pl. 14), and yerba buena (pl. 23). Yerba buena, a low creeper of the mint family, is rarely missing from an oak woods.

Some wildflowers likely to be found in a coniferous forest and others already described in chapter 2, may also be represented. Chief among these are bedstraw (fig. 21), sweet-cicely (fig. 16), and fringecup (fig. 12).

Of the ferns that should be expected in an oak woods, three species are described elsewhere. These are the bracken (pl. 29), sword-fern (pl. 28), and licorice-fern (pl. 28). Licorice-fern is most likely to be found on mossy trunks and branches, or among rocks. A fourth species, which in our region is substantially restricted to oak woods, is the coastal shield-fern, *Dryopteris arguta* (pl. 29). It is an evergreen type, with rather tough, light green leaves 30 or 40 cm long. The blades, widest at the base, have the outline of a tall triangle. They are divided twice, never three times as in the case of the common wood-fern, a close relative that lives in moist coniferous woods. The petiole of the leaf, and the continuation of it into the blade and its side branches, are studded with chaffy scales. The shield-fern is rather regularly associated with the Garry oak in the Willamette Valley, but farther north it is uncommon or absent altogether.

Shrubs, Small Trees, and Vines of Brushy Areas

Situations where shrubs and small trees predominate will usually be found around the edges of coniferous forests and oak woods. But they also occur at the margins of meadows and marshes, as well as on hillsides, in open fields, and along roadsides. Many brushy areas, in fact, are essentially zones of intergradation between one type of habitat and another.

This section deals with small trees, shrubs, and vines typical of brushy places. They are not all necessarily found together. Some of them prefer wet places, whereas others normally occur only in dry situations. The species in the list below should be learned first, for most of them are both widespread and abundant. Poison oak was discussed earlier in this chapter, in connection with Garry oak. The species marked with an asterisk were described in chapter 2, for they are common in coniferous forests. The majority of them, however, grow best in comparatively open habitats. Hardhack, red elderberry, creek dogwood, and Pacific willow are substantially restricted to places that are wet all year long.

*Oregon grape
poison oak
baldhip rose
Nootka rose
serviceberry
*thimbleberry
*blackcap
*salmonberry
ninebark
*ocean spray
hardhack
*osoberry
Western crabapple
red hawthorn (introduced)
*red currant
mock-orange
*snowberry
redstem ceanothus
red elderberry
blue elderberry
creek dogwood
*hazelnut
Pacific willow
Scouler willow

Of the vines found in brushy situations, the more abundant natives are the orange honeysuckle, hairy honeysuckle, and dewberry. The evergreen blackberry and Himalayan blackberry, however, have become so well naturalized in our region that they may look as though they belong in the landscape.

For convenience, the small trees and shrubs will be divided into two groups: those in which the leaves and branches are opposite, and those in which they are alternate. There are so few perennial vines that these require no subheadings.

SHRUBS AND SMALL TREES WITH OPPOSITE LEAVES AND BRANCHES

Snowberry (pl. 11), an important constituent of coniferous woods, is also prevalent in brushy situations. It is, in fact, the shrub that makes many places brushy, even though it does not often grow more than 2 m high. The honeysuckle family, to which it belongs, is also represented in our region by some vines that will be discussed later on, as well as a shrubby type of honeysuckle, two species of elderberry, and the oval-leaved viburnum.

The red elderberry, *Sambucus racemosa* variety *arborescens* (pl. 12), grows up to 5 or 6 m tall. Its leaves generally have five or seven leaflets, and each of these is about twice as long as wide. The small, cream-colored flowers are concentrated in a dense, pyramidal inflorescence. The fruits, of course, are bright red; they are about 5 mm in diameter and ripen in summer. The blue elderberry, *S. cerulea* (pl. 12), rarely exceeds a height of 4 m. Its leaves usually have seven or nine leaflets, which are two and a half or three times as long as wide. The flowers are borne in a nearly flat-topped head. The fruits, about 5 mm in diameter, are basically blue-black, but they are covered by a waxy coating that makes them pale blue.

The two kinds of elderberry do not often mix. The red elderberry grows best near the coast and in wet places in the northern part of the Puget Trough. The blue elderberry is the more common species in the Willamette Valley. Both have a wide distribution, however, even if one or the other is likely to occur in a particular place.

The bush honeysuckle, *Lonicera involucrata* (pl. 11), grows luxuriantly near the coast, reaching a height of 3 or 4 m. Inland, and in drier situations around Puget Sound and the Strait of Georgia, it tends to be small and straggly, except at the edges of marshes. The narrowly oval leaves are mostly about 5 to 8 cm long and have very short petioles. Under especially favorable conditions, they are dark green and almost leathery, but where the bush honeysuckle is struggling to exist the leaves are bright green and thin. The flowers are typically borne in pairs and have pale yellow petals that are joined for most of their length. The free portions of the petals are equal, however, so the flowers are not two-lipped as in most members of the genus *Lonicera*. Beneath each pair of flowers are two pairs of leafy bracts. The upper bracts are at first larger than the lower ones; but as the fruits develop, they all become more or less equal, and eventually turn an attractive purplish red color. The fruits, about 1 cm in diameter, are black when ripe. They are so disagreeably bitter that no one seems inclined to see if they are as poisonous as some have claimed.

The genus *Viburnum,* which has supplied gardeners with many admirable shrubs, is represented in our region by just one species, the oval-leaved viburnum, *V. ellipticum* (pl. 12). It is perhaps most dependably found in the foothills of the Cascades, especially along streams that run down into the Willamette Valley. It does turn up elsewhere, however, although its distribution is a little spotty. This shrub grows to a height of about 3 m. Its leaf blades, on short petioles, are mostly 4 or 5 cm long: they are elliptical, rather stiff, and coarsely toothed, except near the base. The white flowers, a little under 1 cm across, are produced in almost hemispherical clusters. They are succeeded by ovoid, bright red fruits about 1 cm long, which have a hard, slightly flattened pit.

Mock-orange, *Philadelphus lewisii* (pl. 8), is a member of the hydrangea family. In winter it looks more dead than alive, but from late May to July, when it is covered with fragrant white blossoms, it is one of the most beautiful shrubs anywhere. The flowers, borne in clusters of several to about fifteen or more, are regularly about 1.5 or 2 cm across and are rather unusual in having four petals. The many stamens with yellow anthers add to the attractiveness of the flowers. The opposite leaves are light green, narrowly ovate, sometimes very slightly toothed, and generally about 3 to 5 cm long. The ovoid fruits ripen to dry capsules about 1 cm long. The younger twigs, in winter, are a light but somewhat reddish brown; this feature, along with the fact that the stems have no noticeable buds, makes it possible to recognize the shrub when it is dormant. Mock-orange prefers rather open, brushy areas where the soil is rocky. It will almost always be found in situations where poison oak, serviceberry, and ocean spray occur together.

Soapberry, or buffalo-berry, *Shepherdia canadensis* (pl. 12), is abundant around Puget Sound, the Strait of Georgia, and the San Juan Archipelago. It is otherwise rather scarce west of the Cascades. In winter it can be separated from other deciduous native shrubs with opposite leaves by the scurfiness of its younger twigs. The undersides of the leaves are similarly scurfy and also are covered with brownish, microscopic scales. The yellowish green color of the leaf and flower buds when they unfold in April is rather striking. The flowers are small and of two sorts, staminate and pistillate. The almost spherical fruits are about 7 mm long, bright red, very shiny, and usually have light yellow "pock-marks." They are extremely bitter and when crushed they yield a slippery, soapy pulp. Large specimens of this shrub are about 4 m tall. Soapberry is a member of the oleaster family, which includes the so-called Russian olive, a tenacious tree widely cultivated as an ornamental or for windbreaks, especially in areas where the climate is harsh.

The creek dogwood, or red osier, *Cornus stolonifera* (pl. 8), is common along streams, in roadside ditches, and other open, wet situations. It is usually about 2 to 4 m tall and can be recognized in winter by the fact that most of its younger twigs are red or purplish red. The oval leaf blades, generally 5 to 8 cm long, are darker above than below and sometimes strongly wrinkled. The small flowers, only about 5 mm across, have four white petals and are borne in nearly flat-topped clusters. The one-seeded fruits are globular and generally white, but sometimes they become slightly bluish.

Shrubs of the genus *Garrya* are called silk-tassels because the pistillate flowers, crowded into catkins, have little leafy bracts clothed with soft hairs. The staminate flowers, also in catkins, are borne on separate plants. The two species within our region are not fully appreciated because their distribution is limited. *G. elliptica* (fig. 29) is decidedly

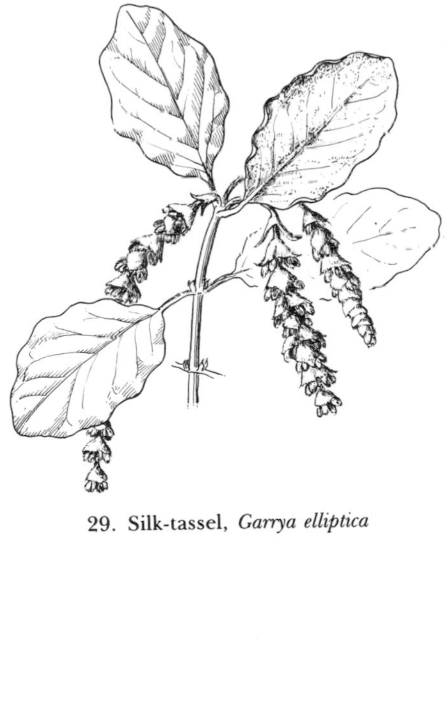

29. Silk-tassel, *Garrya elliptica*

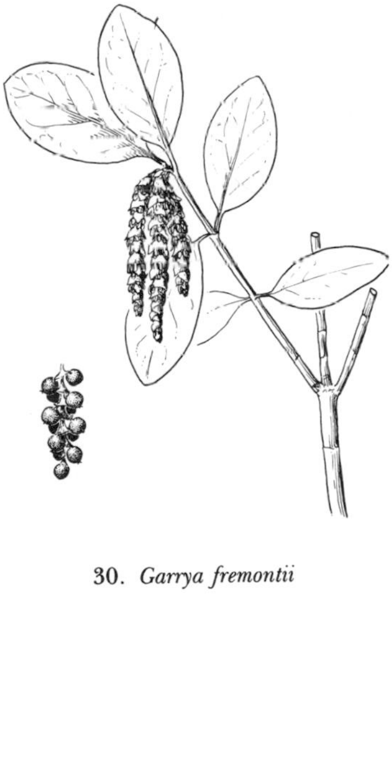

30. *Garrya fremontii*

the more attractive. It grows only at the coast, from Lincoln County, Oregon, to southern California. It is commonly 3 or 4 m tall, sometimes larger. The oval leaves, mostly about 5 to 7 cm long, are nearly leathery in texture, and usually have wavy margins. They are dark green and smooth above, whitish and woolly below. The catkins, up to about 10 cm long, appear in winter or very early spring. The hairy fruits are at first berrylike and about 1 cm in diameter, but they shrivel as they ripen.

Garrya fremontii (fig. 30) grows along the Columbia River Gorge, on both the Oregon and Washington sides, and at lower elevations in the Cascades bordering the southern section of the Willamette Valley. Otherwise, its distribution is largely restricted to southern Oregon and California. In our area this shrub does not often exceed a height of 2 m. Its leaves, about 5 cm long, are yellowish green and lack the wavy margins characteristic of *G. elliptica.* The flower catkins are not often more than 6 or 7 cm long. The purplish fruits, about 5 mm in diameter, are hairy at first, then become smooth.

SHRUBS AND SMALL TREES WITH ALTERNATE LEAVES AND BRANCHES

Of the deciduous species falling into this category, a surprising number are members of the rose family. These include thimbleberry, salmonberry, blackcap, ocean spray, and osoberry, all described in chapter 2. In addition, there are the spiraeas, serviceberry, ninebark, crabapple, and hawthorns, as well as true roses. Of the "nonroses" occurring in brushy places, Oregon grape and poison oak are especially significant, and these have previously been discussed in sufficient detail.

Only three native roses are likely to be found in our region. Two species introduced from the Old World, however, are common on waste land along roadsides, and sometimes they mingle so effectively with native shrubs that they might be mistaken for natives. The introduced roses regularly have stout thorns that are strongly curved downward. *Rosa eglanteria,* the sweetbrier, has leaflets that are rounded at the tip and somewhat hairy and glandular underneath. *Rosa canina,* the dog rose, has leaflets that are pointed at the tip and practically smooth underneath. The flowers of both are about 4 or 5 cm across and usually bright pink, although white flowers are the rule in some populations of *R. canina.*

In our native roses the thorns may be fairly stout or they may be very fine, in which case they are also exceedingly numerous. They are rarely curved to any appreciable extent. The baldhip rose, or small wild rose, *R. gymnocarpa* (pl. 9), is usually easy to recognize because its stems are almost completely covered with delicate prickles and because the five sepals fall away early and so neatly that the ripening fruit is nearly smooth at its free end. The flowers are generally under 3 cm across.

In *R. nutkana* and *R. pisocarpa* the thorns are moderately stout and almost completely restricted to places on the stems where leaves originate, or where leaves originated in previous years. The sepals persist on the fruits. *Rosa nutkana,* the Nootka rose (pl. 9), has bright pink flowers that are regularly at least 5 cm across, and its leaflets tend to be rounded. *Rosa pisocarpa,* the peafruit rose, has flowers that are rarely more than 3 cm across, and its leaflets are typically acute at the tip. This species, more than any other of our roses, is likely to be limited to wet places.

Serviceberry, *Amelanchier alnifolia* (pl. 10), is one of the more important constituents of the flora of relatively exposed situations. It regularly reaches a height of 5 m, and treelike specimens 8 or 10 m tall are occasionally encountered. The leaves of this shrub have bright green, oval blades 2 or 3 cm long, with marginal serrations in the terminal half. The white flowers, borne in clusters at the tips of short side shoots, measure 2 or 3 cm across. The petals are narrow and usually slightly twisted. The fruits, not quite 1 cm in diameter, have several seeds inside. They ripen to a blackish purple color, but are covered with a whitish bloom. They are neither sweet nor juicy, though some birds make use of them.

Ninebark, *Physocarpus capitatus* (pl. 9), prefers the edges of woods that border on meadows, but it may also be found in rather dry, brushy areas. Uncrowded specimens tend to have a rounded profile, and the height may reach 4 m. The leaves are 3 or 4 cm long, serrated, and divided into a few deep lobes. The flowers are concentrated in hemispherical heads and resemble those of blackberries. The petals are white and about 3 or 4 mm long. The stamens are numerous and project outward nearly to the tips of the petals. When the stamens are reddish, the flowers are especially attractive. The fruits of ninebark are inconspicuous, and although they reach a length of about 1 cm, most of this consists of the slender style of the pistil.

There are three rather widely distributed species of *Spiraea* in the lowlands. Hardhack, *S. douglasii* (pl. 9), is common at the edges of marshes, streams, lakes, and roadside ditches. It grows up to about 2 m high and sometimes forms dense thickets. The leaves are oval, mostly about 4 to 6 cm long, and toothed along the margin from the tip to about the middle. The small flowers are bright pink, about the color of strawberry ice cream, and crowded into a dense, elongated inflorescence. This shrub is rather showy during its blooming season in June and July. We have two subspecies in our general area. *Spiraea douglasii* variety *douglasii* is the more widely distributed of the two west of the Cascades and is characterized by leaves that are decidedly woolly underneath. In *S. douglasii* variety *menziesii* the undersides of the leaves are just slightly hairy.

Spiraea betulifolia (fig. 31) is found on rocky, well-drained hillsides in the Willamette Valley. (In other parts of its extensive range, which extends eastward to the Rocky Mountains, it is often seen in wet places.) It grows as a low shrub, less than 1 m tall. Its white or faintly pink flowers are concentrated in nearly flat-topped heads. The leaves, as in the more common hardhack *(S. douglasii)*, are toothed above the middle. They are broadly oval and generally about 3 or 4 cm long. This species is especially common in the northern part of the Willamette Valley, as around Lake Oswego and Oregon City, where it mingles freely with poison oak and other shrubs of open, rocky situations.

Spiraea pyramidata (fig. 32) is often found with *S. betulifolia*. It looks

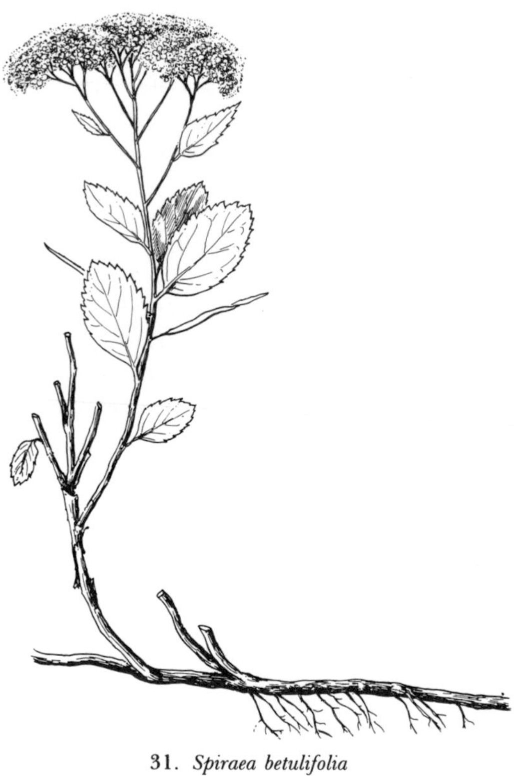

31. *Spiraea betulifolia*

32. *Spiraea pyramidata*

as if it could be a hybrid of *S. betulifolia* and *S. douglasii*, but this idea seems not to have been tested. The flowers are generally pale pink (sometimes white) and are concentrated in an inflorescence whose form is about halfway between that of the other two species. Large plants are only a little more than 1 m high, but they are bushier than most specimens of *S. betulifolia* and have leaves that are commonly 4 or 5 cm long.

The western crabapple, *Pyrus fusca* (pl. 4), often qualifies as a small tree, but it is usually less than 5 or 6 m tall. Very often it has no real trunk, the several main stems branching out into a large bush. In any case, when flowering or bearing fruit, it is one of our more attractive natives. The leaf blades, about 4 or 5 cm long, are approximately oval and are toothed around the margin. The larger ones may have a distinct lobe on one or both sides, about halfway back from the tip. The flowers, in clusters of perhaps ten to twenty, appear in April to June, depending on the elevation. They are about 1.5 cm across and have petals that range from pure white to pale pink. The little apples, ripe by late summer, are 1 or 1.5 cm long and are yellow to purplish red. This tree is abundant in the Puget Trough, especially in the region of Puget Sound, the Strait of Georgia, and the San Juan Archipelago. It also occurs in some places in the Willamette Valley, but is less often seen in more humid areas near the coast.

The crabapple must not be confused with the cultivated apple *(Pyrus malus)* or pear *(P. communis)*, both of which are sometimes found in the wild. Neither has lobed leaves, and their flowers and fruits should be familiar to everyone. The cultivated sweet and sour cherries *(Prunus avium* and *P. cerasus)* have also successfully escaped from cultivation. Even more likely to be mistaken for a native is the so-called mountain ash *(Sorbus aucuparia)*, another deciduous tree of the rose family, deservedly popular as an ornamental. Its compound leaves have thirteen or fifteen leaflets, and these are toothed at the margins. The white flowers, about 1 cm across, are produced in dense, nearly flat-topped clusters. They have a disagreeable odor, but this can be overlooked in anticipation of the gorgeous orange-red fruits, about 1 cm in diameter. The fruits are eaten by birds, and where a seed happens to land there is a good chance that a little mountain ash will soon come up. This tree grows best in a sunny place, and most specimens found in woods are spindly.

The black hawthorn, *Crataegus douglasii* (pl. 4), like the crabapple, may be either a shrub or small tree. Its height rarely attains 6 m. The leaf blades are substantial and leathery, dark green above, paler below. They are usually between 3 and 5 cm long, and their width is about two-thirds the length. There are close-set serrations that extend nearly to the base of the blade. The new twigs generally turn reddish in early summer. Older twigs are provided with stout, sharp spines. The white flowers, about 1 cm in diameter, appear in late spring, and by August the black fruits, each about 1 cm long, are already ripe. As a rule, only a few of the prospective fruits in a cluster materialize. The variety *suksdorfii* has flowers with twenty stamens and is essentially limited to our region. The variety *douglasii,* with ten stamens and leaves that typically have some coarse marginal serrations (in addition to finer serrations) in the apical half, occurs in the San Juan Archipelago, but otherwise its range is primarily east of the Cascades.

The red-fruited hawthorns that are just about everywhere in our region are not natives. There are two species, both thorny, which may grow as shrubs or small trees. They are especially common along country roads and often are encouraged to form fences. In *C. monogyna* (pl. 4) the leaves have from three to seven lobes, and the fruits have just one seed. The leaves of *C. oxyacantha* have three to five lobes, and most of the fruits have two seeds inside. These hawthorns are extremely generous with their flowers, and for a couple of weeks in late spring they are almost completely white. Unfortunately, the flowers smell of urine. The fruits are bright red by mid-September.

Shrubs of the genus *Ceanothus,* members of the buckthorn family, have a variety of common names, including wild lilac and buckbrush. The former is especially appropriate for those whose flowers are both blue and very fragrant. Of the few species found in the Northwest, two are moderately abundant west of the Cascades. One is the sticky-laurel, *C. velutinus* (fig. 33), a rather unimpressive evergreen shrub that regularly grows to a height of 2 or 3 m. The leaves are oval, or oval with a slight tendency toward being heart-shaped, and mostly about 4 or 5 cm long. They are somewhat distinctive in having three main veins that diverge from the base, and also in being a little sticky. The flowers are small, cream-white, and are produced in May and June in crowded, branching clusters. The fruits are three-lobed capsules about 5 mm long; each lobe has a prominent ridge or keel on it. This shrub is found largely in brushy areas. It is widely distributed, but is more abundant on the eastern slope of the Cascades than in our region.

The seeds of *C. velutinus* are heat-resistant, so this shrub often predominates for a few years in an area where there has been a fire. The fact that the roots of this shrub harbor nitrogen-fixing bacteria probably helps to make it a successful colonizer. Nitrogen fixation is discussed later on in this chapter, in connection with Scotch broom and its allies, and also in chapter 2, in connection with red alder.

The redstem ceanothus, *C. sanguineus* (pl. 12), resembles *C. velutinus* but is deciduous, and the lobes of its fruit lack ridges. This rather fragrant shrub is a conspicuous element of the flora in the Willamette Valley, the southern portion of the Puget Trough, and in some other parts of our region.

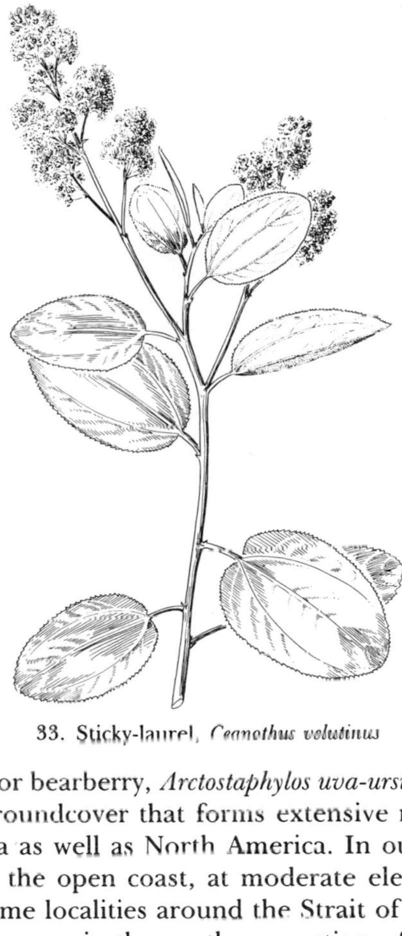

33. Sticky-laurel, *Ceanothus velutinus*

Kinnikinnick, or bearberry, *Arctostaphylos uva-ursi* (pl. 7), is a delightful evergreen groundcover that forms extensive mats. It is found in Europe and Asia as well as North America. In our region it is most abundant along the open coast, at moderate elevations in the Cascades, and in some localities around the Strait of Georgia and Puget Sound. Its occurrence in the southern portion of the Puget Trough and in the Willamette Valley is sporadic. Kinnikinnick is effectively used in landscaping, especially in large rockeries, on sloping banks, and along highways. Its stems, often reddish, are thickly covered with dark green, oblong leaves 1 to 2 cm long. The white flowers, appearing in late spring or early summer, resemble those of salal and madrone, but are smaller. The fruits, nearly 1 cm in diameter, are bright red; they are ripe by late summer and persist into the autumn.

Arctostaphylos columbiana (fig. 34) is a small kind of manzanita that grows in a few places in the lowlands west of the Cascades. It is perhaps most common in parts of Kitsap County, Washington. It forms a shrub 1 or 2 m high, rarely taller. The young twigs are hairy, and the older stems have a reddish bark. The leaves, with oval blades 3 or 4 cm long,

34. Manzanita, *Arctostaphylos columbiana*

are slightly grayish. The flowers, borne in tight little clusters, resemble those of kinnikinnick; they are vaselike, about 6 mm long, and white or pale pink. The dull, orange-brown fruits are not quite 1 cm in diameter, and usually slightly flattened. This shrub sometimes hybridizes with kinnikinnick to produce a plant which has been called *A. media.* This grows as a groundcover, much like kinnikinnick; but it reaches a height of approximately 30 cm, and its appearance is intermediate between that of its parents.

The range of our native western azalea, *Rhododendron occidentale* (pl. 8), is limited to the coastal region of southwestern Oregon and northern California. This is a deciduous shrub that reaches a height of more than 5 m, but usually it is much smaller. The leaves are bright green, and the flowers, borne in dense clusters, have cream-colored petals; the uppermost petal is suffused or streaked with pale orange or pink. The flowers are sweetly fragrant, but the foliage, like that of some garden azaleas, smells a little of skunk.

All willows are deciduous. There are several species in our region, and some of them are difficult to identify positively unless one can study the catkins in late winter and early spring, then look at the leaves and twigs after these have begun to mature. The descriptions given here are greatly simplified. They stress distinctive features and combinations of characters that should enable one to make the right identification at least 90 percent of the time. It is also helpful that certain of the species have a restricted distribution within the area covered by this book.

At the beginning it may be best to state rather flatly that the two species most likely to be seen—and also the ones most likely to develop into trees as tall as 10 m—are *Salix lasiandra* and *S. scouleriana.* They are very different from one another, and each could be readily identified if it were not for the fact that it has some look-alikes.

Salix lasiandra, the Pacific willow (fig. 35), likes to have its feet wet, so it is generally found beside a lake, pond, or stream. It may have a

35. Pacific willow, *Salix lasiandra*

single main trunk or several. It is unmistakable when its catkins are out: the pollen-producing flowers (as in all willows, these are on trees separate from those that bear the seed-producing flowers) have four to nine stamens. Other willows have two stamens or only one. The leaf blades, mostly 10 or 12 cm long, are regularly about five times as long as wide and taper to a slender point. The margins are finely serrated and the surfaces are smooth, at least when the leaves are mature.

Of the species with two stamens, one that might be confused with *S. lasiandra* is the Columbia River willow, *S. fluviatilis* (fig. 36), which is found only along the Columbia River and the northernmost sector of the Willamette River. Its leaf-blades are even more elongate than those of *S. lasiandra,* being sometimes more than ten times as long as wide. *Salix fluviatilis* is a shrubby willow whose height does not often exceed 4 m.

The soft-leaved willow, *S. sessilifolia* (fig. 37), has leaves about the same shape as those of *S. lasiandra,* but they are moderately to decidedly hairy even when mature. (In most of our willows, except for *S. sessilifolia, S. hookeriana,* and *S. sitchensis,* the hairiness characteristic of young foliage typically disappears almost completely.) This is another water-loving, shrubby species; but unlike *S. fluviatilis,* it has a wide distribution.

Salix rigida, represented west of the Cascades by the variety *macrogemma* (fig. 38), is also found in wet places and may be either a large shrub or a small tree. Its leaf blades, mostly 5 to 10 cm long, resemble those of *S. lasiandra* in being almost hairless and drawn out to a slender tip. They are proportionately broader than those of *S. lasiandra,* however, and typically widest below the middle.

The coast willow, *S. hookeriana* (fig. 39), is fairly easy to identify because it is almost strictly maritime in distribution, being found only along the open coast (often on sand dunes) and in the area of Puget Sound and the Strait of Georgia. Its leaf blades, not often as much as three times as long as wide, are hairy above and below when they are young, and the hairiness on the lower surface may not disappear as the leaves mature. The hairiness of the young twigs also persists through the first season.

This brings us to the last three species, which may present problems unless there are flowering catkins to examine. If the pollen-producing flowers have a single stamen instead of two, one can be sure that the specimen in hand is the Sitka willow, *S. sitchensis* (fig. 40). Its leaf blades are generally widest above the middle, and the hairiness characteristic of young leaves usually persists. The twigs also remain velvety for at

36. Columbia River willow, *Salix fluviatilis*

37. Soft-leaved willow, *Salix sessilifolia*

38. *Salix rigida*

39. Coast willow, *Salix hookeriana*

40. Sitka willow, *Salix sitchensis*

41. Piper willow, *Salix piperi*

least a year or two. This species likes moisture, but it is not necessarily limited to the margins of lakes, ponds, or streams.

In the Piper willow, *S. piperi* (fig. 41), and the Scouler willow, *S. scouleriana* (fig. 42), the pollen-producing flowers have two stamens, so it is necessary to look closely at the catkins that consist of seed-producing flowers. In those of *S. piperi* the pistils are hairless, at least by the time they approach maturity; in *S. scouleriana* they are copiously hairy. The leaf blades of *S. piperi,* mostly two or three times as long as wide, are generally broadest near the middle and have bluntly toothed margins. The leaves, hairy when young, are smooth at maturity. The upper surface is dark green, the underside grayish green. This is another species that likes water.

42. Scouler willow, *Salix scouleriana*

In contrast *S. scouleriana* seems to be almost independent of water; in some areas it is common on relatively dry, gravelly hillsides. Its leaf blades are usually widest above the middle, and the margins are smooth or finely toothed. If hairs present on the young leaves persist to maturity, they are restricted to the undersides and may be reddish. *Salix scouleriana* is found throughout our region, where it is undoubtedly the most abundant upland willow. As mentioned earlier, it is one of the few species that regularly develops into a respectable tree as tall as 10 m or more.

Willows are food-plants for the caterpillars of a number of butterflies and moths. Among the more conspicuous and attractive butterflies whose caterpillars feed primarily—or at least to a large extent—on leaves of willows are the western tiger swallowtail *(Papilio rutulus),* the mourning-cloak *(Nymphalis antiopa),* and Lorquin's admiral *(Limenitis lorquini).* All of these are abundant in the Northwest, and the first two are probably known by name to most nature lovers. Lorquin's admiral, like the mourning-cloak, has a wing span of about 5 cm and is mostly brownish black. It can easily be recognized, however, because the front, outer corners of the fore wings are orange. In addition, there is a band of nearly pure-white markings well away from the lateral edges of both the fore and hind wings. The flight of Lorquin's admiral consists of a series of short, rapid strokes that alternates with a gliding motion. This delightful butterfly stops frequently to sun itself, often landing on the ground.

The wax-myrtle, *Myrica californica* (fig. 43), grows only at the coast, usually in soil that is rather sandy. Its range extends from Grays Harbor County, Washington to southern California. The wax-myrtle

43. Wax-myrtle, *Myrica californica*

forms a dense shrub that may be more than 6 m tall. The leaves are evergreen and the blades, mostly about 5 to 8 cm long, are unevenly toothed along the margins. The upper surface is dark green and the underside is yellowish green, often dotted with black. The catkinlike flower clusters, borne in the axils of the leaves, are generally 1 to 2 cm long. Those consisting of pistillate flowers are normally higher on the branch than those composed of staminate flowers. In some clusters both types of flowers may be present. The wax-coated fruits that develop from the pistillate flowers are approximately 6 or 7 mm in diameter and almost spherical.

The so-called Oregon myrtle or California laurel, *Umbellularia californica* (pl. 6), just barely gets into our territory. Its range extends from lower California to the area around Coos Bay, Oregon, and it is not often found more than a few miles from the coast. The beauty of its wood, almost crystalline when finely smoothed and varnished, has been exploited commercially for making bowls, candlesticks, and just about anything that can be turned on a lathe. Unfortunately, many dealers and wholesalers have been somewhat less than candid about the tree, claiming that it is found only in southwestern Oregon and in the Holy Land. This probably helps sell the products, but why a wood so beautiful needs false or uninformed advertising defies comprehension and common sense. We do have some shrubs that are related to myrtles of the Holy Land, but this is not one of them. "Pacific laurel" would be a more fitting name for the tree, because it is in the laurel family, along with the bay tree of gardens. Whatever you choose to call it, it is a beauty. Old trees growing in the open usually have gnarled trunks and a rounded or nearly hemispherical profile. The height may be up to about 20 m. The evergreen leaves are lance-shaped, generally about 10 cm long, and bright green. When torn, they smell strongly of camphor. The small flowers are succeeded by almost spherical fruits up to 2.5 cm long. These have just one large seed.

The chinquapin, *Castanopsis chrysophylla* (fig. 44), is a close relative of oaks and chestnuts. It is evergreen and generally grows as a rather slender tree, although young specimens tend to be bushy. The height may reach 30 m. The bark is whitish and eventually becomes furrowed. The leaf blades, mostly 8 to 10 cm long, are typically lance-shaped. The upper surface is dark green, but the underside is covered with light brown or golden scales. Staminate flowers are borne in clusters of three on long, catkinlike spikes; pistillate flowers are situated within little cups attached to the lower portions of the same spikes, or to separate, shorter shoots. The cups develop into spiny burs about 2 cm in diameter, and these contain from one to three large nuts that resemble chestnuts. In Oregon this handsome tree is found at low and moderate elevations in the Coast Ranges and Cascades. In Washington its distribution is restricted to a few localities along the Columbia River Gorge and in Mason County, west of Puget Sound.

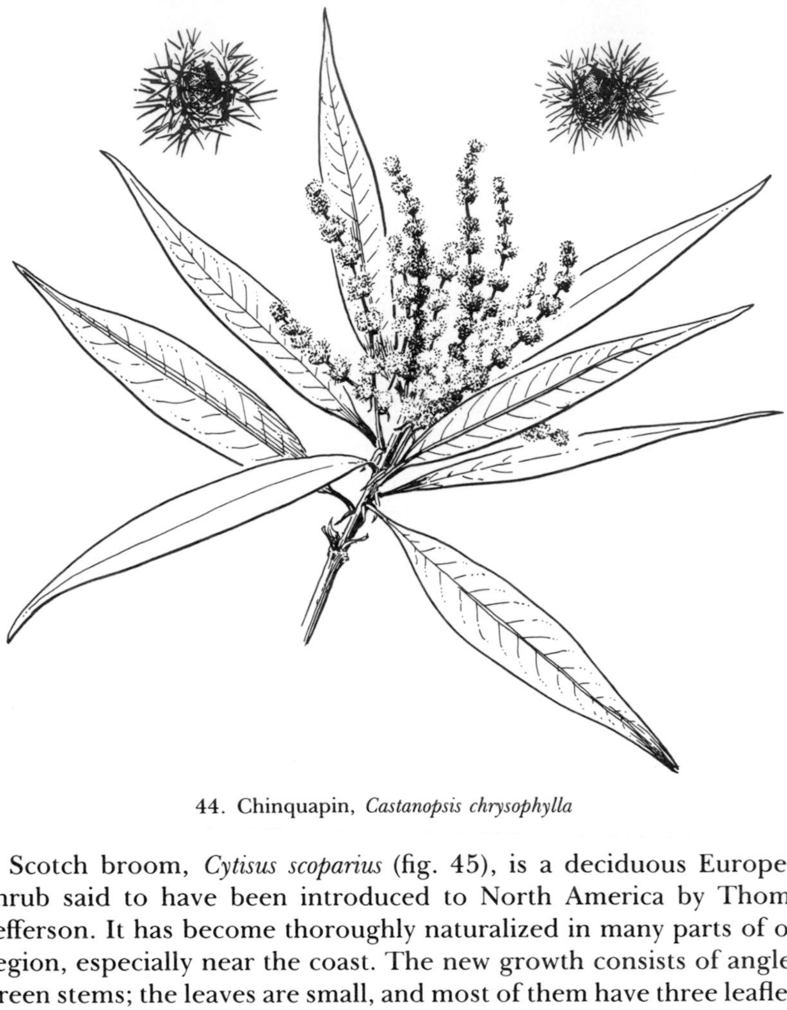

44. Chinquapin, *Castanopsis chrysophylla*

Scotch broom, *Cytisus scoparius* (fig. 45), is a deciduous European shrub said to have been introduced to North America by Thomas Jefferson. It has become thoroughly naturalized in many parts of our region, especially near the coast. The new growth consists of angled, green stems; the leaves are small, and most of them have three leaflets. The flowers, 2 cm or more across, are generally borne singly in the leaf axils; they may be completely yellow or tinged with maroon or purple. There are many horticultural variants that demonstrate differences in flower color.

The seed pods of Scotch broom grow to a length of about 5 cm. The two halves of a pod tend to warp in different directions, and when they finally separate, on a dry day in summer, they do so with an almost explosive snap. The seeds may be catapulted for a distance of several feet. Further dispersal is carried out by ants, which are attracted by an oil-rich appendage on the seeds. The seeds are remarkably heat-resistant, so at least some of them are likely to survive a fire.

Two other European species of broom, with flowers about 1 cm across, are occasionally found growing in the "wild" state. *Cytisus multiflorus* has white flowers, usually produced singly or in pairs. *Cytisus monspessulanus* has yellow flowers borne in clusters. Then there is gorse, *Ulex europaeus* (fig. 46), a close relative of *Cytisus,* which has stout spines all along the branches and at their tips. Its flowers are bright yellow and about 2 cm across. Gorse is a common escape in some places and has been incriminated in the rapid spread of brush fires.

The species of broom and gorse are members of the pea family, which also includes lupines, clovers, and vetches. Plants of this group routinely have nitrogen-fixing bacteria living in nodules on their roots. These bacteria are capable of utilizing atmospheric nitrogen in the

45. Scotch broom, *Cytisus scoparius*

46. Gorse, *Ulex europaeus*

formation of compounds from which proteins are synthesized. They rely on their hosts for sustenance, but make available to them some of the compounds into which they have incorporated nitrogen. This means that plants harboring nitrogen-fixing bacteria are often successful in situations where the soil is poor in nitrates and ammonia, the usual sources of nitrogen exploited by green plants.

PERENNIAL VINES

The common vines of situations that are at least somewhat exposed include several kinds of blackberries, two species of honeysuckles, and two species of *Clematis.* The blackberries are thorny and have alternate leaves, so there is no problem recognizing them. The honeysuckles and *Clematis* have opposite leaves and lack thorns.

Our little native blackberry, the dewberry (pl. 10), was described in chapter 2. It is probably more abundant in brushy places and open woods than anywhere else. Because of its small size and creeping habit of growth, it is not likely to be confused with the two species of Old World blackberries that dominate roadsides and waste land. Both are thorny, coarse, and aggressive, but they are easily distinguished from one another.

47. Evergreen blackberry, *Rubus laciniatus*

The evergreen blackberry, *Rubus laciniatus* (fig. 47), regularly keeps its leaves through the winter. Basically, the blades are divided into five leaflets, but some of these may be completely divided again. The pinkish white flowers of this species are about 2 or 2.5 cm in diameter; the berries are nearly globular and usually under 1.5 cm in diameter.

In the Himalayan blackberry, *Rubus discolor* (fig. 48), many of the leaves may stay on through the winter, but this species is not truly

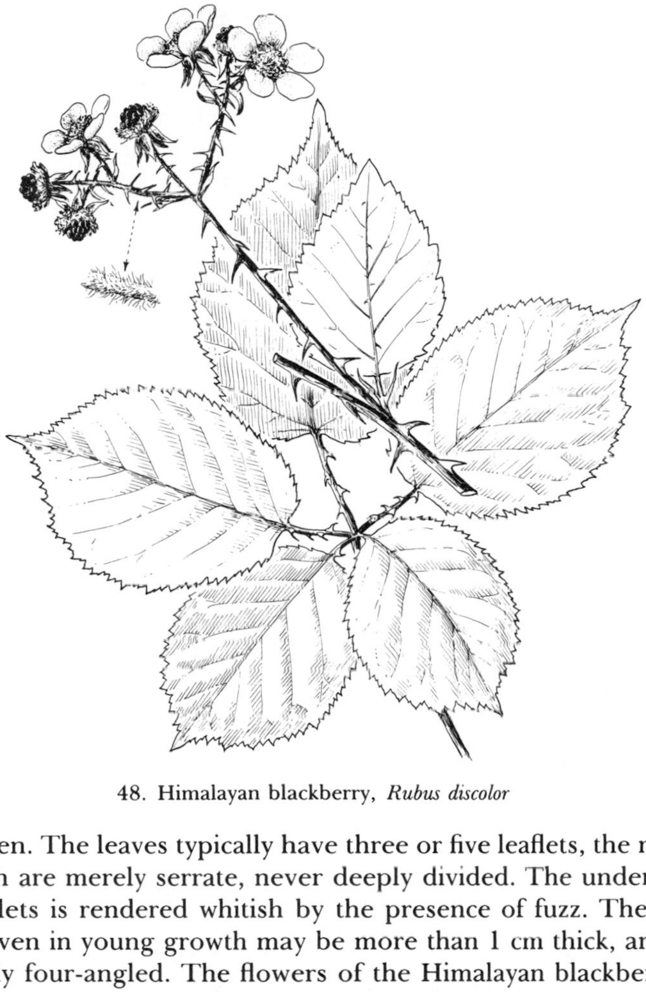

48. Himalayan blackberry, *Rubus discolor*

evergreen. The leaves typically have three or five leaflets, the margins of which are merely serrate, never deeply divided. The underside of the leaflets is rendered whitish by the presence of fuzz. The stems, which even in young growth may be more than 1 cm thick, are often distinctly four-angled. The flowers of the Himalayan blackberry are, on the average, just a bit larger than those of the evergreen blackberry and are white or faintly pinkish. The berries are usually somewhat taller than wide and commonly about 1.5 cm in diameter. This species is the most common introduced blackberry in our region and forms impenetrable thickets. Each year, in late summer, it makes a lot of berry pickers happy.

Two other introduced blackberries, *R. vestitus* and *R. macrophyllus*, occasionally turn up in our area. They are similar to the Himalayan blackberry in having leaves with three or five leaflets that are just serrated instead of deeply divided. *Rubus vestitus* can be distinguished from the Himalayan blackberry because its flower stalks lack sticky glands. The leaflets of *R. macrophyllus* are not decidedly whitish underneath as are those of both the Himalayan blackberry and *R. vestitus*.

Although poison oak sometimes grows as a vine, it is not likely to do so except in a shaded situation. Thus the only vines other than blackberries that need be dealt with here are honeysuckles and *Clematis*. As previously noted, these have no thorns and their leaves are opposite. The orange honeysuckle, *Lonicera ciliosa* (pl. 11), is a tough-stemmed, deciduous vine that clambers over shrubs and up into trees to a height of several meters. It likes sunny places, and is most abundant in brushy areas and at the edges of woods. Its leaves, about 4 to 6 cm long, are approximately oval, dull green above, whitish below. They are smooth, except at the margins, where there is a fringe of delicate hairs. The leaves nearer the flowering tips are joined at their bases, so the stem seems to go through what appears to be a single leaf. The tubular flowers, borne in small clusters, are about 3 cm long. The free portions of the five petals are so nearly equal that the flowers are not decidedly two-lipped, as in the next species. The color is typically orange, but may be nearly red. There is no fragrance, and unlike many honeysuckles that are pollinated by hawk moths at night, this species is pollinated in the daytime by hummingbirds. The red fruits, ripening in late summer, are not quite 1 cm in diameter.

The pink honeysuckle, *L. hispidula* (pl. 11), is less conspicuous than the orange honeysuckle, but it is evergreen. Its somewhat hairy leaves are just 3 or 4 cm long. The pairs near the tips of the stems are joined, and certain of the lower leaves may have accessory lobes that are fused in this way. The flowers, about 1.5 cm long, are strongly two-lipped, as in conventional garden honeysuckles. They are generally a purplish pink, or a mixture of purplish pink and yellow. The fruits are red and not quite 1 cm in diameter. This species prefers exposed places and is most likely to be found where the ground is rocky.

Virgin's-bower, *Clematis ligusticifolia* (fig. 49), is found in the Willamette Valley, but in general its distribution in the Northwest is east of the mountains. It is a tough vine that winds up into trees for several meters. The larger leaves generally have five leaflets, sometimes seven, and some of these are widely spaced. The leaflets are approximately oval to nearly heart-shaped, but they are usually further divided into a few shallow lobes and a number of coarse teeth. The flowers, borne in clusters, are either strictly staminate or strictly pistillate, though the pistillate flowers have stamens on which anthers do not materialize. There are no petals, but the five sepals are cream-white. Each flower is about 1.5 cm across, sometimes larger. The fruits that develop from the numerous pistils may reach a length of 3 cm or more and are covered with white hairs, so that in late summer the vines are as attractive as they are when in flower.

49. Virgin's-bower, *Clematis ligusticifolia*

An introduced species, now widely dispersed through this region, is *C. vitalba* (fig. 50). All of its flowers have both stamens and pistils, and its leaflets are not toothed around the margins, although they may have one or two sharp lateral lobes.

Wildflowers

The wildflowers growing on exposed hillsides, in brushy areas, and in oak woods are mostly different from those typical of coniferous forests. On the whole, they are species that do best where there is ample sunlight and where the soil is well drained. Some of them, however, are regularly found in situations where the ground is soggy in winter and early spring but dries out in summer. Because there is

50. *Clematis vitalba*

considerable intergradation between the habitats with which this chapter is concerned, it seems best to deal with the wildflowers of all the habitats in one section. The list is not exhaustive, and species that are more likely to be found in coniferous forests, weedy fields, and places that are permanently wet are excluded, for they are covered in chapters 2 and 4.

LILY FAMILY

Where the white fawn-lily, *Erythronium oregonum* (pl. 14), grows, it may be so abundant that it is taken for granted. Yet it is among our most graceful flowers. In the Willamette Valley and Puget Trough, it is regularly found where there are oaks, and sometimes it grows in or around open coniferous woods. In general, it prefers well-drained, rocky situations. The bulbs of flowering specimens are at least 10 cm underground, having been pulled deeper and deeper by the roots, which contract as they dry out after each growing season. In early spring the plant pushes up two broad, somewhat fleshy leaves, about 10 or 15 cm long and mottled with brownish green. The nodding flowers, usually produced singly or in pairs on a stalk 15 to 25 cm tall, start to open in mid-April. The three petals and three sepals are identical and soon begin to curve upward. In the Willamette Valley and southern section of the Puget Trough, the petals and sepals are cream-colored, with an orange-yellow blotch at the base of each. The anthers are large and bright yellow. Around the Strait of Georgia and on the islands of the San Juan Archipelago, the petals and sepals are mostly clear white, and there may be a reddish mark bordering the yellow suffusion at the base of each. As the flowers wither, the fruits turn upward and eventually become elongated capsules about 3 or 4 cm long. By mid-July they start to dry and split lengthwise to release their seeds.

The rice-root lily (also called checker lily and mission bells), *Fritillaria lanceolata* (pl. 14), is found almost throughout our area. It may grow up to more than 60 cm high in shaded situations, but plants exposed to nearly full sun are rarely taller than 40 cm. The bulb, generally about 10 cm underground, has little white offsets that resemble grains of rice. The leaves are dull green and rather narrow, and most of them are arranged in whorls of three or more around the upright stem. At lower elevations the flowers appear in April and May. There is usually just one on each plant, but robust specimens often have two or three. The petals and sepals, generally 2 or 3 cm long, are purplish brown, mottled with green or yellow. The nearly globular fruits, characterized by some winglike ridges, are directed upward as soon as the flowers wither, and they crack open in August. The rice-root lily is regularly found with the white fawn-lily, but it grows in many places where the latter does not occur.

Camas, *Camassia quamash* (pl. 14), blooms almost throughout the month of May. Its purplish blue flowers, on spikes about 30 cm tall, are approximately 3 cm across. The lowermost member of the group of six petals and sepals is slightly set apart from the others. The grasslike leaves are folded lengthwise. The bulbs are about 2 cm in diameter and generally are buried to a depth of at least 10 cm.

Camassia leichtlinii is a taller species of camas and is typically found in meadows and other places that are moist almost throughout the year. When its flowers wither, the petals and sepals become twisted around the pistil; this does not happen in *C. quamash.* In large colonies of either species, one is apt to find at least one or two plants with white flowers; and in some populations of *C. leichtlinii,* white-flowered specimens may even be in the majority.

Wherever *C. quamash* is found, the death camas, *Zigadenus venenosus* (pl. 14), will almost certainly be present also. The several leaves arising at the base of this plant are folded lengthwise, and the numerous cream-colored flowers, with three sepals and three petals, are borne on the upper part of a stalk about 20 or 30 cm tall. The fruits are egg-shaped capsules a little more than 1 cm long when ripe. This member of the lily family is moderately toxic to grazing animals. The bulbs and seeds are said to be especially dangerous.

Of the many wild onions found in Oregon, Washington, and British Columbia, just two are common in the lowlands west of the Cascades. Hooker's onion, *Allium acuminatum* (pl. 14), is found on almost every gently sloping, rocky hillside that dries out thoroughly in summer. By the time it blossoms, in June and July, its grasslike leaves have withered. There are usually several reddish purple flowers in each cluster. The three petals and three sepals are essentially alike and about 1 cm long. The flowering stalks are up to about 15 cm high. When any part of the plant is bruised, it smells almost like chives, which is a close relative.

The nodding onion, *Allium cernuum* (fig. 51), is not as widespread as Hooker's onion and seems to prefer situations that are somewhat shaded. It is locally abundant around Puget Sound, on the islands of the San Juan Archipelago, and on Vancouver Island. Its dull green foliage persists throughout the year, and the flower stalk is up to about 20 cm high. The small white or pale pink flowers are tightly clustered in a nodding head.

The brodiaeas, or fool's onions, also bloom in June and July, after their leaves have died down. Four species may confidently be expected in our region, but only two of them are more or less regularly encountered. These are *Brodiaea coronaria,* the harvest lily, and *B. hyacinthina,* the hyacinth brodiaea. *Brodiaea coronaria* (pl. 15) has vase-shaped flowers about 2 cm long, ranging in color from purple to bluish purple. It varies considerably, especially in stature and in the number of flowers produced on the stalk: most often there are three to five flowers; but in some populations it is decidedly unusual to find more than three, and not all of these are necessarily open at the same time. The height does not often exceed 15 cm. In some coastal areas, especially in southern Oregon, the flowers hug the ground, for the stalk is almost nonexistent.

The flowers of *B. hyacinthina* (pl. 15), produced in clusters of a dozen or more on a stem about 50 cm tall, are smaller and more open than those of *B. coronaria.* They are mostly white, except for a bluish or greenish line running the length of each petal and sepal. (In brodiaeas, the three petals and three sepals are generally so similar that the flowers appear to be six-petaled.)

Brodiaea congesta (pl. 15) is found in the Willamette Valley and in some other parts of our range, but is not of general distribution. Its flowers, with petals and sepals about 1 cm long, are bluish purple or pinkish purple and are borne in dense clusters. The flower stalks are tall, like those of *B. hyacinthina,* and are inclined to be a little contorted, especially in their upper portions.

Brodiaea howellii is the species least likely to be seen, although it is fairly common in places, including some of the islands of the San Juan Archipelago. Its flowers are similar to those of *B. congesta,* but are larger, and the color is typically pale blue tinged faintly with purple. The stalks are tall, regularly attaining 50 cm.

The Columbia lily, *Lilium columbianum* (pl. 14), is often called the tiger lily, an acceptable name so long as one understands that the flowers are spotted, not striped. It grows to a height of about 1 m, and its narrow leaves, mostly about 5 to 7 cm long, are arranged in several whorls. The flowers, appearing in June, may number several at the top of a well-established plant. The petals and sepals, 3 or 4 cm long, are bright orange, with reddish brown spots on their inner faces. The six long stamens have impressive yellow anthers. The Columbia lily is most likely to be found in open woods and brushy areas, or in grassy places where bracken grows freely.

IRIS FAMILY

The Oregon iris, *Iris tenax* (pl. 15), is the common species found along roadsides and in brushy places west of the Cascades in Oregon and southern Washington. A pity that its range is not wider, for its flowers, produced in profusion in May and early June, are very showy. About 9 cm across, they range from white to dark violet-blue, being light violet on most plants. Regardless of the prevailing color, there are darker veins on the three spreading sepals, as well as on the narrower, nearly upright petals. The grasslike leaves die back to slender rhizomes just beneath the surface. The rhizomes are conservative in spreading, so that *I. tenax* tends to form compact clumps.

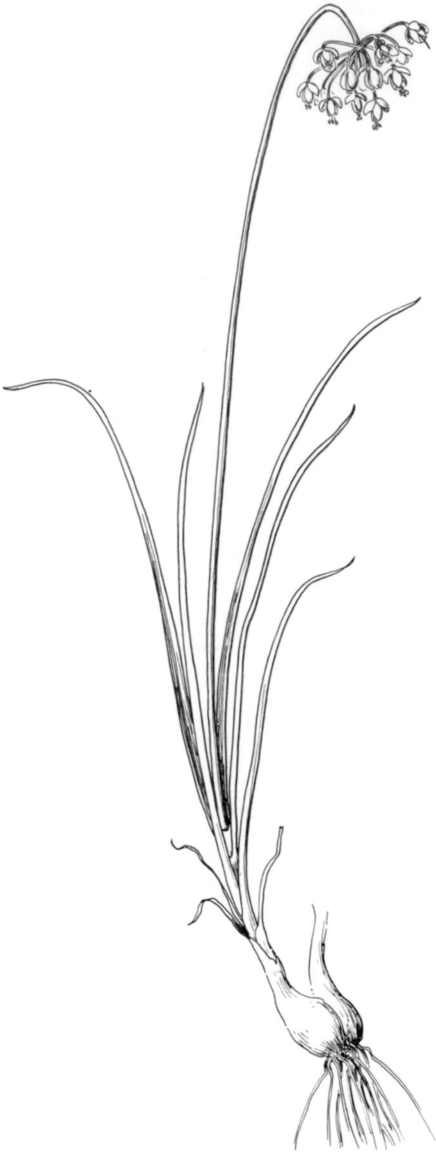

51. Nodding onion, *Allium cernuum*

52. Slender-tubed iris, *Iris chrysophylla*

The slender-tubed iris, *I. chrysophylla* (fig. 52), is a clump-forming type that grows much like *I. tenax,* but the tube of its flower, below the level where the petals and sepals diverge, is very long. As a whole, the flowers are yellowish or whitish, sometimes faintly tinged with blue, and marked with dark veins. This species occurs in the southern part of the Willamette Valley, where it sometimes hybridizes with *I. tenax,* and also at the coast near Coos Bay; but its range is largely outside our region.

Blue-eyed grass, *Sisyrinchium angustifolium* (pl. 15), is found in meadows and on grassy slopes that are moist in spring. In summer it dies back to a rhizome that may get a thorough baking. The flowers, about 1.5 cm across, are blue or violet-blue. The three sepals and three petals are all alike. Some plants bear just one flower; others branch and produce several.

Grass-widows, *S. douglasii* (pl. 15), is found on Whidbey Island, in the southern part of Vancouver Island, and rarely in the San Juan Archipelago. Otherwise, it is a species of the Columbia River Gorge and of open woods, prairies, and scablands east of the Cascades. It forms small clumps and reaches a height of about 25 cm. Each shoot, clasped near its base by a few grasslike leaves, produces from one to three flowers. These are 2 or 3 cm across and have satiny, reddish purple sepals and petals. The intensity of the color varies, and occasionally a plant with completely white flowers is found. Grass-widows is a choice wildflower and deserves special protection, for its occurrence in our region is extremely limited.

ORCHID FAMILY

The rein-orchids, belonging to the genus *Habenaria,* are unmistakable among the less conspicuous representatives of the family, because the base of the lower petal ("lip") of each flower is drawn out into a long, saclike spur. There are a number of kinds in our region, but only a few are widespread. The more common species are *H. elegans* (pl. 16), the elegant rein-orchid, and *H. unalascensis,* the Alaska rein-orchid. Both are partial to brushy places and to dry, open woods. They usually bloom in June and July, after the large, basal leaves that appear in spring have died down. The spikes are generally 20 or 30 cm tall and have numerous small flowers. These are mostly greenish; but in *H. elegans,* which has a slender, pointed spur about 1 cm long, this particular part of the flower is white. The spur in *H. unalascensis* is greenish and not over 5 mm long.

H. greenei is found on islands of the San Juan Archipelago and in some places around Puget Sound, the Strait of Georgia, and the open coast. It has long-spurred flowers similar to those of *H. elegans,* but they are almost completely white, except for some green at the tip of the spur and on the upper sepals and petals. The flower spikes of *H. greenei,* the most attractive of the three species mentioned here, are particularly crowded.

Purslane Family

The small-leaved montia, *M. parvifolia* (fig. 53), is a relative of miner's lettuce and candyflower, both described in chapter 2. It is a small and somewhat leggy perennial that creeps along by an underground rhizome; it also forms new little plants where its almost leafless branches touch the ground and root. The crowded basal leaves are narrow, usually only 5 or 6 mm wide, and the leaves higher up on the flowering stems are alternate. The flowers, about 1.5 cm across, have petals that are uniformly pink, or white with pink lines. There is a coastal variant that has larger flowers and oval or nearly circular blades on the basal leaves.

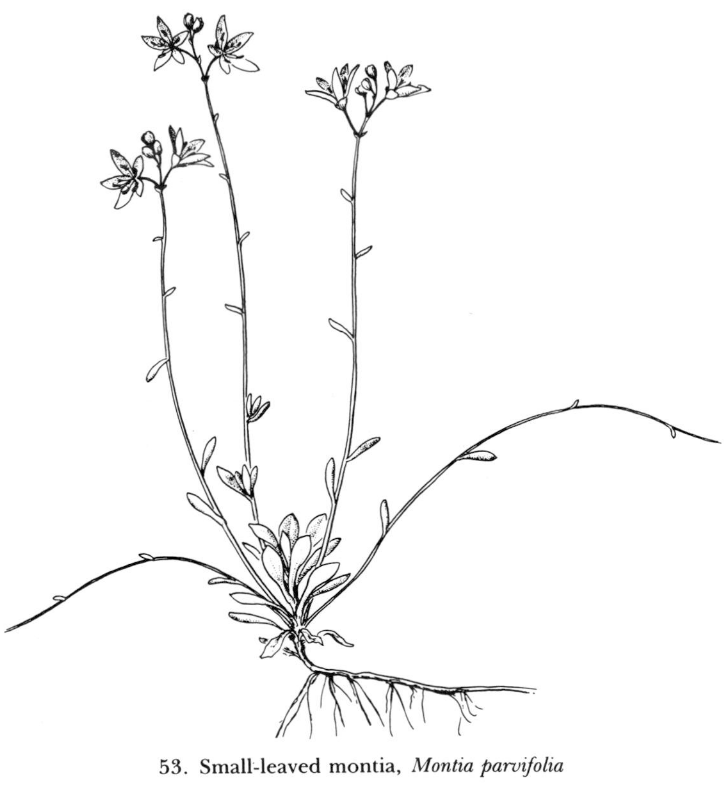

53. Small-leaved montia, *Montia parvifolia*

Miner's lettuce, *M. perfoliata* (pl. 17), is sometimes plentiful in open places; but unless it gets plenty of moisture, it is apt to grow as a dwarf only a few centimeters high. Even though the plants may be yellowed almost from the start and have just a short flowering period before they wither, the pairs of leaves below the flower clusters are united as they are in robust plants from moist, shady situations.

The narrow-leaved montia, *M. linearis* (fig. 54), is still another species that should be expected. It is a small plant, not often more than

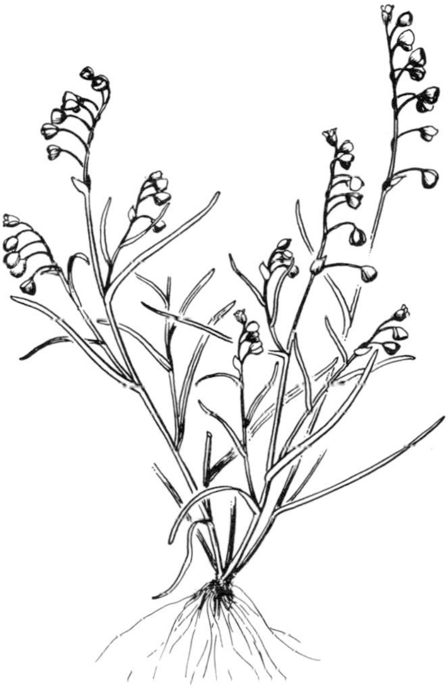

54. Narrow-leaved montia, *Montia linearis*

10 cm high. The leaves are rarely more than 3 mm wide, though they may be as long as 4 cm. Most of the flowers on each shoot are arranged on one side of it and have a tendency to nod. They are white, about 5 or 6 mm across, and do not open widely.

A modest little jewel trying hard not to be noticed is red-maids, *Calandrinia ciliata* (pl. 21). It is a slightly succulent annual that hugs the ground, sometimes forming a rosette of leaves with just one flower in the center, sometimes sending out several prostrate stems, each with one or more blossoms. The flowers, typically with five petals, are deep purplish red. They vary considerably in size, but most of them are between 5 mm and 1 cm across. The basal leaves, generally 3 to 5 cm long, are rather narrow. Their petioles, with bristlelike hairs at their margins, gradually broaden out into the blades.

PINK FAMILY

Chickweed, *Cerastium arvense* (pl. 21), has a long flowering season, lasting from April to June or even July. It is a perennial that forms loose mats. The shoots are mostly about 10 or 15 cm tall and have narrow, opposite leaves. At least some parts are usually hairy. The flowers, produced in loose clusters at the tips of the shoots, are about 1.5 cm across and have five white petals that are cleft at their tips. The flowers of this little native are far more attractive than those of *C. vulgatum* and *C. viscosum,* brought over from the Old World and now thoroughly entrenched in our lawns and pastures. *Stellaria media* is another close cousin that has become a nuisance.

BUTTERCUP FAMILY

The western buttercup, *Ranunculus occidentalis* (pl. 18), is the most common and widespread native species found in open areas, especially on hillsides that are wet in winter and spring, dry in summer. The plant as a whole is rather hairy, and the leaves (the larger of these are basal) have blades that are deeply divided into three approximately wedge-shaped lobes, each of which is subdivided further. The flowers, about 1.5 or 2 cm across, have narrower petals than *R. repens* and most of the other large-flowered species that prefer places that are wet all year long.

The wild larkspurs, which belong to the genus *Delphinium,* bloom in late May and June. Our most widely distributed species is *D. menziesii* (pl. 18), which grows to a height of about 40 cm. Its flowers, about 1.5 cm across, are mostly dark blue, but the pair of small upper petals may be light blue or even white. The spur sticking back from the uppermost sepal is about 1.5 cm long. The leaf blades are divided into several primary leaflets, and these are again divided rather deeply. Some plants are noticeably hairy; others are almost smooth.

In *D. leucophaeum,* which has about the same form and stature as *D. menziesii,* the flowers are largely white or cream, although the basal portions of the petals may be tinged with blue, and the backs of the petals and sepals may also be bluish. This species is found only in the northern half of the Willamette Valley.

A much larger species of *Delphinium,* which grows in the foothills of the Coast Ranges and Cascades in Oregon, and on both sides of the Columbia River Gorge, is *D. trolliifolium.* It may be as tall as 1 m. Its flowers, commonly 4 cm across, are dark blue, except for the upper petals, which are nearly white.

The red columbine, *Aquilegia formosa* (pl. 18), is a choice plant of somewhat open situations. It likes clearings in woods and grassy fields where there is some shrubbery and bracken, and it is often abundant along roadsides in wooded areas. Columbine normally grows to a height of about 50 to 70 cm. The basal leaves, on long petioles, are a little fernlike, as each of the three primary divisions of the blades is again divided into three leaflets, and the leaflets are deeply cut. The graceful flowers, about 3 or 4 cm across, are a mixture of red and yellow, and are pollinated by hummingbirds. They have the form typical of columbine flowers; their sepals are larger than the petals, which have long, saclike "spurs."

55. Whitlow-grass, *Draba verna*

56. Bittercress, *Cardamine oligosperma*

MUSTARD FAMILY

Whitlow-grass, *Draba verna* (fig. 55), is a weed introduced from Europe, but it is so regularly found in exposed places that it might be mistaken for a native. It is generally in bloom at least a few days before spring has officially opened. It is an annual with a basal rosette of simple leaves, mostly about 1 or 1.5 cm long, and one or a few flowering stems not often more than 10 cm tall. The flowers, usually less than 5 mm across, have four white petals. The seed pods reach a length of 6 or 8 mm.

Bittercress, *Cardamine oligosperma* (fig. 56), is native to our region, but behaves as a weed when it gets into gardens. It commonly grows 10 to 20 cm tall and may be branched or unbranched. The elongate leaves, some of which are concentrated at the base of the plant, are completely divided into about seven or nine lobes, of which the terminal one is the largest. The flowers, with four white petals, are less than 5 mm across. The fruits are slender pods that become bumpy as the seeds enlarge. Weeding out this little pest is decidedly unsatisfying, for when its fully ripe pods are touched, they split open and shoot out their seeds, thus spitefully sowing another crop.

POPPY FAMILY

The California poppy, *Eschscholzia californica* (pl. 20), is apparently native to parts of western Oregon and the extreme southern part of Washington, as well as California. It has been widely introduced in other areas within our region. It is a perennial that comes up each spring from a taproot. The height may reach 40 or 50 cm. The much-divided foliage is grayish green. The four-petaled flowers, generally some shade of yellow or orange in wild plants, are usually 4 to 6 cm across. Until a flower is ready to open, the sepals are stuck together to form a tall cone over the rest of it. There are many stamens, and the pistil becomes a long pod that splits open after ripening and drying. The flowers close up at night and on dark days.

STONECROP FAMILY

The broad-leaved stonecrop, *Sedum spathulifolium* (pl. 23), is one of the more distinctive plants of rocky areas, especially cliffs that are shaded for a part of each day. The leaves, 1 to 2 cm long, are crowded, wedge-shaped, and whitened by a powdery coating. There are usually a few red leaves to brighten the clump, but these are nearing the end of their usefulness and will soon drop away. In May and June the tight clusters of bright yellow flowers, each like a little star, make a handsome showing, especially where a large colony of the stonecrop dominates the face of a cliff.

SAXIFRAGE FAMILY

On a worldwide basis, the genus *Saxifraga* is a huge one, and there are many species in the Pacific Northwest. The great majority of these, however, are limited to higher elevations. In lowland areas west of the Cascades, the most common and most widely distributed species is probably *S. integrifolia* (fig. 57). It is variable and has several subspecies that need not be discussed here. It grows in grassy places that are wet in winter and spring, dry in summer, so it is regularly found with camas and shooting stars. This saxifrage is a perennial that comes up every spring, producing a few basal leaves with nearly spade-shaped blades 3 or 4 cm long and a rather stout, fuzzy flowering stalk 20 or 30 cm

57. Saxifrage, *Saxifraga integrifolia*

tall. The flowers, in rather dense heads, are only about 5 mm across and attractive only if examined closely. In most populations found west of the Cascades, the petals are white, but in other areas they may be yellowish or faintly greenish.

The ragged starflower, *Lithophragma parviflora* (pl. 21), is a choice little plant that blooms early in the spring. Its flowers, borne in a group of several at the top of a stalk 20 or 30 cm tall, are about 2 cm across. They are white or pink, and each petal is cut into three or five narrow lobes. The leaves are almost entirely basal and have long petioles. The blades are deeply divided into lobes that are then divided some more. Neither the flowers nor the leaves last long: they wither before summer really gets underway.

Alumroot, *Heuchera micrantha* (fig. 58), sticks close to edges of rocks and to crevices, anchoring itself firmly by a long taproot. Its leaves are all basal and have rather long petioles with scattered hairs. The blades are thin but tough, broadly heart-shaped in outline, and mostly about 4 to 6 cm long; the margin is cut shallowly into several lobes, which

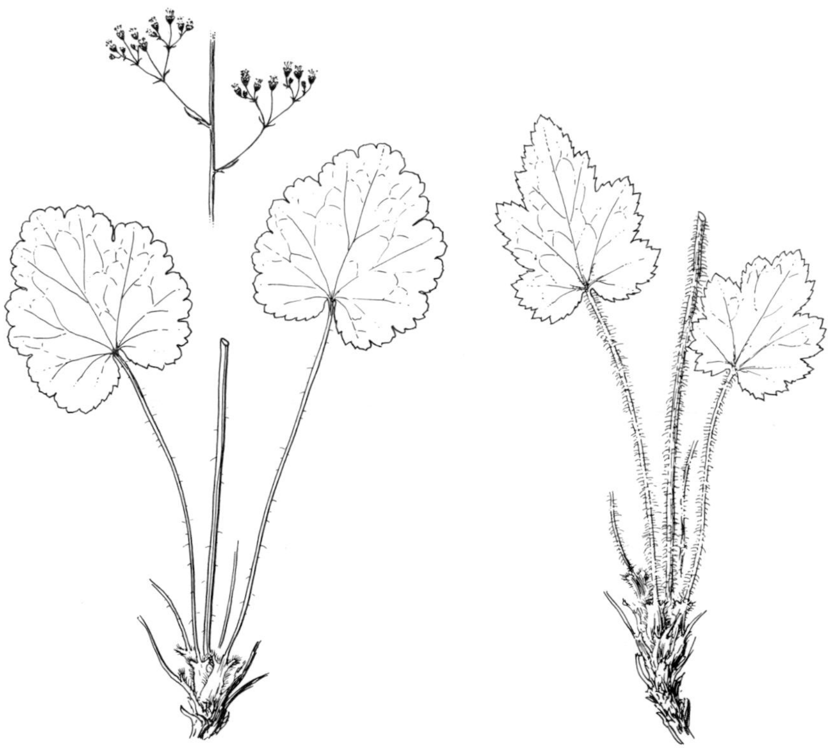

58. Alumroot, *Heuchera micrantha*

are subdivided further by coarse teeth. Although most of the leaves hang on through the winter, some turn red as they get ready to pass out of the picture. The small white flowers are borne on side branches of a stalk that may be 50 cm tall in a large, well-established plant. Alumroot is a close relative of coral bells *(H. sanguinea),* a native of Arizona and Mexico, widely cultivated in gardens.

ROSE FAMILY

Three kinds of wild strawberries grow in our region. One of them, the coastal strawberry, *Fragaria chiloensis* (fig. 59), is restricted to seaside cliffs and the back portions of beaches on the open coast and on

59. Coastal strawberry, *Fragaria chiloensis*

certain islands of the San Juan Archipelago. In this species, the habit of spreading by stolons is especially well developed. The leaves are dark green, thick, and strongly wrinkled.

Fragaria virginiana and *F. vesca* are generally distributed and are sometimes found together. *Fragaria virginiana* (fig. 60) usually predominates in sunny, relatively dry situations. It may be identified by the fact that the terminal tooth on each of the three leaflets is smaller than the one on each side of it. Its leaves are flat and unwrinkled, and

60. *Fragaria virginiana*

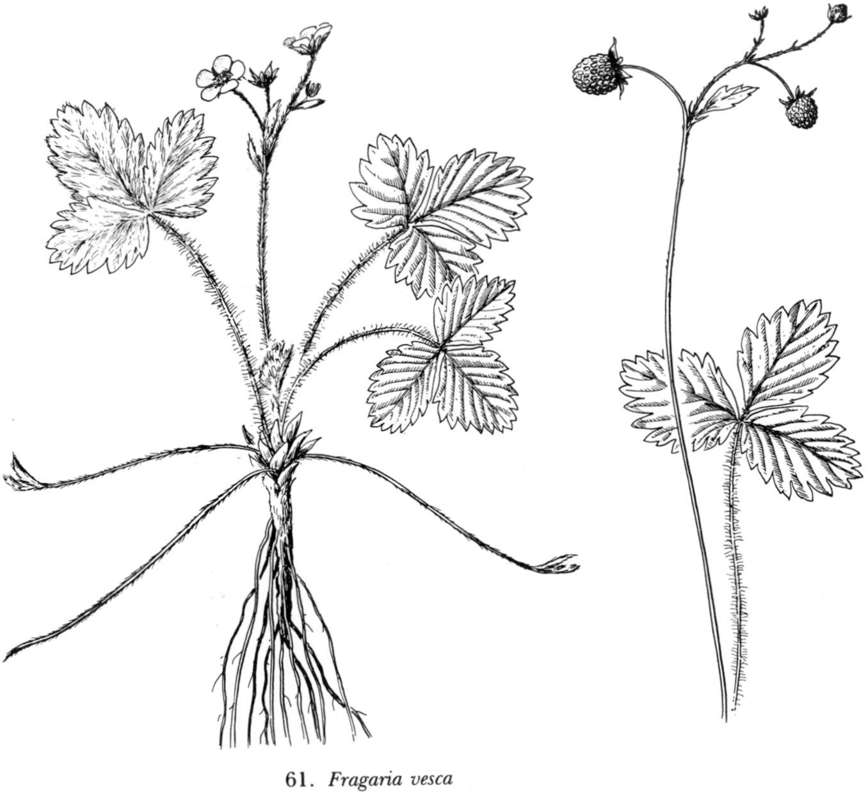

61. *Fragaria vesca*

generally have a bluish cast; in plants that hug the ground in exposed places, the bluish green color of the leaves is particularly pronounced.

In *F. vesca* (fig. 61) the terminal tooth of each leaflet is about the same size as the teeth on each side of it and may project beyond them. The leaves are wrinkled and have no tendency to become bluish. This species is the one most likely to be found in moist coniferous woods, although it will grow in the open in places that do not become parched in summer.

The flowers of all three species are similar. They are mostly between 1.5 and 2.5 cm in diameter, and the petals are white or faintly pinkish. The red fruits are delicious, but it takes time and patience to gather them in satisfying quantities. *Fragaria chiloensis* has figured in the parentage of some varieties of garden strawberries.

PEA FAMILY

The pea family is richly represented in our region. Of the more common vetches, sweet-peas, clovers, and cloverlike plants found on waste land and in weedy gardens, the majority are introductions from the Old World. Some of them are described in chapter 5. The lupines are mostly natives, although certain of them flourish on disturbed ground and along roadsides.

In lupines, the leaves have at least five leaflets radiating from the end of the petiole. Flower color in our native species is usually some shade of blue or purple, often mixed with white. The bushy, yellow-flowered lupine that grows along the coast, especially in Oregon, and in some places around Puget Sound and in the San Juan Archipelago is *Lupinus arboreus*. It was introduced from California to help control shifting sand.

Of the blue- and purple-flowered species, only a few can be mentioned. *Lupinus bicolor* (fig. 62) is a small annual about 20 or 30 cm tall. Its flowers are less than 1 cm long, and the large upper petal, called the banner, usually has a white center. *Lupinus micranthus* is very similar. The most conspicuous of the perennial lupines is *L. polyphyllus* (fig. 63), which grows to a height of about 1 m and has bluish to violet flowers up to 1.5 cm long. *Lupinus latifolius* and *L. albicaulis* should also be expected. *Lupinus littoralis* (fig. 64) is easy to recognize because it is low-growing and found only on beaches and bluffs close to salt water.

Somewhat similar to lupines, and often confused with them, are the buck-beans, members of the genus *Thermopsis*. Although the large, yellow flowers of these plants resemble those of lupines and are arranged in the same sort of upright spike, the leaves are cloverlike, having only three leaflets (plus a pair of leaflike stipules where the

62. *Lupinus bicolor*

63. *Lupinus polyphyllus*

petiole is attached to the stem). There is just one species in our region, *T. montana* (pl. 21). It is most likely to be found in open areas in the foothills of the Cascades.

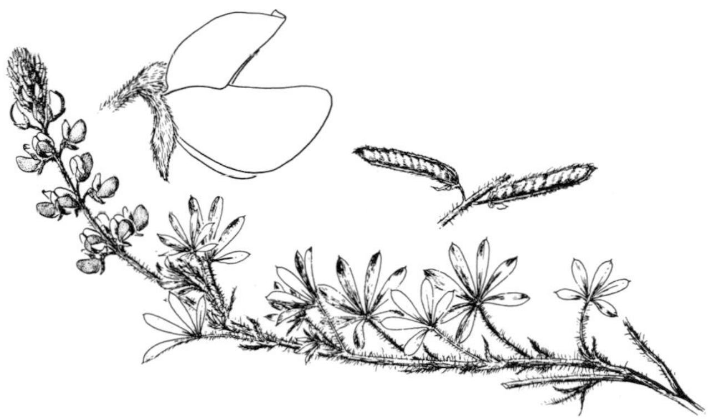

64. *Lupinus littoralis*

GERANIUM FAMILY

Two dwarf annuals related to garden geraniums seem so perfectly adapted to exposed areas that they look like natives. Both, however, are importations from the Old World. Filaree, or stork's-bill, *Erodium cicutarium* (fig. 65), may bloom as early as March in an especially sunny, warm place, and some plants may continue to flower until the end of summer. Typically, it hugs the ground with its basal rosette of fernlike leaves, and the flowers and additional leaves are produced on short, sparingly branched stems. The flowers are about 1 cm across and have five pink or magenta-pink petals. The pistils have very long styles, so the fruits as a whole are about 3 or 4 cm long and resemble storks' bills. As the fruits dry, they split lengthwise into five parts. The slender beak of each part becomes spirally twisted, but when it is thoroughly wet it straightens out. The action of uncoiling helps drive the seed into the ground.

Geranium molle (fig. 66), called crane's-bill, is generally a little less compact than filaree. Its flowers are of about the same size and color, but the petals are broadest near their tips rather than near the middle. The style of the fruit is not over 2 cm long and it does not become twisted. The leaves are also very different from those of filaree: instead of being fernlike, they have blades that are almost circular in rough outline and deeply divided into several radiating lobes, which are coarsely toothed.

Both filaree and crane's-bill may, in certain situations, grow over 30 cm tall; but in the type of habitat under consideration here, they tend

65. Filaree, *Erodium cicutarium*

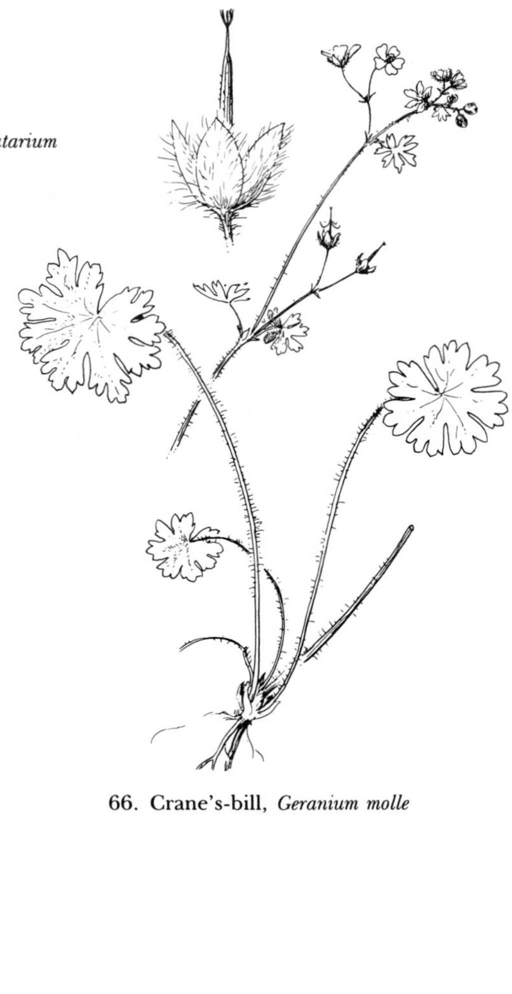

66. Crane's-bill, *Geranium molle*

to be well under 15 cm tall. In addition to *G. molle,* one should expect to find two or three other weedy geraniums, but most of them are coarser and more likely to be found in vacant lots and gardens.

VIOLET FAMILY

There are two widely distributed "blue" violets within our range. In both species, which grow in open woods and brushy areas and on grassy hillsides, the flowers are about 1.5 cm across, and the three lower petals have light bases and dark streaks. The basic color ranges from pale lavender to deep violet. In *Viola adunca* (pl. 20), the saclike spur on the lowermost petal is slender and usually at least half as long as the face of the petal. In *V. howellii* the spur is only about as long as high, and much less than half as long as the face of the petal. The leaf blades of *V. howellii* are more decidedly heart-shaped than those of *V. adunca;* in the latter, the indentation in the blade is often weak or absent.

EVENING-PRIMROSE FAMILY

The genus *Clarkia* includes the delightful annuals called farewell-to-spring and godetia. Some of our species have become important garden flowers, but unfortunately the types promoted nowadays in seed catalogues are mostly "doubles" and other freaks. Clarkias normally have four petals and four sepals (but the sepals may stick together as if there were only one), and in most of the species occurring west of the Cascades the flowers close at night. The fruit, a slender pod that splits into four parts when ripe, develops below the petals, sepals, and stamens. The narrow leaves, generally less than 5 cm long, have short petioles. Of the more common species that occur in our region, the showier ones are *C. amoena* (represented by three varieties), *C. viminea,* and *C. quadrivulnera.* They bloom in early summer, commonly reaching a height of 50 or 60 cm, and in all of them the petals are usually at least 1 cm long. *Clarkia amoena* (fig. 67) has the most attractive flowers: the pink to purplish pink petals, usually with a carmine blotch at their bases, may be up to more than 3 cm long. The sepals almost always stick together, and the seed pods are cylindrical rather than four-angled, as in the other two species. It occurs as far north as Vancouver Island, but is not often seen except in the Willamette Valley, where it makes marvelous displays in late June and July.

The petals of *C. quadrivulnera* (fig. 68), about 1 cm long, are lavender-pink to deep rose. Those that are pale are more likely to show a carmine blotch at the base. The seed pods are four-angled, and the sepals are generally free of one another or form pairs. This is another species that is fairly common in the Willamette Valley; it also occurs on prairies around the southern part of Puget Sound, and in the Columbia River Gorge.

Clarkia viminea, which has flowers almost as large as those of *C. amoena,* is essentially a California species, but it occurs here and there

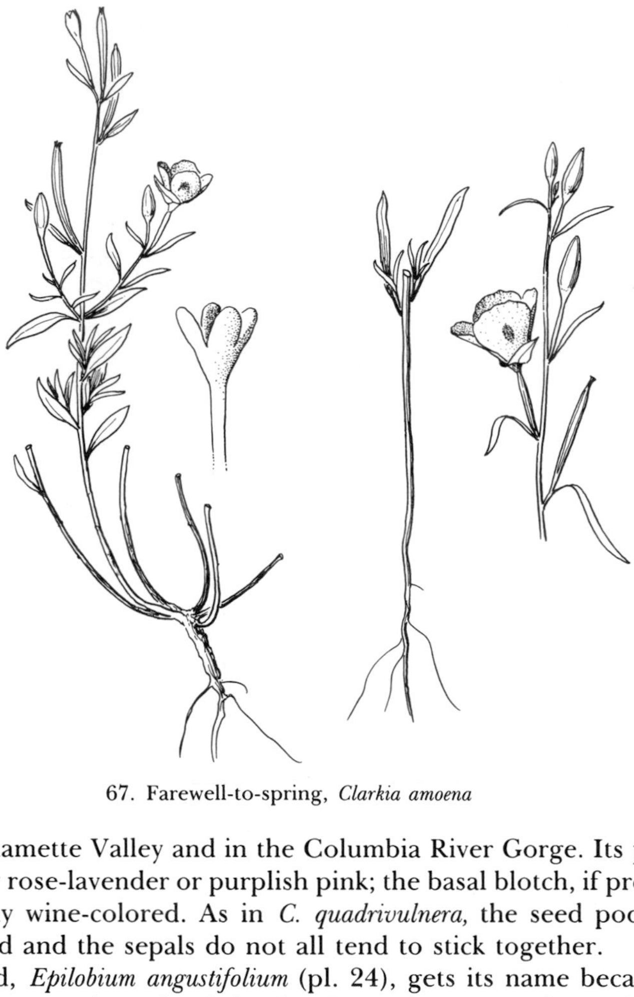

67. Farewell-to-spring, *Clarkia amoena*

in the Willamette Valley and in the Columbia River Gorge. Its petals are usually rose-lavender or purplish pink; the basal blotch, if present, is generally wine-colored. As in *C. quadrivulnera,* the seed pods are four-angled and the sepals do not all tend to stick together.

Fireweed, *Epilobium angustifolium* (pl. 24), gets its name because it often grows eagerly on land that has been clear-cut or burned over. It is a perennial that dies down every autumn, then comes straight up again in spring with stems that may reach a height of more than 2 m. The crowded, narrow leaves are regularly at least 10 or 15 cm long. The bright pink to nearly purple flowers, generally 2 cm across, are produced in profusion in terminal spikes. There are four broad petals, eight stamens, and a deeply four-lobed stigma. The faces of the flowers are directed outward, and the stigma and most of the stamens hang downward. The fruits are slender, four-valved capsules that reach a

68. *Clarkia quadrivulnera*

length of about 8 cm. They crack open in late summer, releasing seeds with tufts of hairs that make them air-borne. The successful colonization of land that has been cleared by cutting or by fire depends on seeds carried in by wind.

PARSLEY FAMILY

Spring gold, *Lomatium utriculatum* (pl. 23), comes up in early spring from a tough taproot, and its much divided, parsleylike leaves normally hug the ground. (In some populations the plants tend to be erect and the leaves are raised.) The bright yellow flowers are small, but there are so many of them in each flat-topped cluster that they are conspicuous during the flowering season, which is generally April and early May in the lowlands.

PRIMROSE FAMILY

The shooting stars, species of *Dodecatheon,* are close relatives of garden primroses and cyclamens. They show at least some resemblance to the latter, if not to the former, because of the way the five petals are turned back. The flowers, in a group of several to many, are held high above the basal leaves. The way the stamens are partially joined together to form a tube of decreasing diameter around the stigma has inspired other common names, such as "birdy-beaks." Shooting stars are among our choicest wildflowers, and where they occur they are usually abundant, brightening up grassy slopes for several weeks in April and May. A number of species in the northwest are limited to mountain meadows or to regions east of the Cascades.

The common species in the lowlands is *D. hendersonii* (pl. 20). Its leaves are fairly thick, with rather broad petioles. The size of the oval or elliptical blades varies considerably, but generally falls into the range of 3 to 8 cm. The flower stalks are around 20 to 30 cm high. The flowers themselves, from tip of the stigma to the tips of the upturned petals, are about 3 cm long. The color of the petals ranges from light purplish pink to nearly magenta; the bases of the petals, however, and also the lower part of the aggregate of stamens, is yellow. The fruits ripen to dry capsules, approximately ovoid in shape and about 1 cm long.

Dodecatheon pauciflorum is occasionally found in grassy areas bordering marshes along the coast. This plant can usually be distinguished from *D. hendersonii* by its leaves, whose blades are about three times as long as wide. There are other differences, too, but any shooting star found in a meadow next to a salt marsh will probably be *D. pauciflorum.*

DOGBANE FAMILY

Spreading dogbane, *Apocynum androsaemifolium* (fig. 69), is a milky-juiced plant with opposite leaves and small clusters of pink or white flowers. It is a much-branched perennial that grows to a height of about 30 or 40 cm and then dies back each winter to a creeping stem. The leaves have short petioles; the blades are oval and usually around 3 cm long. The flowers, in which the five petals are joined into a tube, are up to 1 cm long and not quite as wide. The fruits are slender pods that reach a length of 10 cm or more by the time they are ready to split open and release their seeds, which have tufts of long hairs. Admirers of the periwinkle, *Vinca major,* a European plant much used as a ground cover, will be happy to know that dogbane is in the same family.

PHLOX FAMILY

The skunkweed, *Navarretia squarrosa* (pl. 22), is a prickly little annual that blooms in midsummer. It is generally 15 or 20 cm tall. The basal

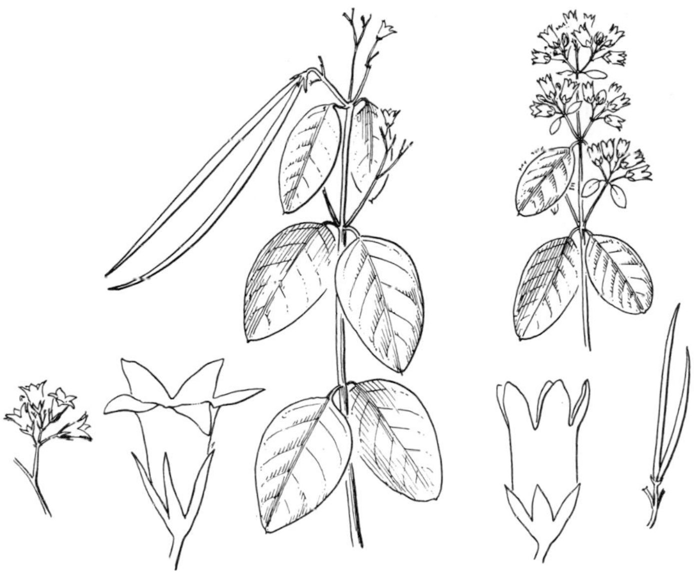

69. Spreading dogbane, *Apocynum androsaemifolium*

leaves are divided into many narrow lateral lobes, after the fashion of a feather, but the leaves higher up on the stem usually branch twice. The lobes are tipped with spines. The bright blue flowers, about 5 mm across, are produced in a tight cluster at the top of the plant. Where *N. squarrosa* is really abundant, its skunklike odor may be strong enough to be noticed in a moving automobile.

BORAGE FAMILY

Although this family includes some common wildflowers and weedy relatives, the distinction between species—and even between certain of the genera—requires attention to minute details. The simplified treatment provided here should enable a beginner to get off to a good start. As a rule, but not always, a plant of the borage family can be picked out because of its superficial appearance. If the flowers are arranged in a curved spike that resembles the neck and scroll of a violin, and if the five petals are fused basally to form a tube, the plant in hand is almost certainly one of this group. The genera most likely to be found in the wild are *Amsinckia, Cryptantha, Plagiobothrys, Myosotis, and Cynoglossum.*

Amsinckias, or fiddlenecks, are easy to recognize on account of their orange or yellow flowers. Our most widely distributed species is *A. menziesii* (pl. 21), with flowers about 5mm across.

Species of *Cryptantha* (white forget-me-not) and *Plagiobothrys* (popcorn flower) have white flowers, though these may have yellow centers. The distinction between the two genera is based largely on the form of the seed. If the seed has a keel running along much of its length,

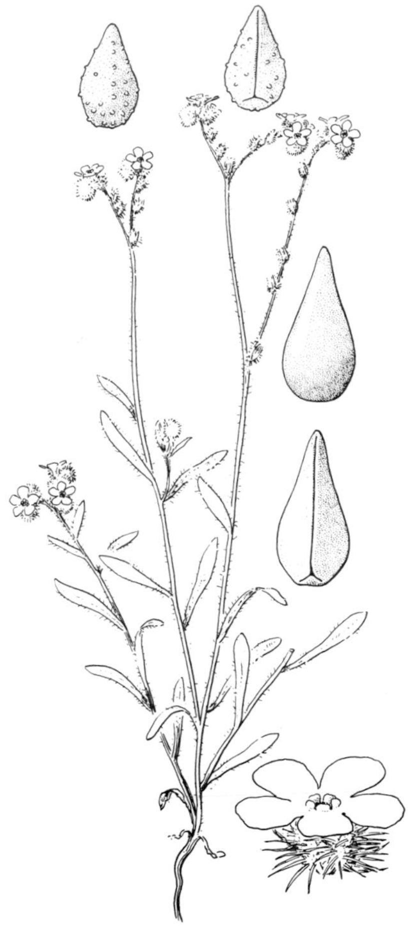

70. White forget-me-not, *Cryptantha intermedia*

it belongs to a *Plagiobothrys.* If, on the other hand, it has a groove, it belongs to a *Cryptantha.* Some common and widespread species of each genus are illustrated: *C. intermedia* (fig. 70), *P. figuratus* (fig. 71), and *P. scouleri* (fig. 72).

The real forget-me-nots belong to the genus *Myosotis.* Our most abundant species is *M. discolor,* an introduced weed. It usually has some flowers that are pale blue, others that are dull yellow. There are other species, mostly imported, which generally have blue flowers.

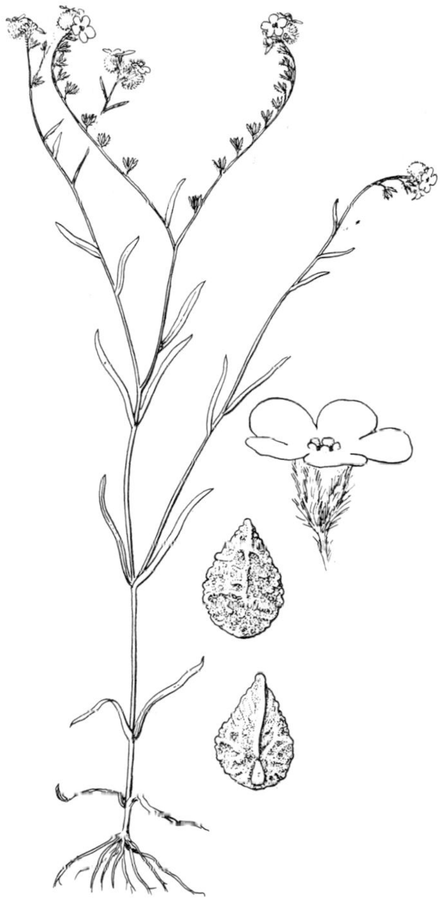

71. Popcorn flower, *Plagiobothrys figuratus*

72. *Plagiobothrys scouleri*

Pacific hound's-tongue, *Cynoglossum grande* (fig. 73), is a tall plant, regularly more than 50 cm high, that is more likely to be found in brushy places and open woods than in completely exposed areas. Its flowers, about 1 cm across, are deep blue or violet-blue, and the spike in which they are concentrated has no tendency to curve. The largest leaves, with blades 10 or 15 cm long, are near the base of the plant.

MINT FAMILY

Yerba buena, *Satureja douglasii* (pl. 23), belongs to the same genus as the kitchen herb called savory, or basil-thyme. It is a typical mint in having a squarish stem, opposite leaves, and an irregular corolla. Yerba buena is a low creeper, sending out long runners that are rooted at intervals. The bright green leaves are oval, usually about 1.5 cm or 2 cm long. The flowers, generally not quite 1 cm long, are white or faintly purplish and arise singly from the leaf axils. When crushed between the fingers, yerba buena gives up a fragrance that is fairly strong but pleasing. This plant is a regular feature of brushy or wooded habitats that have good drainage. It is commonly found with oaks and madrones, and in dry coniferous forests.

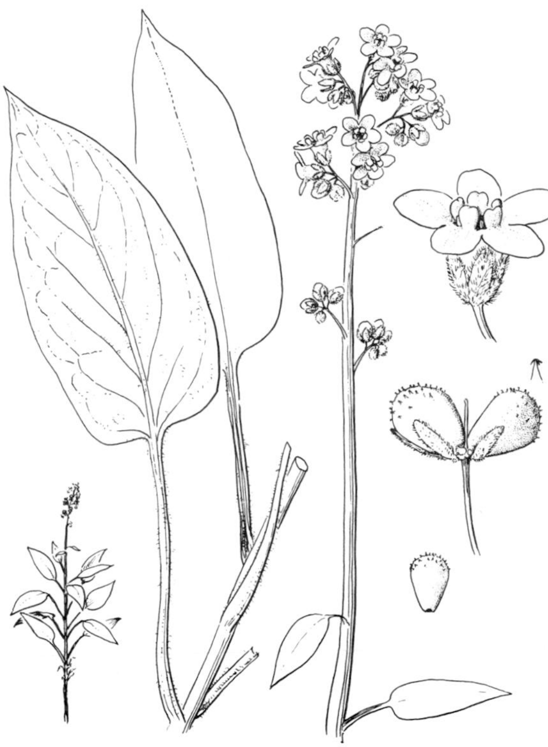

73. Pacific hound's-tongue, *Cynoglossum grande*

FIGWORT (SNAPDRAGON) FAMILY

Mimulus alsinoides (pl. 22) is a tiny monkeyflower that grows between rocks and in crevices, often with *Rhacomitrium* and other mosses. Its height does not often exceed 10 cm, and its flowers are only about 1 cm long. These are so striking, however, that the plant cannot be overlooked. They are bright yellow, and the lower lip is marked with a reddish brown blotch.

Blue-eyed Mary, *Collinsia parviflora* (pl. 22), is one of the earliest spring wildflowers in open, sunny situations. It is not often more than 10 or 15 cm tall, and some specimens are not even 5 cm high. The flowers, mostly about 6 to 8 mm long, have a strongly two-lipped corolla that is humped on its upper side near the base. The color is blue and purplish blue, except for the large upper lip, which is white or nearly so.

The Indian paintbrushes, of the genus *Castilleja,* are partial parasites. They have leaves and chlorophyll and are apparently able to make much of their own food, but underground they are attached to other plants. The flowers of paintbrushes, having a two-lipped corolla, are basically much like those of snapdragons; but they are much less conspicuous than the colored bracts, generally divided into three lobes, that accompany the flowers. Of the few species occurring in the lowlands west of the Cascades, *C. hispida* (pl. 22) and *C. miniata* are the most common. Both are perennials about 40 cm tall and branch mostly from the base. The bracts are bright red or orange-red. In *C. hispida* the bracts and at least many of the upper leaves are deeply divided into three or more lobes. In *C. miniata* the bracts are scarcely lobed, and some may not be divided at all; few, if any, of the leaves are lobed. Both species have hairy stems; the leaves are regularly hairy in *C. hispida,* sometimes hairy in *C. miniata.*

BROOMRAPE FAMILY

The broomrapes, cancerroots, and their allies are root parasites of other flowering plants. They are leafless, except for a few scales at the base of the stem, and have no chlorophyll, so all of their nourishment must come from their hosts. Our most common species is *Orobanche uniflora* (pl. 20), generally attached to the broad leaved stonecrop or some saxifrage, particularly *Saxifraga integrifolia.* In old gardens where introduced stonecrops (such as the European *Sedum album*) run wild, this *Orobanche* is occasionally found growing on them. Each stem, about 5 cm tall, bears a pretty, snapdragonlike flower approximately 1 cm across. The corolla is bluish or purple, with a yellow blotch on the lower lip and a white patch deep inside, on the ceiling of the portion that is fused into a tube. The fine seeds are produced in a small capsule that cracks open in late summer, and are eventually washed into the soil. They must germinate in contact with the roots of a suitable host if they are to establish a connection with it.

The ground cone, *Boschniakia hookeri* (pl. 20), is such an interesting plant that its somewhat restricted distribution is disappointing. In the area of the Strait of Georgia, Puget Sound, and the San Juan Archipelago, it is yellowish and is attached to salal; along the open coast, it may be either yellowish or purplish, and parasitizes both salal and kinnikinnick. The portion that appears above ground, in May and June, consists almost entirely of flowers inserted between scalelike bracts resembling those of a pine cone. The height of this inflorescence is generally about 6 to 8 cm. The individual flowers are about 1 cm long and have two-lipped corollas. The capsular fruits that succeed the flowers crack in late summer to liberate the small seeds.

CUCUMBER FAMILY

Bigroot, *Marah oreganus* (pl. 23), is a perennial that sprouts up each spring from a swollen, woody root that may weigh more than 10 kilograms (22 pounds). Its stems spread out over the ground like those of its cultivated relatives, the cucumbers, canteloupes, squashes, and gourds, and they also climb onto shrubs. The leaves of bigroot have blades about 15 cm across, which are irregularly and rather shallowly divided into several pointed lobes. Coiled tendrils for gripping twigs are produced at intervals along the stems. The pollen-producing flowers, borne in groups of ten or more on short side shoots, have five to eight white petals and are approximately 1 cm across. The seed-producing flowers are greenish and arise singly on short stalks. Each fruit, containing several large seeds, may be more than 5 cm long and usually has at least a few spinelike outgrowths.

VALERIAN FAMILY

Where corn-salad, *Plectritis congesta* (pl. 23), grows, it usually is so abundant that its flower heads make the ground pink in late spring. The plants normally do not branch, growing straight up to a height of 15 to 20 cm or more. The stems are four-angled, and the leaves are opposite. Those at the base may have petioles, but the ones on the upper part of the shoot hug the stem tightly. The individual flowers, decidedly two-lipped, are only about 5 mm across, but there are generally at least 20 or 30 in each head.

ASTER (SUNFLOWER) FAMILY

Oregon sunshine, *Eriophyllum lanatum* (pl. 24), is a woolly little sunflower that is common in well-drained, open situations in the Willamette Valley and Puget Trough. On the islands of the San Juan Archipelago and in some areas around the Strait of Georgia, it grows in rocky habitats close to the shore. Most plants are about 30 or 40 cm high and form rather compact bushy growths. The leaves are mostly 12 to 14 cm long; and in varieties found west of the Cascades, they are typically divided into several narrow lobes. The leaves, stems, and bracts beneath the flower heads are covered with long hairs, some portions thus becoming almost white. The flower heads, about 2 cm across, are both showy and attractive because of the bright yellow rays. A careful observer will note that the inner portion of each ray is more deeply colored.

Asters start to bloom in late summer, and their flowers generally last all through September. *Aster chilensis* is perhaps the most widely distributed species in the lowlands of our region. It is a perennial that comes up each year from an underground rhizome and grows to a height of up to 1 m. The flower heads are about 1.5 cm across and have blue, pale purple, pink, or white ray flowers. The leaves, up to approximately 10 cm long, are rather narrow and have smooth margins. This aster is most commonly found in brushy areas and open woods.

Aster subspicatus (pl. 24) is similar, but its leaves are usually toothed and its flower heads frequently reach a diameter of 2 cm. The bracts that enclose the lower part of the flower head of *A. subspicatus* are mostly about the same size; in any case, the smallest are about two-thirds as long as the largest. (In *A. chilensis* the bracts are graduated in size, the upper ones being much larger than the lower ones.) *Aster subspicatus* often grows at the seashore and in moist situations, but it is fairly versatile.

There are some other asters in our region, and certain of them could be confused with *A. chilensis* or *A. subspicatus.* For positive identification, it is essential to get help from a comprehensive guide to the flora.

The common species of goldenrod in our region is *Solidago canadensis* (pl. 24). Like the asters, it flowers in late summer, livening up fields and roadsides at a time when most other plants are busy with seed production. By way of creeping rhizomes, goldenrod builds up large colonies which can be very impressive when in full bloom. The height of the flowering stems is generally between 50 cm and 1 m, but may be taller. Most of the leaves that amount to anything are found along the upper half of the stems. They are commonly about 5 to 10 cm long, rather elongated, and sometimes toothed at the margins, although the teeth are usually widely spaced. The flower heads, concentrated in a terminal spike, are individually only 3 or 4 mm across. The disk flowers, as well as the dozen or so ray flowers, are a rich yellow.

About the only other goldenrod that can dependably be found in our region is *S. spathulata.* It does not tend to creep so much as *S.*

canadensis, is shorter, and has leaves at the base; in fact, these leaves are usually the largest on the plant. In addition, the rays of the ray flowers of *S. spathulata* are only about three times as long as wide; in *S. canadensis* the rays are decidedly narrower than this. Any goldenrod found around sand dunes near the coast will almost certainly be *S. spathulata.*

The gum plant, *Grindelia integrifolia* (pl. 24), is found on some rocky hillsides close to salt water in Puget Sound and the Strait of Georgia, as well as around salt marshes in this area and along the open coast. There are also inland populations in the Puget Trough and Willamette Valley. The gum plant is a perennial that comes up afresh each spring and grows to a height of about 50 cm. It blossoms from midsummer to early autumn, and the flower heads of maritime forms may be up to 4 cm across. The green bracts beneath the flowers themselves are very sticky. The leaves produced at the base of the plant are mostly 10 to 20 cm long and have distinct petioles; the blades are approximately oblong. Elsewhere the leaves are much smaller and clasp the stems.

Yarrow, *Achillea millefolium* (pl. 25), is in almost every field and along every roadside, but it also grows in brushy places. Typically it is about 40 or 60 cm tall and has woolly stems, but the height and other characters vary a good deal. The leaves, most of which are concentrated near the base, are elongate and basically featherlike, but the branches are further divided into tiny segments. The flower heads are concentrated into flat or slightly convex clusters. Each head, about 1 cm across, is basically like that of a daisy, for it consists of a group of disk flowers in the center and ray flowers around the margin. The latter look superficially like petals, but the petallike portion actually results from the fusion of five petals. The petals of the disk flowers are very small. The number of rays is not constant, but generally there are five or fewer; they are normally white, but plants with pink rays are frequent in some populations.

Pearly everlasting, *Anaphalis margaritacea* (pl. 25), comes up in spring from an underground rhizome and by early summer reaches a height of 50 or 60 cm or more. The leaves, scattered almost evenly along the stem, are mostly about 5 to 7 cm long; they are narrow and typically covered with long hairs that are matted into a white wool. The flower heads are borne in rather tight clusters at the tips of the stems. Each head is about 1 cm across and is composed mostly of pearly white bracts; the real flowers form a compact mass in the center. If the inflorescences are brought into the house, the bracts retain their form and texture, just as cultivated everlastings do.

Ferns and Fern Allies

Most of the ferns that grow in exposed situations are found at the bases of rocks or in crevices, or are rooted in moss that covers rocks. The chief exception to this rule is the bracken, *Pteridium aquilinum* (pl. 29), a versatile deciduous species that grows in open, grassy areas as well as in woods and brushy habitats.

The licorice-fern, *Polypodium vulgare* (pl. 28), has been discussed in connection with coniferous woods, where it is usually found on mossy logs and tree trunks. In rocky areas, its stems creep under carpets of moss and between rocks. On shaded, moist cliffs it may grow as luxuriantly as it does in the woods; but in severely exposed areas where moisture disappears quickly and is almost nonexistent in summer, the leaves of the licorice-fern may not exceed 10 cm. This species may be almost evergreen except where it dries out in summer. New foliage is added in the autumn, after the rainy season has begun.

The sword-fern, *Polystichum munitum* (pl. 28), is an evergreen woodland species that regularly braves the rigors of living on open, rocky hillsides. In such situations it tends to be small, and its leaves are usually much stiffer than those of plants growing in moist woods. In especially compact forms, the leaflets may be so crowded that they overlap.

Now for the ferns that are essentially limited to rock crevices. With one exception (the brittle bladder-fern), these are evergreen. The maidenhair spleenwort, *Asplenium trichomanes* (pl. 29), is a miniature species whose leaves rarely exceed a length of 10 cm. They arise from a creeping stem, but are so close together that they appear to come from a crown. The petioles are blackish brown, and the spore-bearing structures are concentrated in oval groups on the undersides of the small leaflets.

The gold-back fern, *Pityrogramma triangularis* (fig. 74), also has blackish brown petioles, and its stem creeps to some extent. The leaf blades, mostly a little under 10 cm long, have an approximately triangular outline, although they are divided three times near the base and twice above the base. The upper surface is green, but the lower surface is covered with a yellow powder, which accounts for the common name. The spore-producing structures are concentrated along the veins on the underside.

The pod-fern, *Aspidotis densa* (*Cheilanthes siliquosa*) (fig. 75), although widely distributed, is less likely to be found in our region than on the sunny sides of ravines running toward the Columbia Gorge and on exposed rocky hillsides at moderate elevations in the Cascades. It

75. Pod-fern, *Aspidotis densa*

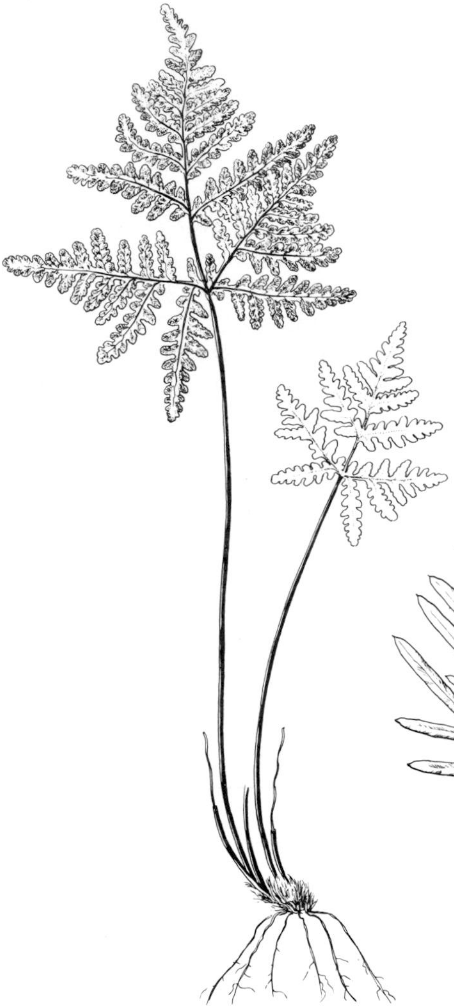

74. Gold-back fern, *Pityrogramma triangularis*

should be looked for, however, wherever there are rock slides. It is a compact species, usually with crowded leaves. The petioles are glossy and dark brown, usually slightly longer than the thrice-divided blades, which reach a length of about 5 or 6 cm. The leaflets are elongated, dark green above, and have stiff tips; not all of the leaves in a clump produce spores, but the spore-bearing sacs of those that do are partly covered by infolded margins of the leaflets. Each leaflet thus resembles a pod that has started to split open lengthwise.

The parsley-fern, *Cryptogramma crispa* (fig. 76), is superficially similar to the pod-fern because its leaves are about the same size and similarly clustered. The petioles are green or yellowish, however, and the leaflets are light green. There are, besides, two very distinct kinds of leaves: those that bear spores and those that do not. The spore-bearing leaves last a single season, their leaflets are elongated, and the sacs in which the spores are produced are partially covered by inrolled margins on the underside, as in the pod-fern. The parsleylike, sterile leaves are usually shorter, and their ultimate leaflets are less distinctly separate from one another. This species is most likely to be found on rock slides and generally grows in association with the pod-fern.

The brittle bladder-fern, *Cystopteris fragilis* (fig. 77), dies back in winter. It prefers rocky areas that are partially shaded by shrubs or trees. The rhizome creeps, and the petioles of the closely spaced leaves range from the color of straw to blackish brown. The light green blades, which are usually divided twice (three times near the base), are mostly about 10 to 15 cm long. The clusters of spore-bearing sacs are covered by a hoodlike indusium ("bladder"), but as the sacs ripen and get ready to discharge the spores this structure is thrust back and withers.

The selaginellas constitute a group of plants that resemble mosses but are more closely related to ferns. Remember that in ferns and their allies the persistent, leafy generation reproduces by spores and is thus comparable to the temporary and leafless spore-producing phase in the life history of a moss. Some selaginellas, especially compact desert species sold in curio shops and dime stores, are called "resurrection plants." Clumps so dry that they appear to be dead revive almost miraculously when watered.

Our most common species, *Selaginella wallacei* (pl. 29), can qualify as a resurrection plant, too. It grows in exposed rocky places that become parched for long periods in summer. Even when withered, however, it can be recognized because the more nearly upright terminal portions of some of its branches are four-angled. In these portions, which are about 2 or 3 mm in diameter, the leaves fit together more

76. Parsley-fern, *Cryptogramma crispa*

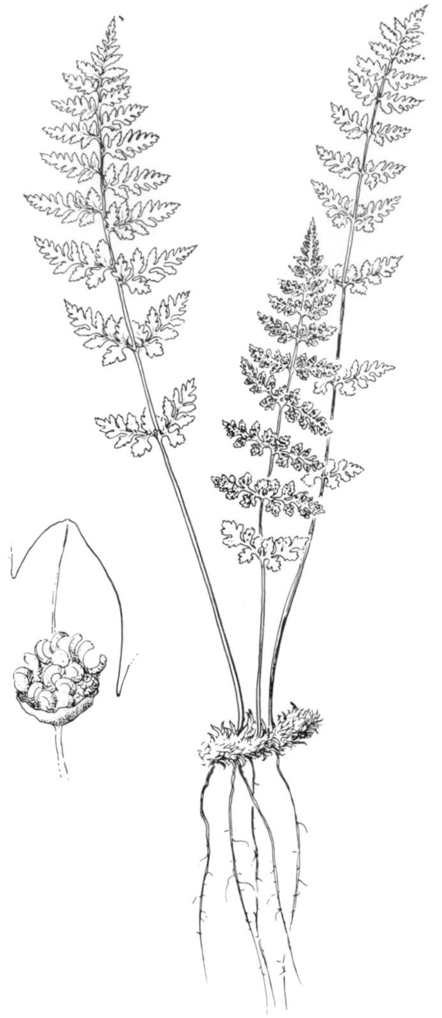

77. Brittle bladder-fern, *Cystopteris fragilis*

tightly than they do elsewhere on the plant. They are specialized for the production of spores. The sacs in which spores have developed are bright orange and can be seen between the leaves. The running stems of this species, rooted at intervals, may be more than 10 cm long, but the subsidiary branches tend to be short. The needlelike leaves are about 2 or 3 mm long and are deep green when moisture is plentiful, becoming grayish green as they dry out.

Selaginella oregana (pl. 29) is a more slender species found in humid areas near the coast. It is usually mixed with mosses that grow on trees, especially big-leaf maple.

Mosses

Most of the mosses that grow luxuriantly in exposed situations are different from those typical of shady habitats. Some species are almost completely restricted to rocks on which a little soil has collected; others are more common on the ground; and certain kinds grow chiefly on wood, including fence posts and the bark of trees. Any mosses found on stone walls, steps, and roofs, and on relatively bare ground in gardens and along roadsides, are apt to be among those described in this section.

The dominant moss on exposed, rocky outcrops is usually *Rhacomitrium canescens* (pls. 21, 32). It forms extensive, yellowish green mats that turn to an almost ashen color when they dry out. Although this species creeps, the new shoots tend to be upright. The leaves, about 2 mm long and 1 mm wide at the base, taper gradually to a slender, whitish tip that has a few marginal teeth. The sporophyte stalk, usually about 1.5 cm tall, is reddish brown; the upper part of it becomes twisted as it dries. The capsule is 2 mm long and is directed upward; only a small part of it is covered by the calyptra, the "dunce cap" that persists for a short time.

The hair-cap moss, *Polytrichum juniperinum* (pl. 30), is perhaps the most nearly worldwide of all mosses. It is common throughout our area and is so easy to recognize that a beginner should learn it right away. It is especially abundant on and between rocks, on gritty soils, and on wood that has accumulated some dirt. It tends to form thick mats, often mixed with *Rhacomitrium* or other mosses, and it can survive harsh droughts. *Polytrichum juniperinum* also grows on rocks and logs in shady places, and even in situations that are almost continually moist. The leaves of the hair-cap moss, except when dry, are usually a dull bluish green. They may be up to 1 cm long and have smooth margins. There is a broad, sheathing base, then a sword-shaped portion that tapers rather abruptly to a hairlike prolongation. The sporophyte has a glossy, reddish brown stalk up to 4 or 5 cm long, and the upright capsule is conspicuous because of its large size and because the calyptra that completely covers it is densely hairy. The male plants are very attractive when they are sexually active: the tips of the stems, where the sperm-producing organs are concentrated, are bright pinkish red.

Two other species of *Polytrichum* are fairly common in our region and might be confused with *P. juniperinum.* In *P. piliferum* the hairlike prolongation at the tip of each leaf is whitish. In *P. commune* the leaves taper so gradually to the apex that there is no obvious prolongation, and the margins have prominent teeth.

Pogonatum contortum (pl. 30) looks much like a *Polytrichum* because it is of comparable size and because the calyptra covering the capsule of the sporophyte is conspicuously hairy. In the leaves of *P. contortum,* the principal portion of the leaf blade is not distinctly set off from the clasping basal portion. In addition, they have toothed margins and do not taper to a slender prolongation, so that although they slightly resemble the leaves of *P. commune,* they cannot be confused with those of *P. juniperinum* or *P. piliferum.* The sporophyte stalk of *P. contortum* is about 3 cm tall and the capsule is 4 or 5 mm long. This species typically grows on soil, but it is not likely to be found in areas that are much exposed and that become parched in summer. It is mentioned here, however, because it is so similar to polytrichums. *Pogonatum contortum* is characteristic of humid areas and is partial to situations that have been disturbed within the last few years. It is sometimes abundant in road cuts and on soil clinging to the root systems of fallen trees.

The two common species of *Tortula* also have upright capsules, but the calyptras on these are smooth. The leaves of tortulas taper abruptly to white hair-points; they are otherwise bright green, except at the base, which is colorless. In *T. princeps* (pl. 32) the leaves are about 5 mm long and have toothed hair-points; the sporophytes are up to 3 cm tall. In *T. muralis* (pl. 32) the leaves are about 4 mm long and there are no teeth on the hair-points; the sporophytes are not often more than 1.5 cm tall. The sporophyte stalks of tortulas are reddish and become twisted when they dry. These mosses grow on rock, soil, and tree trunks, but only in exposed situations.

Dicranoweisia cirrata (pl. 32) is the most abundant moss on bare wood, as that of fences; but it also grows on tree trunks, rocks, roofs, and soil. It grows erect and forms dense, dark green or light green tufts. The leaves are up to only about 3 mm long, and the absence of hair-points enables one to distinguish it easily from *Tortula muralis,* a superficially similar species. The sporophytes are approximately 1 cm tall. As in tortulas, the capsules are held upright, and the stalks become twisted when they dry.

Grimmia pulvinata, which forms small cushions on rock, can usually be picked out from among other mosses by its grayish green color. The leaves, 5 or 6 mm long, are basically dark green, but their white hair-points make the colonies appear grayish. The sporophyte stalks, mostly about 2 cm long, are so strongly bent that the capsules may be partly pushed down into the cushions formed by the leafy gametophytes. The stalks become twisted as they dry, and the capsules become distinctly grooved.

Plagiomnium

Leucolepis menziesii

Hornwort, *Anthoceros*

Conocephalum conicum

Marchantia polymorpha

Lunularia cruciata

Porella

PLATE 33

Aleuria aurantia

Bird-nest fungus, *Crucibulum vulgare*

Gyromitra infula

Witches' butter, *Dacrymyces palmatus*

Varnished bracket fungus, *Polyporus oregonensis*

Dryad's saddle, *Polyporus applanatus*

Polyporus sp.

PLATE 34

Old man's beard, *Usnea hirta*

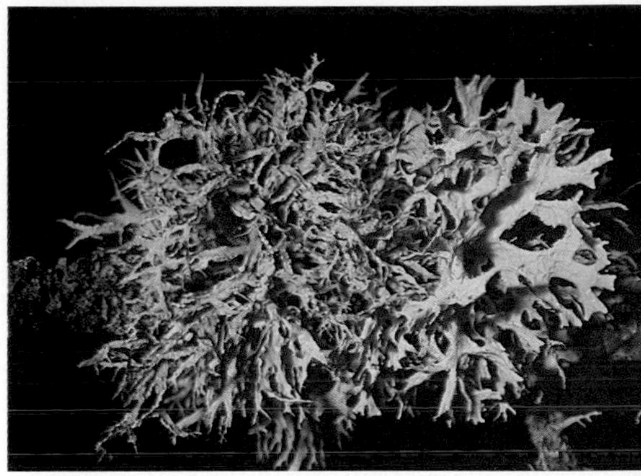
Ramalina farinacea (left) and *Evernia prunastri* (right)

Ramalina farinacea

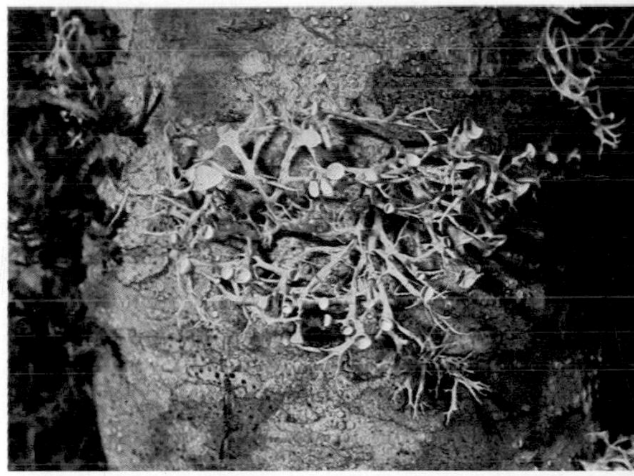
Ramalina digitata

Sphaerophorus globosus

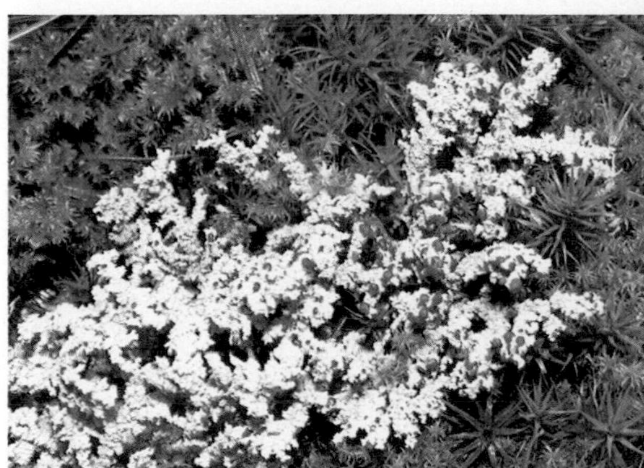
Stereocaulon tomentosum

PLATE 35

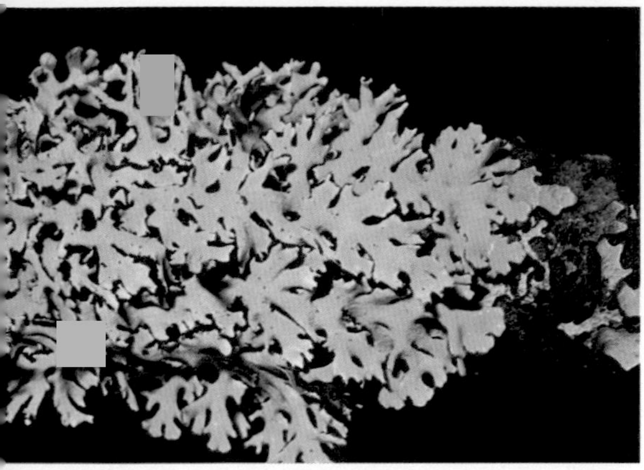

Hypogymnia physodes

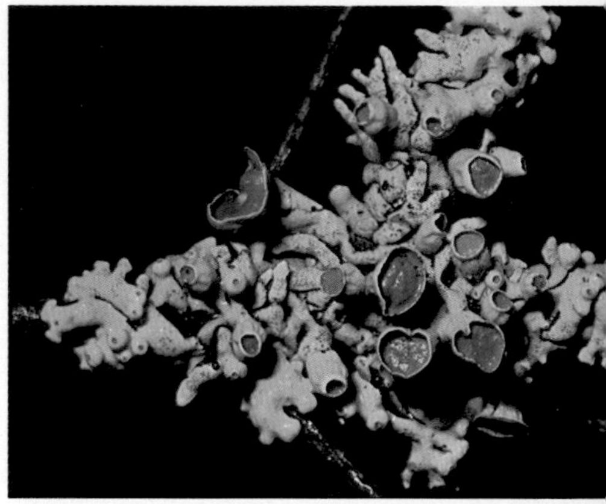

Hypogymnia enteromorpha

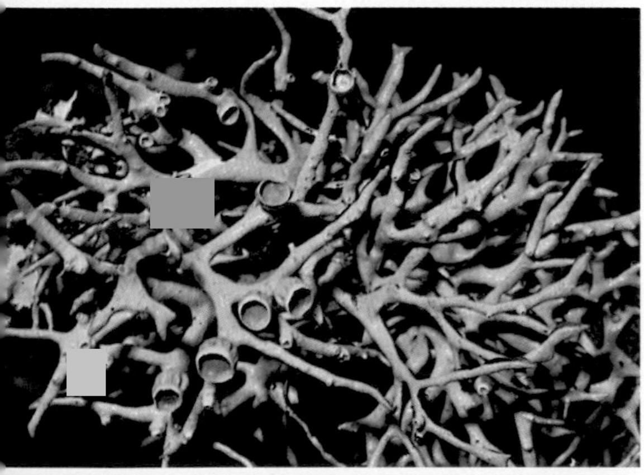

Hypogymnia vittata

Parmelia sulcata

Platismatia glauca

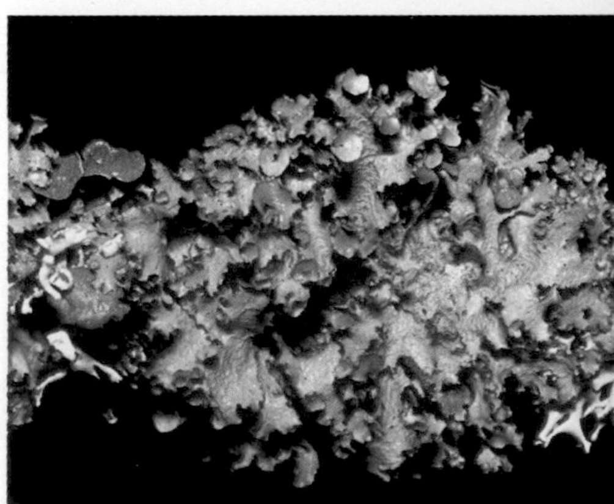

Platismatia stenophylla

PLATE 36

Xanthoria candelaria

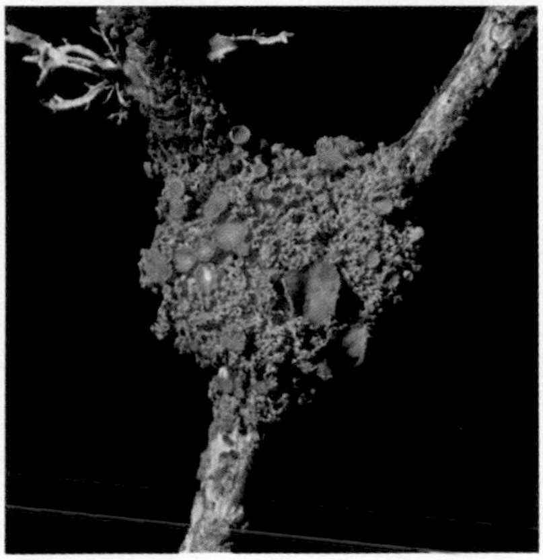
Xanthoria polycarpa

Cetraria canadensis

Peltigera canina

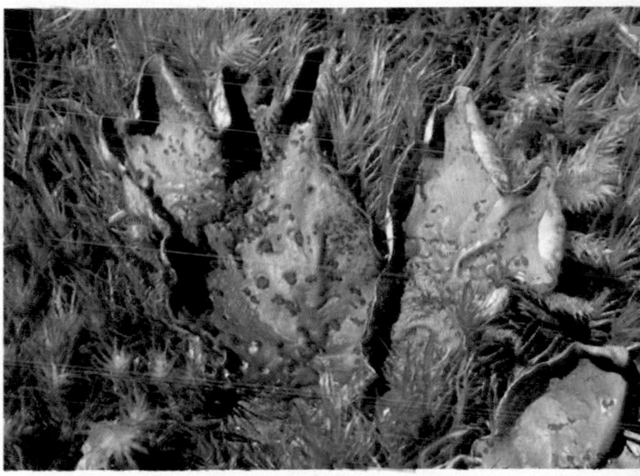
Peltigera aphthosa

Umbilicaria

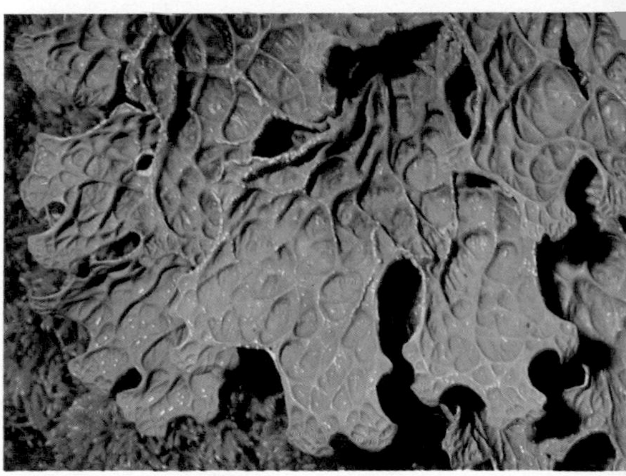
Lungwort, *Lobaria pulmonaria*

PLATE 37

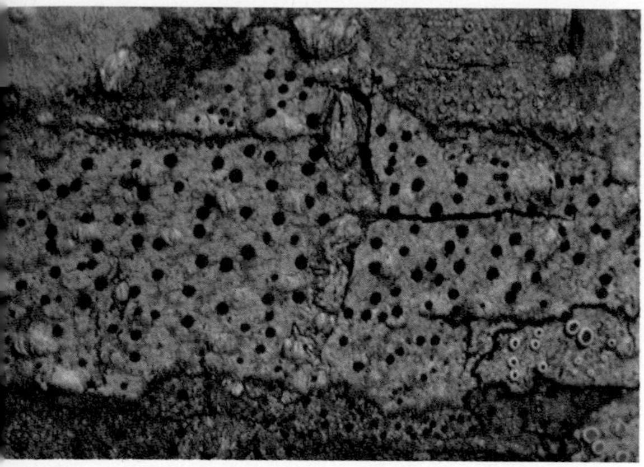

Clot lichen, *Mycoblastus sanguinarius*

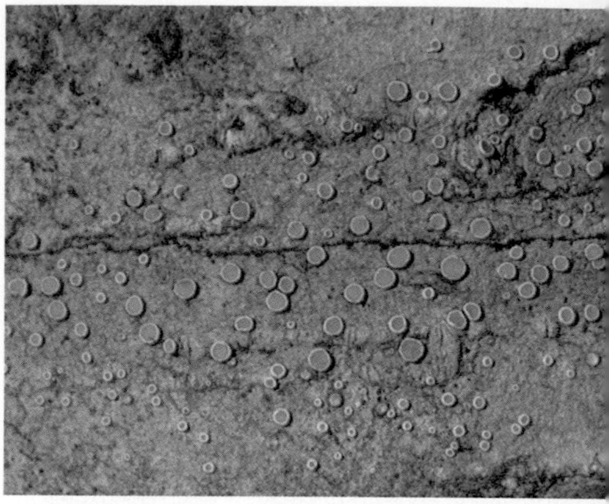

Ochrolechia pallescens

Lecidea cinnabarina

Pertusaria amara

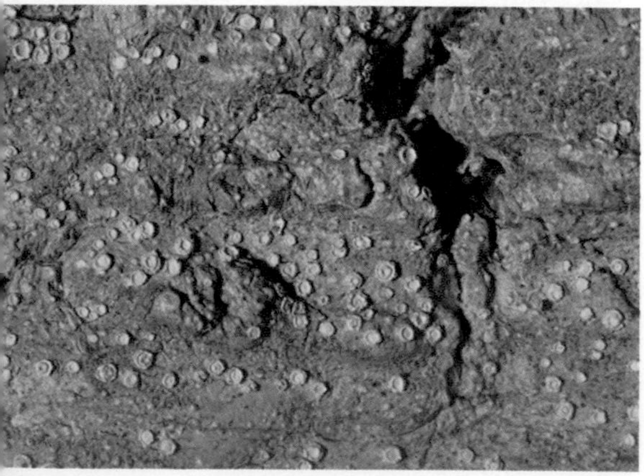

Pertusaria ambigens

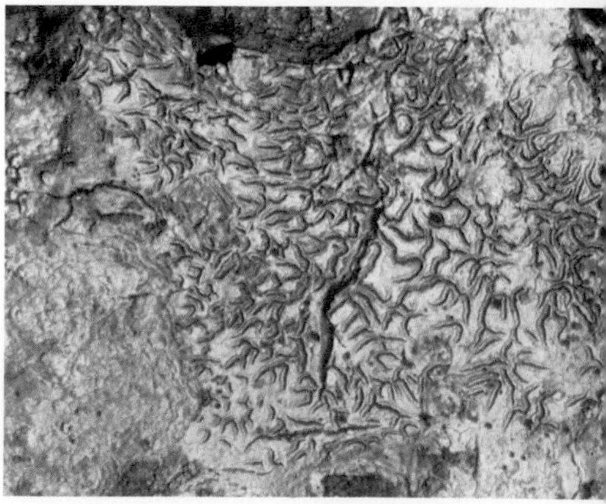

Graphis scripta

PLATE 38

Cladonia pyxidata

Cladonia bacillaris

Cladonia bellidiflora

Cladonia furcata

Cladonia rangiferina

Pilophoron aciculare

PLATE 39

Physcia stellaris

Caloplaca

Lecidea

A common lichen that forms thin yellow coati
on bark and wood

A one-celled green alga ("protococcus")
that forms green coatings

Letharia vulpina

PLATE 40

Monadenia fidelis

Haplotrema sportella

Vespericola columbiana

Allogona townsendiana

Helix aspersa

Oxychilus alliarius

PLATE 41

Banana slug, *Ariolimax columbianus*

Prophysaon andersoni

Hemphillia malonei

Arion ater

Milky slug, *Agriolimax reticulatus*

Limax maximus

PLATE 42

European centipede, *Lithobius forficatus*

Millipede, *Harpaphe haydeniana*

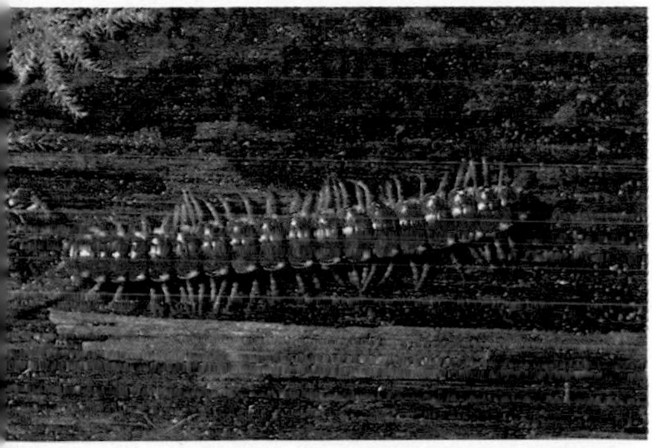

Kepolydesmus pungo

A millipede of the cylindrical type

Pillbug, *Armadillidium vulgare*

Sowbug, *Oniscus asellus*

Carnivorous ground beetle (carabid)

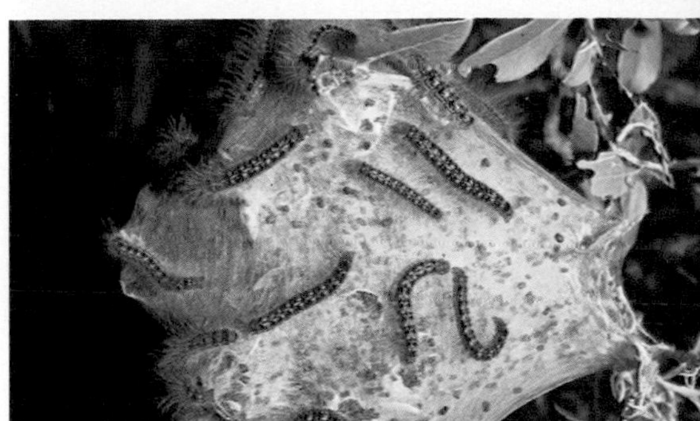

Coast tent caterpillar,
Malacosoma californicum pluviale

PLATE 43

Oregon salamander,
Ensatina eschscholtzii oregonensis

Western red-backed salamander,
Plethodon vehiculum

Clouded salamander, *Aneides ferreus*

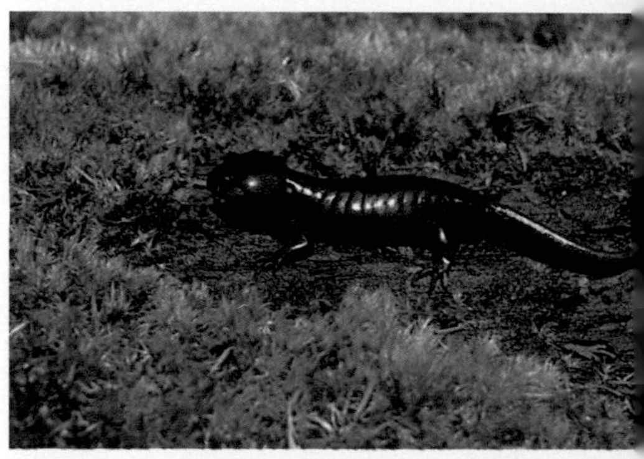

Brown northwestern salamander,
Ambystoma gracile gracile

Western long-toed salamander, *Ambystoma macrodactylum*

PLATE 44

Rough-skinned newt, *Taricha granulosa*

Olympic salamander,
Rhyacotriton olympicus olympicus

Pacific treefrog, *Hyla regilla*

Northern red-legged frog,
Rana aurora aurora

Cascades frog, *Rana cascadae*

Bullfrog, *Rana catesbeiana*

PLATE 45

Northwestern toad, *Bufo boreas boreas*

Tailed frog, *Ascaphus truei*

Northern alligator lizard,
Gerrhonotus coeruleus principis

Western skink, *Eumeces skiltonianus*

Northwestern fence lizard,
Sceloporus occidentalis occidentalis

Northwestern ringneck snake,
Diadophis punctatus occidentalis

PLATE 46

Northwestern garter snake,
Thamnophis ordinoides

Red-spotted garter snake,
Thamnophis sirtalis concinnus

California mountain kingsnake,
Lampropeltis zonata

Pacific rubber boa, *Charina bottae bottae*

Sharp-tailed snake, *Contia tenuis*

Pacific gopher snake,
Pituophis melanoleucus catenifer

PLATE 47

Northwestern pond turtle,
Clemmys marmorata (underside)

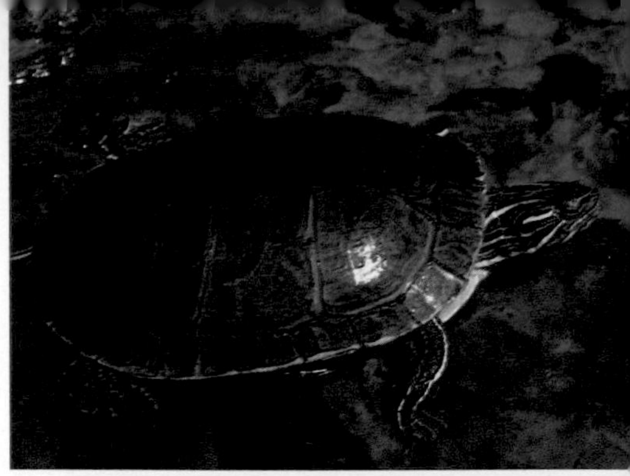

Painted turtle, *Chrysemys picta*

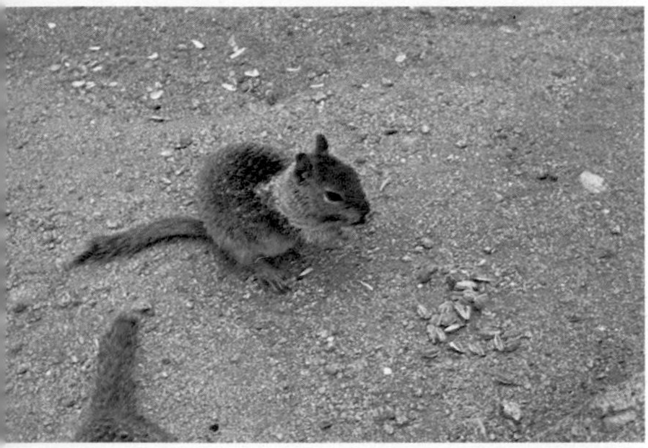

Beechey ground squirrel, *Otospermophilus beecheyi*

Little brown bat, *Myotis lucifugus alascensis*

Trowbridge shrew, *Sorex trowbridgii*

Coast mole, *Scapanus orarius*

Shrew-mole, *Neurotrichus gibbsii*

PLATE 48

Species of *Bryum* have plump, nodding sporophyte capsules and typically grow on soil, especially between rocks. The leaves of *B. capillare* (pl. 32), only about 3 mm long, resemble those of a *Tortula* because they have hair-points. In some other bryums, hair-points are lacking, but the general form of the plants is similar to that of *B. capillare.*

Funaria hygrometrica (pl. 32) slightly resembles *B. capillare,* but the stalks of its sporophytes freely bend and coil in response to changes in humidity. The plump capsules, 2 or 3 mm long, may be oriented in almost any direction, and the chaffy, beaklike calyptras do not fall off until the capsules are nearly mature. The gametophytes are rarely more than 5 mm high, and the leaves do not have hair-points. *Funaria* is most likely to be found on disturbed soil and in situations that have been burned over.

Lichens

Perhaps the simplest way to start sorting out the more common lichens of exposed and partially exposed situations is to group them according to their habitat preferences. Unfortunately, some species that most typically colonize rocks also grow on bark or bare wood. Nevertheless, most of the really distinctive lichens of our region can rather definitely be associated with a particular substrate.

The following species occurring on the branches and trunks of trees and shrubs in the marginal, more open portions of coniferous woods are even more likely to be found in comparatively open places: *Usnea hirta* (pl. 35), *Evernia prunastri* (pl. 35), *Ramalina farinacea* (pl. 35), *Parmelia sulcata* (pl. 36), *Mycoblastus sanguinarius* (pl. 38), and *Ochrolechia pallescens* (pl. 38). All of these were described in chapter 2. However, some of the more common and distinctive lichens growing on trees and shrubs in sunny places are not likely to occur where there is shade during most of the day.

Xanthoria candelaria (pl. 37) is a small foliose lichen abundant on trunks of deciduous trees, especially Garry oak and big-leaf maple. Its thallus is usually yellow-orange when dry, greenish yellow when wet, and consists of finely divided lobes that are mostly free of the bark. The fruiting bodies, up to about 3 mm in diameter, are bright orange. This species, which may almost completely cover a tree trunk, also grows on rocks.

Xanthoria polycarpa (pl. 37) is similar, but is less inclined to grow on tree trunks than on twigs of deciduous trees and shrubs. It is typically concentrated where a twig branches. Its colonies are generally very compact and cushionlike, and there may be so many fruiting bodies that the rest of the thallus is nearly obscured.

Letharia vulpina (pl. 40) is a fruticose species plentiful east of the Cascades, especially on branches of yellow pine and junipers. It is rather uncommon in our region, although it is occasionally found on living trees, dead snags, or fence posts in exposed situations. This is a striking species, yellow-green or chartreuse in color, that forms much-branched growths 10 cm or more in diameter. The branches are usually flattened, and their surfaces are typically marked by elongate pits and ridges, as well as by granular reproductive bodies. The blackish brown fruiting cups, up to 7 or 8 mm in diameter, are fringed by outgrowths that are often slightly branched. West of the Cascades this lichen rarely produces fruiting cups of consequence. *Letharia vulpina* is highly toxic and has been used in Europe to poison wolves and foxes.

Cetraria canadensis (pl. 37) might be confused with *L. vulpina* because of its yellow or yellow-green color. Its colonies are foliose rather than fruticose, however, and its fruiting cups are more nearly chestnut brown than blackish brown. In our area this species is most likely to be found on branches of dead conifers.

Of the lichens found on otherwise nearly bare rocks, one of the more common is a foliose species, *Physcia stellaris* (pl. 40). Its growths are sometimes irregular. Large patches may be more than 15 cm across. The color is usually gray or yellowish gray. The fruiting bodies are slightly concave disks up to about 5 mm in diameter and dark brown to nearly black in color. Other species of *Physcia* are found in our area, but most of them are not generous in producing fruiting bodies.

Species of *Umbilicaria* (pl. 37) form thin sheets attached only near their centers. The growths are basically circular, but they are usually contorted, cut into lobes, or otherwise irregular. The color is brown or blackish brown. The fruiting bodies are little disks scattered over the upper surface, but some of the species in our area almost never show them. Umbilicarias grow on very exposed rocks and boulders that are devoid of moss or even a little soil. The only plants that can grow with them are encrusting lichens.

Most of the orange or orange-brown lichens that form thin encrustations on rock are species of *Caloplaca* (pl. 40). Several kinds occur in our region, and certain of them are partial to rocks at the seashore, just above the high water mark. The fruiting bodies of caloplacas are small disks stuck directly to the thallus. They are not often more than 2 mm in diameter, but their color is often brighter than that of the thallus as a whole.

If you find a thin gray or whitish encrustation with black fruiting bodies, this could be a species of *Lecidea* (pl. 40). There are several genera, however, including *Lecanora* and *Pertusaria,* that form similar growths. In some species the thallus has a tendency to crack, like dry mud; in others, it remains almost homogeneous in texture. Not all lichens of this general type have dark fruiting bodies, and not all are restricted to rock. Some live on bark, or on both bark and rock.

Pilophoron aciculare (pl. 39) is a pleasant surprise on occasion. Its primary thallus is a gray crust, from which arise cylindrical stalks about 1.5 or 2 cm tall. These are capped by little black beads that glisten when they are wet. After a dry spell, the stalks become so stiff that they feel almost like the bristles of a wire brush. They may grow upward, outward, or downward, depending on the orientation of the rock surface where the lichen happens to be attached. There is no other lichen in our area that can be mistaken for this species.

A rich variety of lichens is found on rocky soil and on rocks where there is an accumulation of dirt and growths of moss. Most of these lichens bear fruiting bodies on upright stalks, which arise from a less conspicuous primary thallus that is applied to the substrate. The primary thallus may be scaly, foliose, or of the encrusting type, and may disappear by the time the fruiting bodies are well on the way.

Several species of the large genus *Cladonia* may be expected. Not all of these grow on soil—some are partial to old wood in exposed situations—but it will be convenient to discuss the several easily recognized species of *Cladonia* together.

The stalks of *Cladonia pyxidata* (pl. 39) are up to about 3 cm high and typically have broad, shallow cups at their tips, so they look like golf tees. The inner surface of each cup, especially near the rim, usually has many small disks stuck tightly to it. The color of the stalks—and of the upper surface of the scalelike lobes that constitute the primary thallus—ranges from pale green to yellowish gray and depends to some extent on the moisture content of the lichen. *Cladonia pyxidata,* which could be called "pixie goblet," may be common on rock walls and stone steps in gardens, and is sometimes found on tree trunks. Other species of *Cladonia* are so similar that it is not possible to separate them without detailed microscopical and chemical study.

Several cladonias in our region have bright red fruiting bodies. The two species most likely to be found are *Cladonia bacillaris* (pl. 39) and *C. bellidiflora* (pl. 39). The former is the more graceful. Its fruiting stalks, up to about 2 cm high, are generally smooth, except perhaps for a few scales near the base. The fruiting bodies are rather compact, often almost beadlike, and usually under 3 mm in diameter. This species commonly grows on stumps, logs, and on fence posts. If the wood is barkless and has been lightly charred by fire at some time in the past, so much the better. *Cladonia bellidiflora* is a coarser species. Its stalks may be up to nearly 4 cm high and are regularly scaly, especially in their lower portions. The fruiting bodies are sometimes up to almost 1 cm in diameter and usually are lumpy and deeply lobed. *Cladonia bellidiflora* may occasionally be found on barkless wood, but it is more abundant on mossy logs and among mosses on gritty soil. It may form crowded beds more than 15 cm in diameter.

In certain cladonias the upright stalks that arise from the primary thallus are extensively branched. *Cladonia furcata* (pl. 39) is representative of a group characterized by rather open colonies. It regularly grows with mosses in somewhat shaded habitats and reaches a height of about 5 cm. Small, brown fruiting bodies adorn many of the ultimate branches. In another group the colonies form especially dense, low mounds. In *C. rangiferina* (pl. 39), called "reindeer moss" because it is one of the lichens eaten by reindeer in Arctic regions, the ultimate branches typically arise in fours and end in blunt, often brownish tips. *Cladonia mitis* and *C. arbuscula* are similar, but their ultimate branches are more likely to arise in threes and to be somewhat pointed at the tips. These last two species are difficult to separate without chemical tests, although *C. arbuscula* has a tendency to point its ultimate branches in one direction. In any case, if you find lichens of this sort—and they are often common on sandy or gravelly soils—it is probably wiser just to identify them as belonging to the reindeer moss group.

Stereocaulon tomentosum (pl. 35) and *S. paschale* are often abundant on gritty soil or on rocks that have a coating of moss. These lichens may be more than 4 or 5 cm high, but generally they are just 1 or 2 cm tall. In color, they are almost white. The fruiting bodies are reddish brown or blackish brown, up to about 2 mm in diameter. The stalks on which they are borne may be branched and are typically at least partly obscured by flaky outgrowths. *Stereocaulon tomentosum* may be distinguished from *S. paschale* on the basis of the fact that its stalks, wherever they are not covered by flakes, have a woolly surface.

4

Wet Places

This chapter is concerned mostly with plants that grow where there is seepage or standing water. It is not always reasonable, however, to state flatly that a particular species is restricted to wet places. A number of plants that thrive where the ground is saturated with water will, if protected by shade, succeed admirably in situations where the amount of moisture is only moderate. There are also species that typically grow where the soil is soggy in winter and spring but almost bone-dry during much of the summer.

In general, plants that are not strictly limited to wet places and that have been covered in some other part of this book will not be discussed here. Grasses and submerged aquatic vegetation are routinely excluded; anyone interested in these will find helpful guides listed in the bibliography. Amphibians and reptiles that are more or less permanently aquatic, or that go to water to breed, hunt food, or escape from enemies, are described in chapter 6.

Groves of Alder, Cottonwood, Ash, and Birch

This category is something of a catch-all, devised to cover a variety of situations in which deciduous trees with a preference for wet ground are concentrated. Three of the five species that will be discussed here are distributed through much of our region; the other two are not likely to be encountered except in the northern part of the Puget Trough, and even there they are not widespread.

The red alder (pl. 3) has been described in connection with coniferous forests and should already be known to everyone. Soon after a forest is cut or burned, seedlings of alder usually come up almost like grass. They grow rapidly, and for a number of years this species constitutes a large part of the total vegetation. Eventually, the alders are diluted and succeeded by coniferous trees and other deciduous species, such as the maples and cascara. Along streams and in other wet places, however, alders may predominate indefinitely.

The black cottonwood, *Populus trichocarpa* (pl. 5), is typically found in bottomlands bordering rivers, streams, lakes, and marshes. As a rule it is a rather slender tree, less than half as wide as tall. The height may reach 30 m. The leaf blades, up to about 8 cm long, are bright green and shiny above, brownish and resinous below. They have a nearly heart-shaped outline, although an indentation where the petiole is attached may be lacking or scarcely noticeable. The margins are finely toothed. The leaf buds of the cottonwood are covered with a sticky, fragrant substance that sweetens the air delightfully for a few days in spring. The pollen-producing and seed-bearing catkins are borne on separate trees. In summer the small fruits, having ripened, split open and release their seeds, which are covered with cottony hairs that make them easily carried by wind. Groves of cottonwood are a beautiful sight in the autumn, when the leaves turn bright yellow.

A close relative of the cottonwood is the quaking aspen, *P. tremuloides* (pl. 5). Reputed to grow in more states than any other tree, it is plentiful in some parts of the Northwest, especially at lower and moderate elevations in the mountains; but on our side of the Cascades its distribution is spotty. It occurs in a few places in the Willamette Valley, around Puget Sound and the Strait of Georgia, and on some of the islands of the San Juan Archipelago. Quaking aspen, not often more than 10 m tall, generally forms thickets and is easily recognized. Its bark is powdery white, and the powder can be rubbed away with a finger. The leaf blades, up to about 5 or 6 cm long, are mostly heart-shaped or close to it, and they have fine serrations all around the margins. Because the petioles are flexible and strongly flattened at right angles to the blades, the leaves quiver in even the gentlest breeze.

The Oregon ash, *Fraxinus oregana* (fig. 78), is another tree that prefers exposed bottomlands and stream banks. Like the cottonwood, it often forms nearly pure stands, especially at the borders of swales. The ash is easily recognized at any time of the year. It has opposite leaves and branches. The compound leaves consist of five or seven leaflets that are approximately oval and generally 5 to 10 cm long. The foliage is olive green or yellowish green and turns yellow in the autumn. The small, inconspicuous flowers are arranged in a cluster of branching stalks. The flowers that produce pollen are borne on trees separate from those that produce the distinctive, flattened fruits, each about 3 cm long and resembling tongue depressors or stirring paddles. Even in winter a few fruits are likely to be seen on the trees. If not, many of the stalks to which they were attached will still be present. The almost hairlike fineness of the terminal branches of these stalks is characteristic. The bark of the ash is grayish and closely furrowed, and it generally supports an interesting assortment of lichens, most of which make the bark appear lighter than it actually is. Large specimens of this tree may reach a height of more than 20 m.

78. Oregon ash, *Fraxinus oregana*

Birches, which belong to the same family as alders, do not occur west of the Cascades in Oregon. The paper birch, *Betula papyrifera* (pl. 5), however, is abundant on the east side of Puget Sound north of Seattle, and also along the Strait of Georgia. It is not often encountered anywhere else in our region. The paper birch is partial to moist situations unshaded by larger trees, and it may form dense stands. It grows to a height of about 20 m, and is a typical birch in having a papery, white bark that peels away in strips. The leaf blades are about 4 cm long, and their margins are rather coarsely toothed. The pollen-producing and seed-producing catkins of birches are basically similar to those of alders.

Shrubs and Small Trees

Of the widely distributed shrubs and small trees of our region, the ones most likely to have wet feet are salmonberry (pl. 10), hardhack (pl. 9), red elderberry (pl. 12), creek dogwood (pl. 8), bush honeysuckle (pl. 11), and several kinds of willow. Salmonberry was described in chapter 2, for it is generally present in woods that are moist throughout or that have some wet spots. It is not restricted to shady situations, however, and in open areas where water is plentiful, it may form almost impenetrable thickets.

The remainder of the shrubby plants on the list were considered in chapter 3, partly because they contribute to brushy areas and partly because it was convenient to describe them together with some other shrubs and small trees. Red elderberry and bush honeysuckle are the only ones likely to stray far from wet places, and even they grow most luxuriantly along ditches, in seepage areas, and at the borders of streams, ponds, and marshes.

Although the Pacific willow, *Salix lasiandra* (fig. 35), is almost routinely present where there is standing water, or at least wetness, other species of *Salix* should be expected. *Salix piperi, S. rigida, S. sitchensis,* and *S. sessilifolia* are fairly widespread in the region west of the Cascades. *Salix fluviatilis* has a very restricted distribution, being found only along the Columbia River and the northernmost sector of the Willamette River. *Salix scouleriana,* which is common, often grows in wet places, but it is versatile enough to be successful in some relatively dry, well-drained habitats. All of the willows just mentioned have been described and illustrated in chapter 3.

Cat-tails, Rushes, Sedges, and other Grasslike Plants

Among the more conspicuous herbaceous plants of wet places are representatives of several families that superficially resemble grasses. The more important of these are cat-tails, bur-reeds, sedges, and rushes.

Cat-tails are easily recognized. Their flowers are organized into compact, solid spikes. Our only species, *Typha latifolia* (pl. 26), is a perennial that comes up each spring from a creeping rhizome buried in mud. Especially robust specimens may be more than 2 m tall. The long leaves are up to 2 cm wide, and the flower spikes, which turn dark brown in summer, are usually about 15 cm long and 2.5 cm thick.

In bur-reeds the flowers are produced in tight, globular clusters. Of the several species that might be encountered, *Sparganium emersum* (fig. 79) is probably the most common. It normally reaches a height of 30 or 40 cm, and its flower clusters are about 2 cm in diameter. Those that consist entirely of pollen-producing flowers are above the ones composed of seed-producing flowers.

79. Bur-reed, *Sparganium emersum*

Sedges and rushes may be confused with one another and with grasses. In grasses the stems are typically cylindrical and the leaves are in two rows. The sheath of each leaf, which clasps the stem below the blade, is usually open. In addition, there is a little collar (ligule) encircling the stem above the base of the blade. Rushes have cylindrical stems, but their leaves are arranged in three rows, the sheaths are

80. Rush, *Juncus effusus*

81. *Juncus ensifolius*

closed, and there is no collar. Sedges are distinctive in having three-angled stems. They are like rushes, however, in having three rows of leaves. The leaf sheaths of sedges are almost always closed and a collar is present above the blade only in one genus, *Carex*.

The rushes are represented in our region by many species, but *Juncus effusus* (fig. 80) is perhaps the most easily recognized common species. Although it varies considerably, the height generally falls into the range of 20 to 80 cm. The leaf blades are reduced to small, bristlelike structures. The flowers are produced in fairly compact clusters a few centimeters below the pointed tips of the stems. *Juncus ensifolius* (fig. 81), which is also common, has well-developed and neatly folded leaf blades, and its flower clusters are even more compact than those of *J. effusus*.

The sedges and their close allies are also represented by many species. *Carex aquatilis* and *C. obnupta* are of rather general occurrence. Both are fairly large—regularly 50 or 60 cm tall, and sometimes taller than 1 m. The flowers are in elongated spikes. In *C. aquatilis* (fig. 82) the spikes are up to about 5 cm long and stand erect; in *C. obnupta* (fig. 83) they are usually at least 10 cm long and droop a little.

Bulrushes belong to the sedge family, and most of them are similar to sedges in having stems that are noticeably, if not conspicuously, three-angled. To be sure that a plant is in the sedge family rather than the rush family, one will have to look closely at the organization of the fruits. The fruits of rushes eventually split open and contain at least three seeds; in sedges the fruits do not split open and are single-seeded. In any case, of the many kinds of bulrushes in our region, *Scirpus microcarpus* (fig. 84) is perhaps the most frequently encountered. Its flower spikes, each only about 5 mm long, are concentrated in numerous small groups within a loose cluster. The stems are just barely three-angled.

Other Herbaceous Plants, Mostly with Broad Leaves

The species covered in this section represent a number of diverse families. Although most of them require considerable wetness, they do not all prefer the same kind of habitat. Some, as the skunk-cabbage, grow best in marshes, very wet meadows, and at the edges of ponds and streams; their roots are in standing water almost all year. Others, as the little orchid called ladies-tresses, are much less nearly aquatic, although they are normally found in meadows and grassy areas where there is ample moisture, as near a shallow pond that is filled in winter and spring. Still others are typical of places where there is seepage, even if the presence of a more than average amount of water is not obvious at the surface.

82. Sedge, *Carex aquatilis*

ARUM (CALLA-LILY) FAMILY

The yellow skunk-cabbage, *Lysichitum americanum* (pl. 26), is the only representative of this family native to the Northwest. The bright yellow spathes that partially enclose the fleshy flower spikes are modified leaves. The other leaves, which generally do not unroll completely until after the spathes are full-blown, may reach a length of more than 1 m. The odor of the plant does resemble that of a skunk, but it is not

83. *Carex obnupta*

84. Bulrush, *Scirpus microcarpus*

offensive. In the skunk-cabbage of eastern North America, *Symplocarpus foetidus,* the inflorescence produces a rather disagreeable stench; and in various Old World relatives, the inflorescences smell like dead animals, horse manure, dog dung, and stale urine. The odors attract carrion beetles, blowflies, or other insects that normally lay their eggs on smelly things that can be eaten by their larvae. While the insects are muddling around among the flowers, they pick up pollen that they carry to other flowers. The insects drawn by the inflorescences of our skunk-cabbage include such diverse types as honeybees and certain beetles.

WATER-PLANTAIN FAMILY

Wapato, *Sagittaria latifolia* (fig. 85), is common along sloughs of rivers and in ditches, swamps, and at the edges of ponds and lakes. Its leaves, with arrowhead-shaped blades, stand to a height of about

85. Wapato, *Sagittaria latifolia*

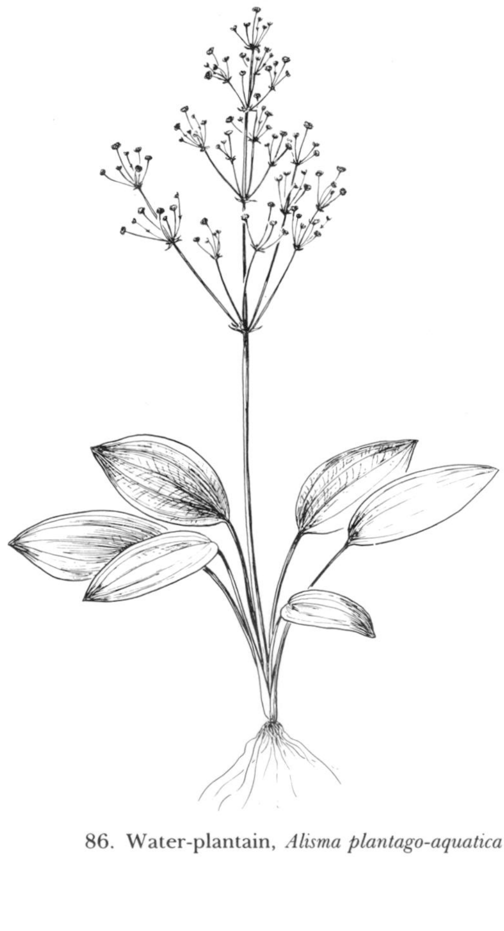

86. Water-plantain, *Alisma plantago-aquatica*

40 or 50 cm. They come up each spring from a starchy tuber that Indians use for food. The flowers, with three white petals, are about 2 cm across; they are borne in loose spikes, with three flowers generally arising at each node. As the numerous dry fruits developing from each flower ripen, they form a head about 2 cm in diameter.

Water-plantain, *Alisma plantago-aquatica* (fig. 86), is widespread in the Northern Hemisphere, but its distribution in our region is spotty. The leaf blades, on long petioles, are oval to nearly heart-shaped and up to about 15 cm long. There is usually just one flower stalk to each plant, but this is extensively branched in whorls and may be taller than 50 cm. The flowers, with three green sepals and three white or pink petals, are about 5 mm across. Numerous one-seeded fruits, tightly packed together, develop from each flower.

LILY FAMILY

The false hellebores, belonging to the genus *Veratrum,* tower above most plants with which they grow. Their thick stems, regularly 1 to 1.5 m tall, bear broad leaves that are strongly ribbed lengthwise, and terminate in inflorescences consisting of many flowers. In *V. californicum* (fig. 87) the branches of the inflorescence stand stiffly upright, and the flowers are mostly about 2 or 2.5 cm across. The three sepals and three petals are white or sometimes greenish, especially near the base. In *V. viride* (fig. 88) the branches of the inflorescence droop, and the flowers are generally about 1.5 cm across. The petals and sepals are green or yellowish green.

ORCHID FAMILY

Spiranthes romanzoffiana (pl. 16), called ladies-tresses, is common in some meadows and moist, grassy fields. It usually starts growing in May and blooms in June and July, producing a spike about 20 or 30 cm tall. The only leaves of consequence are a few narrow ones near the base; those higher up are reduced to mere bracts. The flowers, about 1 cm long, are numerous, crowded, and arranged in rows that spiral around the stem. They are whitish, but not really pure white; individually they are not particularly attractive, but their arrangement is interesting.

NETTLE FAMILY

The stinging nettle, *Urtica dioica* (represented in our region by the variety *lyallii,* fig. 89), is a perennial that creeps by underground stems and forms dense colonies. Its shoots, which regularly surpass a height of 1 m, die back in winter. The leaves are opposite, and their coarsely toothed blades, mostly 5 to 10 cm long, are oval or narrowly heart-shaped. The small, greenish flowers are formed on drooping clusters that arise at the leaf axils. Those that produce seeds are nearer the top of the shoot than those that produce only pollen. When this nettle produces sprouts in early spring, it could be mistaken for a hedge-nettle or some other mint because of the form and arrangement of the

87. False hellebore, *Veratrum californicum*

88. *Veratrum viride*

leaves. One brief encounter with the stinging hairs that cover the plant will clear up the confusion. The tingling usually lasts for several hours. Stinging nettle is not strictly limited to wet places. Because of a preference for nitrate-rich soils, it is often found around barnyards and past or present human habitations.

The leaves of nettle are eaten by caterpillars of some well-known butterflies. Most notable of these in our region are the red admiral (*Vanessa atalanta*), painted lady (*Cynthia cardui*, or *Vanessa cardui*), and the West Coast lady (*Cynthia annabella*, or *Vanessa carye*). They have other food plants, too, but the red admiral relies chiefly on nettle. It is a handsome butterfly, about 5 cm across; the color is mostly blackish brown, but there is a red border on each hind wing and a red band running diagonally across each fore wing.

89. Stinging nettle, *Urtica dioica* variety *lyallii*

WATER-LILY FAMILY

The yellow pond lily, *Nuphar polysepalum* (pl. 26), usually grows in water less than 1 m deep. Its thick rhizome creeps through the mucky bottom and sends up leaves with spongy petioles and large floating blades. The flowers, produced singly, have butter-yellow petals surrounding numerous stamens and a central group of united pistils. There is no other native plant that can be confused with it. The fragrant, white or pink-tinged water-lily found in some lakes is *Nymphaea odorata*, introduced from eastern North America. One other species should perhaps be mentioned. *Nymphaea tetragona*, which has been found not far north of Bellingham, Washington, resembles *N. odorata*, but has fewer petals (not more than fifteen) and is not fragrant. The range of *N. tetragona* is discontinuous. It grows in eastern Asia and in North America northward and eastward from Michigan; the localities where it has been seen in Washington and Idaho are exceptional.

BUTTERCUP FAMILY

The most common buttercup of wet places, especially roadside ditches, is the creeping buttercup, *Ranunculus repens* (pl. 18). It was introduced from the Old World, but is now thoroughly naturalized. It is usually (but not always) at least moderately hairy and creeps along by runners that root at intervals. The basal leaves, on long petioles, have three leaflets, each of which is further divided incompletely into three coarsely toothed lobes. The flowers, about 2 cm across, have glossy, deep yellow petals. Normally there are five petals, but sometimes there are more, and variants with double flowers are occasionally found. This buttercup is pleasant enough when growing more or less wild, though it is undoubtedly tough competition for some native plants. It may become a very tenacious weed in lawns.

Ranunculus orthorhynchus, the swamp buttercup, is an indigenous species that could be confused with *R. repens.* It does not spread by creeping stems, however, and its leaf blades may have as many as seven principal lobes.

Among several other species of *Ranunculus* that should be expected, *R. flammula* (fig. 90) is perhaps the most common. This is a native and is typically found in or around shallow ponds, including those that dry

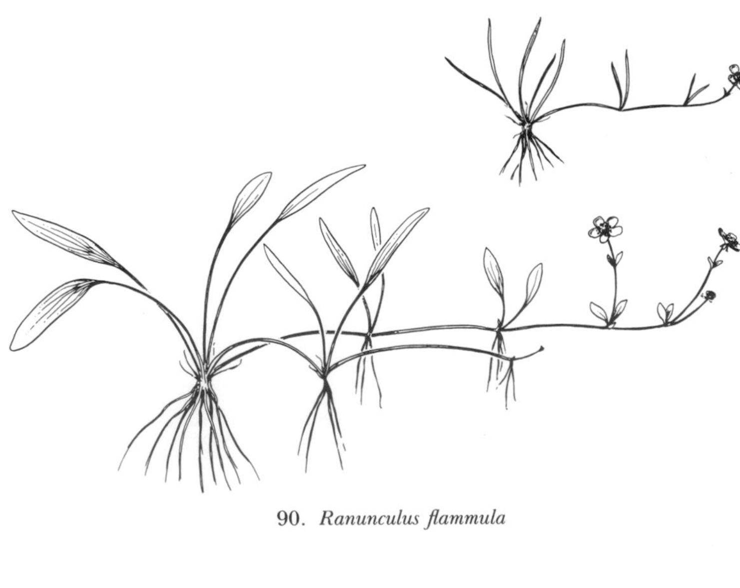

90. *Ranunculus flammula*

out in summer. It spreads by slender runners, and its upright branches are usually only about 10 or 15 cm tall. The leaf blades, up to 5 cm long, are narrow and not lobed as they are in most of our buttercups. In plants that are permanently aquatic the blades may be only 2 or 3 mm wide. The flowers are 1.5 to 2 cm across. *Ranunculus alismaefolius* is somewhat similar to *R. flammula,* but it does not have creeping stems and it is often taller than 30 cm. Its leaves and flowers are decidedly larger than those of *R. flammula.*

PARSLEY FAMILY

Water-parsley, *Oenanthe sarmentosa* (fig. 91), practically fills up many of our shallow, sluggish streams and roadside ditches. It is a perennial that may grow as tall as 1 m, but it falls down, takes root, and keeps spreading. The leaf blades, about 20 or 30 cm long, have an approximately triangular outline and are deeply cut from one to three times

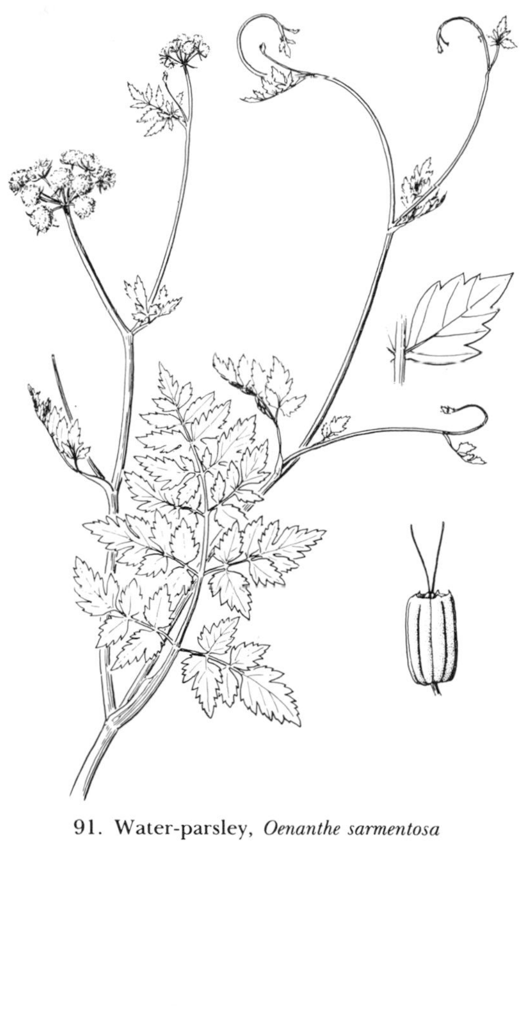

91. Water-parsley, *Oenanthe sarmentosa*

into toothed leaflets. The small, white flowers are arranged in clusters that collectively form a nearly flat-topped inflorescence. The ripe fruits, with rather prominent lengthwise ribs, are about 3 or 4 mm long and appreciably flattened.

Cow-parsnip, *Heracleum lanatum* (fig. 92), is another perennial that comes up every spring and grows exuberantly, its flower stalks sometimes reaching a height of 2 m or more. The leaf blades are routinely at least 20 cm across; typically, they are divided into three completely separate leaflets, and these are in turn deeply cut into several toothed lobes. The bases of the petioles are much inflated and clasp the stems. The white flowers are produced in dense, flat-topped clusters. When bruised, the plant gives off a pungent and somewhat disagreeable odor remotely similar to that of its relatives, the carrots and parsnips. Inland, this species is almost completely restricted to ditches and borders of marshes, but along the coast it often grows on bluffs facing the sea.

92. Cow-parsnip, *Heracleum lanatum*

FIGWORT (SNAPDRAGON) FAMILY

Just about every roadside ditch or cliffside seepage area, if it is exposed to sunlight, will have the monkeyflower, *Mimulus guttatus* (pl. 22). Although it creeps along by stolons, and often forms extensive colonies, it is an annual. It may be puny or robust, depending at least to some extent on circumstances. Most plants are 40 to 50 cm tall. The leaves are opposite, generally smooth, and have oval, toothed blades about 4 to 6 cm long. Some of the leaves have petioles, but the upper ones usually clasp the stem. The yellow flowers, 2 or 3 cm long, are borne singly in the axils of the upper leaves. The petals are organized

93. American brooklime, *Veronica americana*

94. Marsh speedwell, *Veronica scutellata*

into a strongly two-lipped corolla, as in snapdragons and most other members of the figwort family, and the hairy, puffed-out part of the lower lip is spotted in maroon.

The speedwells and brooklimes, members of the genus *Veronica,* are represented in our region by more than ten species. Some of them are annoying weeds, especially in lawns. A few, however, are regularly found in ditches, marshes, bogs, and other wet situations. In *Veronica* the organization of the corolla is appreciably different from that in most other genera of the figwort family. The tube forming the basal portion is short, and the rest of the corolla is expanded into four unequal lobes. The two stamens are attached to the sides of the uppermost lobe.

The American brooklime, *V. americana* (fig. 93), is perhaps the most common and most attractive of the species that grow in wet places. It is a creeping annual not often more than 30 or 40 cm tall, with short-petioled, opposite leaves up to 5 or 6 cm long. The flowers, produced in short racemes, are nearly 1 cm across and typically bright blue, sometimes pink.

Other veronicas that are likely to be encountered and that might be confused with *V. americana* are *V. anagallis-aquatica, V. catenata,* and *V. scutellata.* The leaves of these are without petioles; and in the case of *V. scutellata,* the marsh speedwell (fig. 94), the blades are very narrow. In all three species the flowers are on the whole slightly smaller than those of *V. americana.* A perennial species, *V. serpyllifolia,* is decidedly different from any of the preceding. It is usually less than 10 cm tall, and its flower racemes are slender and condensed. The leaf blades are oval and only about 1 cm long. There is a native variety, *humifusa,* with blue flowers, and an introduced variety, *serpyllifolia,* with flowers that are white to pale blue and have dark veins. The latter is apt to be a pest in lawns. One had best consult a comprehensive guide to the flora before attempting to sort out the veronicas.

MINT FAMILY

The hedge-nettle, *Stachys cooleyae* (pl. 23), is a hairy perennial that dies down in winter. It is a typical member of the mint family in having four-angled stems, opposite leaves, and two-lipped flowers; but the pungent odor it gives off when bruised is more fetid than mintlike. It grows to a height of 1 m or more. The larger leaves have blades about 10 cm long. These are narrowly heart-shaped and have coarsely toothed margins. The smaller leaves, higher up on the stem, are more slender and lack an indentation where the petiole joins the blade. The reddish purple flowers, about 1.5 or 2 cm long, are produced in terminal spikes. The flowering season lasts from June to late summer.

Any hedge-nettle that does not quite fit the description of *S. cooleyae* could be one of a few other species that occur in our region. None of them is as widespread as *S. cooleyae.*

ASTER (SUNFLOWER) FAMILY

Coltsfoot, *Petasites frigidus* (pl. 24), is a rather low perennial that comes up in March and April from thick, creeping stems. It often flowers before its foliage is well developed. The leaf blades, deeply divided into several lobes, are commonly 15 or 20 cm across. The flower heads, almost 1 cm in diameter, are concentrated at the tops of stout stalks whose lower portions are covered by scalelike leaves. In general, the corollas of the individual flowers are white. In some flowers, however, especially those that produce only pollen, the corolla is drawn out into a ribbon, as in the ray flower of a daisy or sunflower, and this may be pinkish. The lowland variety of coltsfoot, to which the foregoing description is applicable, is *palmatus.* The variety *nivalis* grows at higher elevations in the Olympic Mountains and in the Cascades of British Columbia, Washington, and northern Oregon. Its leaf blades are typically longer than wide and not so deeply lobed as those of *palmatus.*

Ferns and Fern Allies

The most common fern of really wet places is the lady-fern (pl. 28), described in chapter 2. Although it is typical of shady woods, it can stand exposure to summer sun if it is rooted in mucky soil. Deer-fern (pl. 28) requires a situation where moisture is plentiful, but it is less inclined than the lady-fern to grow out in the open, except in very humid areas near the coast. Bracken (pl. 29), which is successful under a variety of conditions, is sometimes found in seepage areas and bogs.

An unobtrusive oddity occasionally encountered in wet, grassy meadows and open, moist woods is the leathery grape-fern, *Botrychium multifidum* (fig. 95). It has just one leaf, but this consists of two entirely different portions. One part of the blade is dissected into thick leaflets and slightly resembles a sterile blade of the parsley-fern, although it is much stiffer. The other part, which stands upright generally to a height of about 20 cm, terminates in a number of narrow segments that bear the "grapes." Within these globular structures the spores are produced. The sterile part of the leaf persists through the winter and does not wither until the succeeding summer, by which time a new leaf has appeared.

The Virginia grape-fern, *B. virginianum* (fig. 96), is a primarily eastern species that has been found in moist woods and brushy areas in western British Columbia and Washington. It is rare, however. The sterile portion of its leaf, which dies down in winter, is thin and flexible compared with that of *B. multifidum,* and it is also much larger. The plant as a whole may be taller than 50 cm. In mountain meadows of the Pacific Northwest there are several other species of *Botrychium,* all of them smaller on the average than *B. multifidum.*

The horsetails and scouring-rushes, members of the genus *Equise-*

95. Leathery grape-fern, *Botrychium multifidum*

96. Virginia grape-fern, *Botrychium virginianum*

tum, are among the plants collectively called "fern allies," because their life histories indicate that they are reasonably close to ferns. All equisetums are impregnated with silica and thus have an abrasive quality, which has made some of them useful for scouring pots and pans. They have creeping underground stems and may spread vegetatively to form extensive colonies. The shoots seen above ground are hollow, jointed, and delicately ribbed. The leaves are reduced to mere scales arranged in rings at the joints.

In most horsetails, including the only ones likely to be found in our region, there are two types of stems: those that are bright green and have whorls of branches arising at the joints, and those that are neither green nor branched but have "cones" at their tips. The green shoots, concerned with the manufacture of food, last from spring until fall. The nongreen shoots last but a few weeks, just long enough for their cones to mature and produce reproductive spores. As a rule, the fertile stems come up a bit ahead of the green shoots, or at least with the earliest of them. Horsetails are almost ubiquitous on open roadsides, banks, and waste land, especially where there is seepage. The two species we have may mingle to some extent, but generally they form separate populations.

The green shoots of the common horsetail, *Equisetum arvense* (pl. 30), with main stems up to about 5 mm thick, are regularly 30 to 40 cm high and have about 10 or 12 ridges. The fertile shoots, with stems about 5 to 7 mm thick, do not often exceed a height of 30 cm. The cones are 2 or 3 cm long.

The giant horsetail, *Equisetum telmateia* (pl. 30), is a much coarser plant. Its green shoots frequently reach a height of 70 or 80 cm, and in some situations they may be taller than 1 m. The diameter of the stems may exceed 1 cm, and the number of ridges is usually between 20 and 40. The fertile shoots, up to 30 or 40 cm high, are very stout, and their cones are commonly at least 6 or 7 cm long.

In scouring-rushes, the cones are borne at the tips of green stems that are normally unbranched. One species, the common scouring-rush, *E. hyemale* (pl. 30), is often abundant in slightly marshy places, where it may form dense stands. Its dark grayish green stems, about 1 cm thick and sometimes 1 m tall, persist for a number of years. Thus a bed of the scouring-rush can be recognized at any season. The cones, around 2 cm long, are prettier than those of horsetails and are pointed at the apex.

An engaging little fern ally occasionally found growing in mud that is just barely covered with water is the so-called clover-fern, or pepperwort, *Marsilea vestita* (fig. 97). Its slender rhizomes give rise, at intervals, to the distinctive leaves, which are about 10 or 15 cm long and have four leaflets, arranged like those of a four-leaf clover. The leaflets are approximately 1.5 cm long, pale green, and decidedly hairy. The spores of this plant are produced within elliptical, almost nutlike bodies borne on short stalks. These bodies are 6 or 7 mm long, usually hairy, and break apart into two valves when they are ripe. Unfortunately, this choice plant, a favorite of all botanists who are inspired by oddities, is uncommon in our region. Perhaps the best place to look

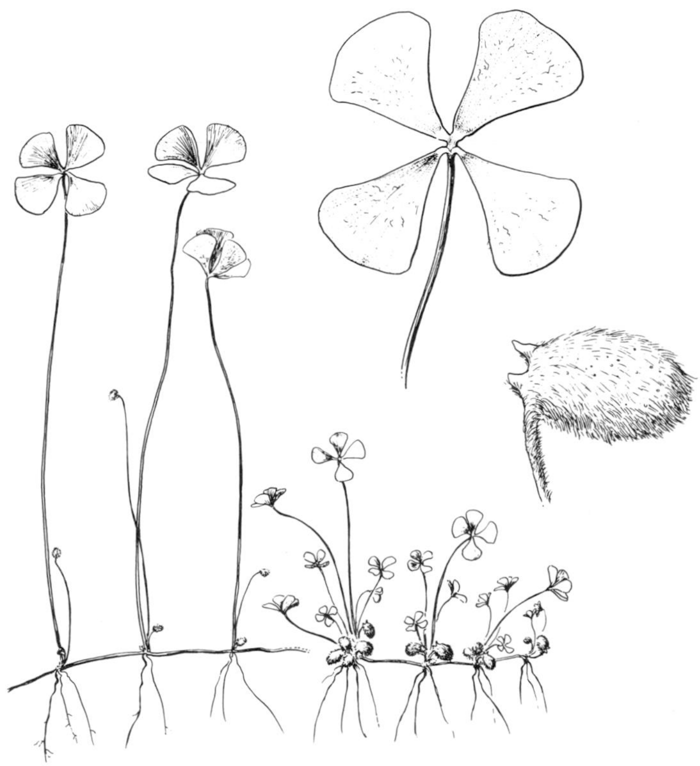

97. Clover-fern, *Marsilea vestita*

for it is in bottomlands along the Columbia River west of Portland, Oregon, and Vancouver, Washington. Where it is happy, it may form nearly pure stands almost as luxuriant as beds of clover.

Water-fern, *Azolla mexicana,* will be mentioned in the next section, which deals with an assortment of plants that float on the surface of ponds and lakes.

Small Floating Plants

Duckweed, *Lemna minor* (pl. 26), looks a little like a thalloid liverwort, but it is a flowering plant rather closely related to the arums. It has neither definite leaves nor a definite stem. The floating portion, up to about 4 mm long, has an oval outline and is bright green. It sends down a single hairlike root. Duckweed multiplies rapidly by budding, so that the surface of a pond or lake where it grows may be completely covered by it. Flowers, which are rarely produced, are practically microscopic and usually arranged in groups of three in a little marginal cleft. Two of the three flowers are pollen-producing and consist of a single stamen; the other flower is pistillate and eventually produces seed.

A similar species, *Spirodela polyrhiza,* is up to about 8 mm long and is dark green above, purplish below. Each plant produces a number of roots. This type of duckweed does not often grow so luxuriantly as to form a nearly continuous cover at the surface.

The water-fern, *Azolla mexicana* (pl. 26), is a floating fern ally that often competes with duckweed for surface area. It is usually a pale bluish green color, but during periods of strong illumination it may become decidedly reddish. *Azolla* has a branching stem and distinct leaves, and a large plant may reach a diameter of about 2 cm. Roots are produced at intervals along the stem. The leaves consist of two lobes, one of which is submerged, the other held up out of the water. The latter regularly contains filaments of a symbiotic blue-green alga, *Anabaena azollae,* which is capable of fixing atmospheric nitrogen in much the same way as bacteria associated with the roots of alder and plants of the pea family. *Azolla* reproduces by fragmentation, as well as by spores produced singly or in clusters within little capsules. (The single spores become short-lived female plants, the others become male plants, and sexual reproduction leads to development of the more conspicuous sporophyte generation just described.)

Ricciocarpus natans (pl. 26) is a common liverwort found floating on shallow water or growing on wet soil and mats of decaying leaves at the water's edge. The thick thallus is dichotomously lobed and produces crowded, short roots on the underside. Floating plants are usually triangular or butterfly-shaped, a little more than 1 cm across. Those out of water tend to form almost circular rosettes 2 cm or more in diameter.

Another common type of liverwort is *Riccia fluitans* (pl. 26). The elongated lobes of its light green thallus are only about 1 mm wide. They show, however, the dichotomous pattern of branching characteristic of most thalloid liverworts. In luxurious growths of *Riccia,* the thalli are interlocked to form a nice refuge for insect larvae and other small animals.

Bogs

A bog is not just another marsh or swamp. It is a specific situation, characterized by high acidity, a poverty of nutrients, and a distinctive assemblage of plants. First of all, there must be mosses of the genus *Sphagnum* (pl. 27), which form a spongy turf in which the upright stems are so crowded that they support each other. *Sphagnum,* because of the way it grows, is admirably suited to drawing up water from below by capillarity, as well as to absorbing water that falls as rain. This quality is, in part, what makes it possible for the turf of living moss, growing on top of a thick accumulation of dead *Sphagnum* ("peat"), to be considerably higher than the original water level. The acidity of the bog is largely due to the fact that *Sphagnum* withdraws positively charged ions of metals, which it needs for its metabolism, and replaces them with hydrogen ions.

One of the more unusual flowering plants characteristic of lowland bogs in our area is a carnivorous plant, the round-leaved sundew, *Drosera rotundifolia* (fig. 98). Its leaves, concentrated in a basal rosette, are adapted for catching small insects. After the sticky, knobbed hairs on the upper surface and along the margins snare a victim, the longer hairs at the leaf edge slowly bend inward, and the prey is soon hopelessly trapped. Then the glands on the hairs release enzymes that initiate digestion of the insect's proteins. Some other little glands on the leaf surface absorb the products of digestion. Carnivorism is a splendid solution to the problem of living in a bog where nitrogen is scarce. The sundew produces a few six-petaled white flowers, each about 5 mm across, on a stalk that forks once or twice. The flowers open for a relatively short time near midday and thus are likely to pass unnoticed.

The California pitcher-plant, or cobra-plant, *Darlingtonia californica* (fig. 99), is found in sphagnum bogs in extreme northern California, in the Siskiyou Mountains, and along the coast of Oregon to a point a few miles north of Florence. At Darlingtonia Wayside, a protected bog on the main highway near Florence, it is abundant and makes a nice display. This amazing plant is the only western representative of the pitcher-plant family. The leaves, up to more than 50 cm tall in robust specimens, arise from the creeping stem. They are so remarkably constructed for trapping insects that a brief explanation of their structure is in order. They are essentially tubular, becoming gradually

98. Round-leaved sundew, *Drosera rotundifolia*

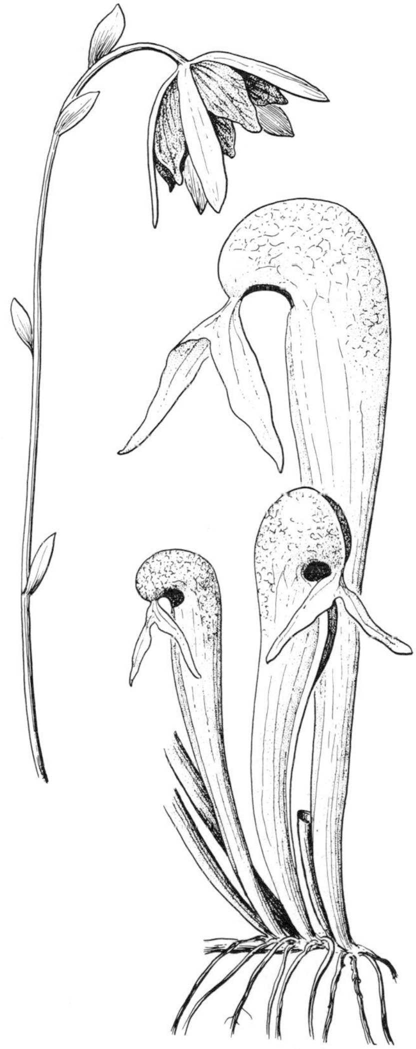

99. California pitcher-plant, *Darlingtonia californica*

wider upward to the hood that lies above the opening. The hood has a number of glassy "windows," and hanging from its tip is an appendage that looks like a fishtail. There are nectar glands on this appendage, as well as within the tubular cavity; there are also downward-directed hairs in the cavity, so that insects that have been lured into it tend to keep moving toward the bottom of the trap. The leaf secretes fluid into the trap, and the insects that drown in it are digested by bacteria. Some of the soluble products of digestion are absorbed and used by the pitcher-plant. The flowers of *Darlingtonia,* borne singly on stalks a little taller than the largest leaves, appear in spring. They are usually about 5 cm across; the narrow, yellowish green sepals are longer than the purple petals. The fruit is a capsule approximately 3 cm long.

The sedges and their allies are regularly found in wet places, but the so-called cotton-sedges or cotton-grasses, members of the genus *Eriophorum,* are an attractive and characteristic feature of true bogs. Our common lowland species is *E. chamissonis* (pl. 27). Its single flowering stalk, arising from a tuft of inconspicuous, grasslike leaves, is usually 30 or 40 cm tall. The clusters of small flowers are inconspicuous; but in summer, after the fruits have ripened and the cottony bristles (equivalent to petals and sepals) have lengthened, the heads are 3 or 4 cm across.

Trientalis arctica (pl. 27), a bog-loving relative of the starflower, *T. latifolia,* has white flowers, a little more than 1 cm across, with a varying number of petals (usually six or seven). This species is not often more than 10 cm tall, and its appearance is different from that of *T. latifolia* because it has well-developed leaves along the lower part of the stem.

Potentilla pacifica, the Pacific cinquefoil (pl. 27), a member of the rose family, is not limited to bogs, for it is found also on sand dunes, on beaches, at the borders of coastal marshes and mud flats, and in other wet places. Its flowers resemble those of a buttercup: they are 2 or 2.5 cm across, bright yellow, and borne on stalks around 20 cm long. The leaves are divided into about 13 or 15 major leaflets, the largest of which are nearest the tip. There are usually a few tiny leaflets scattered among the principal ones. This cinquefoil sends out runners that root at intervals and give rise to new plants.

Most of the shrubs typically found in bogs are members of the heath family. Labrador tea, *Ledum groenlandicum* (pl. 27), is the largest of these, reaching a height of 1 m or more. It has leathery, elongated leaves, mostly about 5 cm long, whose margins are turned under. The undersides of the leaves are woolly with rust-colored hairs. The flowers are pure white, 1 cm across, and borne in clusters of around fifteen or twenty. The dry fruits, about 5 mm long, are ovoid, but noticeably five-lobed.

A different species, *L. glandulosum,* is sometimes encountered in bogs along the coast of southern Washington, Oregon, and northern California. (It is otherwise a plant of mountain bogs, in eastern as well as western North America.) It can be distinguished from *L. groenlandicum* because the undersides of its leaves do not have rust-colored hairs; instead, they are whitish or grayish and somewhat mealy. In other respects, however, coastal plants of *L. glandulosum* (belonging to the variety *columbianum)* are similar to those of *L. groenlandicum.*

The swamp laurel, *Kalmia occidentalis* (pl. 27), forms low, tangled mats. Its leaves, 1 or 2 cm long, are dark green above, grayish below, and the margins are turned under as in Labrador tea. The flowers, about 1.5 cm across, have deep pink petals with the texture of crepe, and 10 conspicuous stamens. The fruits are nearly round capsules about 3 mm long.

The wild cranberry, *Vaccinium oxycoccos* (fig. 100), is a tiny shrub whose trailing stems are woven into tangled masses. Its leaves, mostly

100. Wild cranberry, *Vaccinium oxycoccos*

just a little under 1 cm long, are appreciably pointed at the tip. The nodding, deep pink flowers, with only four petals, are very pretty, though they are only about 1 cm across when first open, before the petals turn up. The berries, ripening in late summer, are nearly round, generally less than 1 cm in diameter, and bright red. The cultivated cranberry, *V. macrocarpon,* a native of eastern North America, is grown commercially in some coastal bogs. Its fruits regularly exceed a diameter of 1 cm.

The sweet gale, *Myrica gale* (fig. 101), is a deciduous shrub representing the myrtle family. It grows to a height of about 1.5 m. The leaves, which do not appear until after the plants have begun to flower in spring, are broadest above the middle and up to approximately 6 cm long. Both surfaces are dotted with waxy, yellow glands. Rather well-defined marginal teeth are generally limited to the upper portion of

101. Sweet gale, *Myrica gale*

102. Swamp birch, *Betula glandulosa* variety *hallii*

the blade. There are two types of flowers, both usually covered with a yellowish wax, borne on separate plants. The staminate flowers are in clusters 1 to 2 cm long; the clusters of pistillate flowers are not often more than 1 cm long. The fruits that succeed the pistillate flowers are about 3 mm in diameter and basically smooth, except for the glands that produce wax. Sweet gale is something of a rarity and is practically limited to the margins of sphagnum bogs.

The wax-myrtle (fig. 43), an evergreen species of *Myrica,* is common at the coast in Oregon and southern Washington, but it is not a bog plant. It is discussed in chapter 3.

The swamp birch, *Betula glandulosa,* is represented in our region by the variety *hallii* (fig. 102). It is rare, however, and found only in a few bogs in the Puget Trough. For a birch it is small, not often growing taller than 2 m. Although it is deciduous, it can be recognized while dormant by its flexible branches and by the fact that the younger twigs are fuzzy and conspicuously dotted with glands. The oval leaf blades, mostly 2 to 3 cm long, are widest at or above the middle and are toothed along the margins except in the basal portion, which has a wedge-shaped outline. The staminate and pistillate catkins are similar to those of the paper birch, described near the beginning of this chapter.

5

Backyards, Vacant Lots, and Roadsides

MOST of this book is concerned with native animals and plants. But our region, like almost every other part of temperate North America, has many alien species. Some were introduced intentionally, others by accident. The dandelion, house sparrow, and hundreds more are now thoroughly naturalized. In general, it is fair to say that the introduced species include most of our noxious weeds and animal pests. This does not mean that all native species are blameless. Termites of the kinds that may be eating up your front porch were doing a great job of recycling fallen timber long before the first explorers came to the Northwest. Is it their fault that we have tempted them with fence posts and split-level houses?

Anyway, this chapter is concerned mostly with weedy plants and with a variety of little animals that live in cozy places, as under old boards and flower pots. Even if your yard is the showplace of the precinct, look around you. Isn't there a loose brick or a forgotten piece of firewood somewhere? This is all you need to get into the slug-and-sowbug business.

A Few Common Weeds

A weed may be defined as a plant that is a nuisance when it grows where it is not wanted. Some native plants, such as bittercress, qualify as weeds, but the vast majority of species that fit into this category were introduced from other parts of the world. A few weeds have been discussed in previous chapters because they have become integrated into situations where most of the vegetation is indigenous. Fireweed and filaree are good examples. The species selected for description here are mostly types that are colorful or that attract attention for other reasons. The bibliography lists some books that are concerned entirely with weeds, and the comprehensive guides to the flora of this region include introduced species along with native plants.

PEA FAMILY

This large group is represented by many introduced weeds, especially vetches, sweet-peas, clovers, and some plants that resemble clovers. Of the vetches commonly encountered along roadsides and in gardens, most are both alien and annual. They cling by tendrils, which are modified terminal leaflets of the compound leaves. *Vicia sativa* (pl. 21), the common vetch, is fairly easy to recognize. Its flowers, generally borne singly or in pairs, have very short stalks; they are also relatively large—about 2 cm long. The petals, on the whole, are purplish rose, although the largest one, which is uppermost, may be more nearly purple than the others. The leaflets, of which there are about ten to fourteen (plus the tendril), appear to have been cut off near the tip, even though the midrib is continued as a short, slender projection. A variety of *V. sativa,* called *angustifolia,* is similar, but its flowers are only about 1.5 cm long, and its leaflets are narrower and not cut off.

Vicia tetrasperma, the slender vetch, produces flowers in pairs or threes, but they are at the end of long peduncles. The bluish flowers do not often exceed a length of 7 mm. *Vicia cracca,* the cow vetch, is a perennial with deep blue, purple, or sometimes white flowers about 1.5 cm long. There are generally more than thirty of them crowded into a one-sided raceme.

Vicia americana, also perennial, is a native, but it often behaves as a weed. Its rose and purple flowers, borne in groups of four to ten on a long peduncle, are usually 1.5 or 2 cm long. The several varieties of this species differ in the form of the leaflets and in the extent to which the plants are hairy. They intergrade so much, however, that it is often difficult to tell where one variety begins and another leaves off.

So much for the vetches. If you encounter any that do not seem to fit the descriptions of the few that have been mentioned, get help from a book on weeds or from a comprehensive guide to the flora of this region.

The sweet-peas, which belong to the genus *Lathyrus,* can be distinguished positively from vetches on the basis of one telltale character. In the flower of a pea, the style—the little snout on the pistil, which survives until the pod is ripe—is appreciably flattened and hairy only on its lower side near the tip. In vetches the style is not flattened, and it is more or less uniformly hairy close to the tip. Some of our peas are indigenous, others alien. Of the species found along roadsides and on waste land, *L. latifolius* (fig. 103) is decidedly the most obvious, and probably the most common. A perennial introduced from Europe, it has flowers about 2 cm long. The petals are generally deep pink, but they may be pale pink or white, with or without darker pink streaks. The leaves are unusual in having just two large leaflets, plus the tendril. The stems are equally distinctive because of their winglike expansions.

103. Perennial pea, *Lathyrus latifolius*

The clovers belong to the genus *Trifolium.* There are many native species, as well as introduced kinds. The two that are most common in fields and along roadsides are perennials that were brought in from the Old World. The red clover, *T. pratense* (pl. 21), is a bushy species with a taproot and regularly grows to a height of 30 or 40 cm. Its spherical or slightly conical flower heads are compact and about 3 cm tall. The individual flowers, approximately 1.5 cm long, are typically rose-pink. The leaflets are narrowly oval; the largest are usually 3 or 4 cm long.

The white clover, *T. repens* (fig. 104), creeps by stolons and tends to be low in stature compared with the red clover. Its flowers, whitish or cream, sometimes with a pinkish or purplish tinge, form a rather loose head about 1.5 or 2 cm tall. The leaflets are generally broadest above the middle and may have a slight indentation at the tip. This is perhaps the most common of the clovers found in lawns.

There is room to mention just one more introduced species, a very striking annual, the crimson clover, *T. incarnatum.* It is usually at least 40 cm tall and rather hairy throughout. The crimson flowers are concentrated in elongated heads that may be more than 4 cm long. This species is not as widespread as either of the two previously discussed and is more likely to be found at the edge of a cultivated field than in waste places or along roadsides.

Close allies of clovers are the sweet-clovers *(Melilotus)* and medicks *(Medicago).* In the former the flowers, either white or yellow, are in long spikes, and the plants as a whole are often a meter or more in height. None of the true clovers rises to that stature. In medicks the seed pods

104. White clover, *Trifolium repens*

are distinctive in being coiled or at least sickle-shaped, and they may also be prickly. The flowers, either yellow or purplish, are usually in dense heads. Common medicks in our region include alfalfa *(M. sativa)* and bur-clover *(M. hispida),* a yellow-flowered weed of gardens.

ST. JOHN'S-WORT FAMILY

Klamath weed, *Hypericum perforatum* (pl. 18), introduced from Europe, is a weedy relative of St. John's-wort, widely cultivated as a ground cover. It grows to a height of 50 cm or more, branching mostly from the base and dying back each winter. The flowers, about 2 cm across, have five bright yellow petals, dotted along their margins with little black glands. A distinctive feature of the flowers is the large number of stamens, concentrated in several groups. The fruit becomes a dry capsule not quite 1 cm long.

PARSLEY FAMILY

Queen Anne's lace, *Daucus carota* (fig. 105), is just a wild, weedy version of the cultivated carrot. In its first year it stores enough food

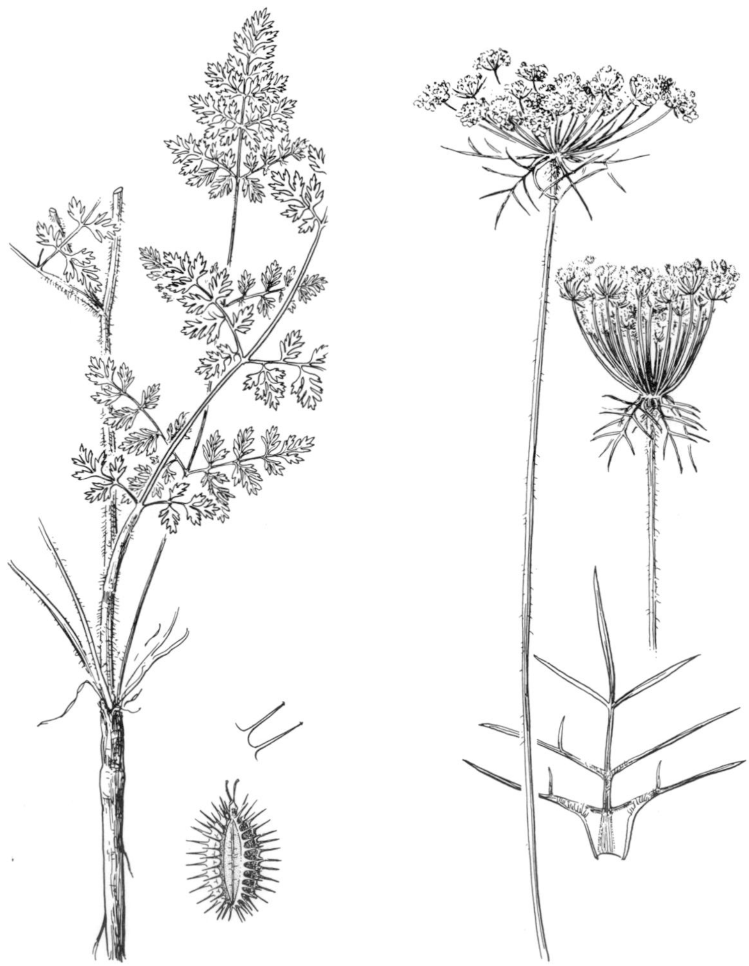

105. Queen Anne's lace, *Daucus carota*

in its taproot to enable it to bloom and produce seed in the second year. Then it dies. Most flowering specimens are between 50 cm and 1 m tall. The basal leaves are quite similar to those of a cultivated carrot, being divided repeatedly into small leaflets. The inflorescence, at the top of the stem, is a flat-topped cluster about 5 to 10 cm across. The flowers are tiny and normally white, sometimes a little yellowish; however, one flower in the center of the inflorescence may be pink or purple, and in some plants all of the flowers are pink. The ovoid fruits that succeed the flowers are about 3 mm long. The appearance of the inflorescence, together with the much-branched leafy bracts that form a kind of foil beneath it, is decidedly reminiscent of lacework.

GENTIAN FAMILY

Centaury, *Centaurium umbellatum* (pl. 21), was introduced from the Old World and has become successful in meadows and grassy fields that are reasonably moist. It regularly grows to a height of 30 to 40 cm, sometimes without branching, sometimes branching from the base. There is a rosette of basal leaves, plus pairs of opposite leaves scattered along the stem. The flowers, less than 1 cm across, typically borne in rather dense heads of twenty or thirty or more, have yellow anthers that contrast prettily with the pink or purplish pink flowers. (Occasionally, the petals are yellow or reddish.) After the anthers crack to liberate their pollen, they become spirally twisted. The fruit is a slender capsule about 1 cm long, and the seeds are hardly larger than specks of dust.

A native species, *C. muhlenbergii*, is found in the Willamette Valley and along the Columbia Gorge. The leaves near the base of the plant are sufficiently spaced out that they do not form a rosette, and the number of flowers in a head does not often reach twenty.

MINT FAMILY

Of the weedy mints, self-heal, *Prunella vulgaris* (pl. 23), is almost ubiquitous. This is a low perennial that creeps by underground stems, and its leafy, upright shoots are generally not more than 15 cm tall. As in other mints, the stems are squarish and the leaves are opposite. The flowers, crowded into a short inflorescence, are purplish blue (rarely pink or white) and a little more than 1 cm long. The lower lip of the corolla is shorter than the upper one and is divided into three lobes, the middle one being the larger and conspicuously fringed.

Ground-ivy, *Glecoma hederacea* (fig. 106), is another creeping type. It is attractive enough to be cultivated, but may get out of hand. The leaf blades are somewhat heart-shaped or kidney-shaped and have bluntly toothed margins. The flowers, produced along much of the length of each upright shoot, are purplish blue and usually about 1.5 cm long. In some plants the anthers are nonfunctional and the flowers are therefore strictly pistillate. Unlike most weeds, ground-ivy often grows well in shady situations and when found in woods, it could be mistaken for a native.

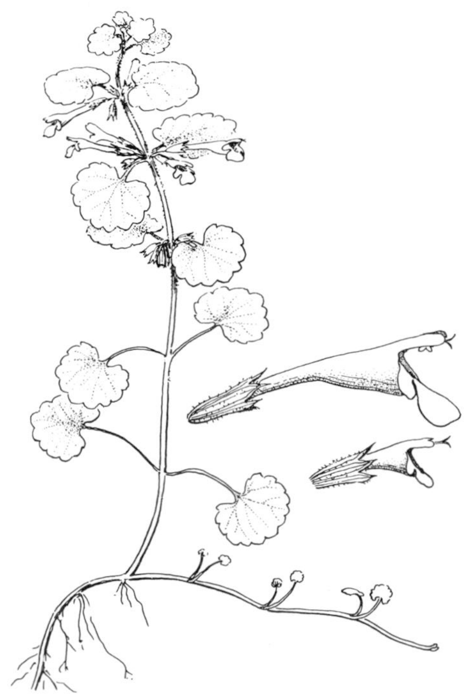

106. Ground-ivy, *Glecoma hederacea*

FIGWORT (SNAPDRAGON) FAMILY

Foxglove, *Digitalis purpurea* (pl. 22), having escaped from gardens, is pretty enough to tolerate even when it becomes established where it is not wanted. It is typically a biennial, and in the second year produces a leafy shoot that ends in a long flower raceme. Many plants are more than 1 m tall. The corolla is tubular, slightly two-lipped, and 3 or 4 cm long. The color ranges from white to deep rose or purple, and there are almost invariably dark spots with white halos all over the floor of the tube.

Mullein, *Verbascum thapsus* (pl. 22), is a densely woolly plant that sometimes reaches a height of more than 2 m. Like foxglove, it is a biennial. Its bright yellow flowers, about 1.5 cm across and with only a short tube, are individually attractive, but only a few of the many that develop on a single raceme during the season are open at any one time. The largest leaves, 20 to 30 cm long, are near the base of the plant; toward the raceme the leaves become progressively smaller.

Certain veronicas were mentioned in chapter 4 because they are typical of wet places. There are other kinds in lawns and weedy fields. Perhaps the most attractive of these is *Veronica chamaedrys* (fig. 107). It is a creeping perennial with oval, toothed leaves about 2 cm long and bright blue flowers not quite 1 cm across. If you are tempted to take home a start of this little jewel, think twice. You will have a hard time keeping it where you want it.

Parentucellia viscosa (pl. 22) was introduced from the Mediterranean region and is partial to moist fields. It regularly grows to a height of 20 or 30 cm and is almost completely covered with sticky hairs. The leaves, mostly 2 or 3 cm long, are opposite and light green. The

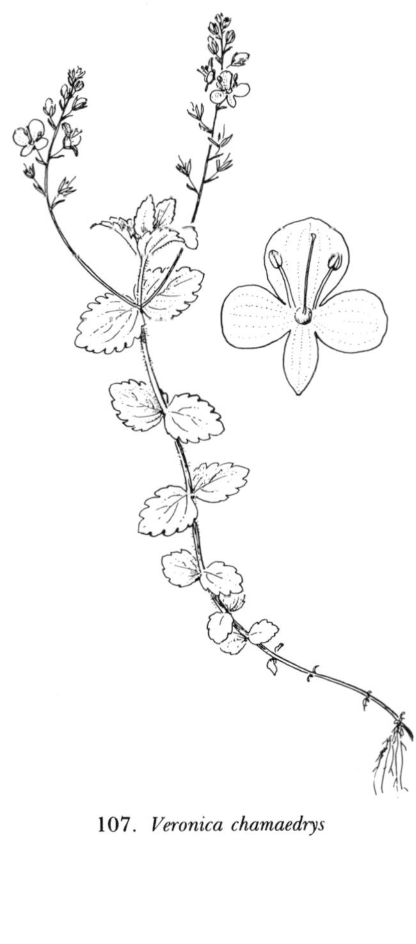

107. *Veronica chamaedrys*

flowers, alternating with green, leafy bracts, have two-lipped, yellow corollas about 1.5 or 2 cm long. The upper lip is shorter than the lower and decidedly hairy. *Parentucellia* slightly resembles yellow-flowered species of owl's clover, especially *Orthocarpus castillejoides,* which is often found around salt marshes. In owl's clovers, however, the bracts and sometimes the upper leaves are divided into three or more lobes, and the bracts are at least tipped with the same color as the corolla.

ASTER (SUNFLOWER) FAMILY

The common dandelion, *Taraxacum officinale,* is such a familiar lawn weed that it need not be discussed here. A similar plant, the cat's ear, *Hypochaeris radicata* (pl. 25), is also common in lawns and is the most abundant of its clan along roadsides, in pastures, and in vacant fields. Like the dandelion, this species has milky sap and basal leaves; the leaves, however, are stiff and rather hairy. The flower heads are borne singly or in loose groups of several on each flower stem. They are bright yellow and usually 2.5 or 3 cm across. All of the flowers, as in dandelions, have ribbonlike corollas and thus resemble ray flowers of daisies. The fruits, with their featherlike plumes, are admirably fitted for dispersal by the wind.

Chicory, *Cichorium intybus* (pl. 25), is another weed with milky sap. Its flower heads, usually blue, sometimes pink or white, are so pretty that the aggressiveness of this plant in taking over waste places may be overlooked. The heads open in morning sunshine and are about 2.5 or 3 cm across. Chicory is a perennial that grows from a taproot, and the only substantial leaves, resembling those of a dandelion, are basal. The flowering stem branches a number of times and may reach a height of 1 m or more. The roots of this plant, after being dried, thoroughly roasted, and ground-up, are sometimes used for making a hot brew, and more commonly for "stretching" coffee or for adding an extra flavor to it.

The Canada thistle, *Cirsium arvense* (pl. 25), is perhaps the best reason for the invention of chemicals for killing weeds. It is large, aggressive, and tenacious, and has a prodigious capacity for seed production. It looks like an annual, but it has creeping roots from which new shoots sprout in spring. In short, it is misery in the form of a plant, even though its flower heads are pretty and fragrant enough to attract bees. Usually the heads are about 1.5 cm across, and the numerous small flowers crowded into them are ordinarily purplish pink or pale purple, sometimes white. The plants grow to a height of 1.5 m or taller, and the elongate leaves, cut into shallow or deep lateral lobes, are spiny all around the margins. The upper surfaces of the blades are nearly

108. Ox-eye daisy, *Chrysanthemum leucanthemum*

109. Dogfennel, *Anthemis cotula*

smooth, but the lower surface is white because of woolly hairs. In spite of its common name, this thistle, like the following, is a native of the Old World.

The bull thistle, *C. vulgare* (pl. 25), has very sweet-smelling flowers packed into heads about 3 cm across. The flowers are usually a bright purplish pink, but white-flowered plants are occasionally noted. Bull thistle grows to a height of 1 m or more, but is on the average not quite so tall as the Canada thistle. The pointed lateral lobes of the leaves are tipped by stout spines, but there are spines all along the margins and bristly hairs on the upper surface. The stems, unlike those of Canada thistle, are so spiny that it is painful to pull up a plant without gloves. This species is a biennial, dying back after the first year's growth and then blooming in the second summer.

Of the weedy species with white ray flowers, the ox-eye daisy, *Chrysanthemum leucanthemum* (fig. 108), and a smaller cousin, the dogfennel, *Anthemis cotula* (fig. 109), are the most widespread in our region. The former is a perennial that usually dies down in winter. Its stems are nearly erect, have few if any branches, and bear single flower heads. Most plants are about 50 cm tall. The leaves are coarsely toothed; those at the base of the plant tend to have distinct petioles, whereas

110. Pineapple weed, *Matricaria matricarioides*

those higher up generally clasp the stems. The flower heads are usually 3 or 4 cm across and have approximately twenty or twenty-five white rays whose length just about equals the diameter of the disk.

The dogfennel is an unpleasantly scented annual, generally under 50 cm high, that typically branches several times. The leaves are divided and redivided into many hairlike lobes, so they are almost fernlike. The flower heads, about 2 cm across, have fewer than twenty rays, but otherwise resemble those of the ox-eye daisy.

Pineapple weed, *Matricaria matricarioides* (fig. 110), has no ray flowers at all. The many disk flowers are arranged in a conical cluster. This is a low annual, not often more than 15 cm tall, with much-dissected leaves that resemble those of the dogfennel. It is a minor nuisance and the most charitable thing that can be said about it is that it does smell like a pineapple.

Mosses and Liverworts

Most of the common mosses found on soil in rockeries and other situations where the ground has recently been disturbed were described in chapter 3. *Bryum capillare* (pl. 32), *Funaria hygrometrica* (pl. 32), *Pogonatum contortum* (pl. 30), and *Tortula muralis* (pl. 32) are among the more regularly encountered species. On rocks, including those of which steps and walls are constructed, and also on roofs, *Dicranoweisia cirrata* (pl. 32), *Grimmia pulvinata, Tortula muralis, T. princeps* (pl. 32), and *Rhacomitrium canescens* (pl. 32) should be expected. There will almost certainly be others not covered in this book.

Lawns, especially those on soil that is acid or poor in nutrients, often have heavy growths of mosses, mostly creeping types. *Rhytidiadelphus triquetrus* (pl. 31), described in chapter 2, is sometimes prevalent. A related species, *R. squarrosus* (pl. 31), is more likely to be found in lawns than in the wild, where its occurrence is generally limited to a narrow zone just above the high-tide line along maritime marshes and lagoons, or on the banks of lakes and streams. Sometimes its shoots are upright, sometimes trailing. On the whole it is yellowish green, but the stems are reddish brown. The leaves on the main stems, about 4 mm long and 2 mm broad near the base, taper gradually to a pointed tip. The leaves on branch stems tend to be narrow. Sporophytes are almost never found on this moss, except when it grows near salt water. They have reddish stalks about 2 cm long and nodding capsules 2 mm long; the stalks become twisted as they dry.

Two thalloid liverworts, *Marchantia polymorpha* (pl. 33) and *Lunularia cruciata* (pl. 33), are partial to packed soil, especially that which is heavy and clayey. They will colonize ground that is gritty and well-drained, however, if adequate moisture is present. Both species are sometimes all too successful in rockeries and greenhouses, where their continuous growths may make it difficult for seedlings or the leaves of bulb plants to come up. *Marchantia* is often found in nature, as on stream banks and at the edges of other wet places. *Lunularia* is an introduced species that is almost completely restricted to gardens, rockeries, and greenhouses.

The thallus of *Marchantia* branches dichotomously, and the larger lobes are about 1 cm wide. The fine rhizoids on the lower surface keep the plant in contact with the soil. Little cups on the upper surface produce tiny buds called gemmae, which eventually fall out of the cup and form new plants.

Marchantia also reproduces sexually. The eggs and sperm develop on stalked, umbrellalike structures. In female plants the umbrellas have nine lobes; in male plants they are disks with scalloped margins. A drop of water landing on the top of the disk of a male plant causes sperm to be released, and another drop may splash them in the direction of a female plant. In any case, water is required for fertilization to be accomplished, because the sperm must swim for at least a short distance to reach the eggs. After an egg is fertilized, it grows into a yellowish mass on the underside of the umbrella. This eventually ruptures and liberates spores that germinate into the familiar liverwort phase again. The spore-producing structure, though attached to the umbrella, is a separate plant, because it develops from a fertilized egg and because its spores lead to a new generation of sexual plants. It is thus comparable to the stalked sporophyte growing out from the leafy sexual generation of a moss.

The thallus of *Lunularia* is smaller and more delicate than that of *Marchantia.* The cups within which it forms its gemmae are crescent-shaped. On this continent, *Lunularia* apparently does not reproduce sexually. In Europe, however, its pattern of sexual reproduction and the subsequent maturation of the sporophyte are comparable to those of *Marchantia.*

Some Insects, Slugs, and Other Small Animals

The richness of the fauna in your backyard and in vacant lots nearby will depend on where you live and on your attitude toward piles of old lumber, flattened-out cardboard boxes, and other debris. Most of the little animals that will be discussed here need moisture and are partial to situations where something solid is in fairly tight contact with soil. In summer, as the ground dries out, many of them must seek refuge below the surface.

Out in the country and in wooded suburban areas, an accumulation of rotting boards or a stack of firewood will almost certainly harbor some of the native snails, slugs, centipedes, and millipedes described in chapter 2. The Oregon salamander, red-backed salamander, and northwestern garter snake, dealt with in chapter 6, should also be expected. In cities and towns, however, the natives have been mostly replaced by species introduced from the Old World. This section deals with some of these, as well as with a few indigenous types that prosper in urban situations. Most notable among the latter are termites, for whom a two-by-four in just the right place is as nourishing as a fallen tree in a forest.

INSECTS

The number of insects that live in or under debris, even in cities, is huge. The few that are accorded special consideration here are either almost universally present or noteworthy in some other respect. There are many others that deserve mention and that may be more common in certain places than the ones described. Fortunately, for those who wish to know more about insects, there are helpful guides for recognition of major groups, as well as books and monographs for identification of species that occur in our region.

Earwigs

Earwigs are strange insects characterized by forceps at the hind end. Some of them are wingless. Our most common kind, the European earwig, *Forficula auricularia* (fig. 111), has short wings, and also leathery covers for the hind pair. The color is on the whole dark brown, but the antennae, legs, and wing covers are lighter. In males, which reach a length of about 1.5 cm, the forceps are proportionately longer and

111. European earwig, *Forficula auricularia*

112. A nymph of *Zootermopsis angusticollis*

more strongly curved than in females. Earwigs live under boards, under bark, and in similarly tight places in barns and dwellings. They come out at night to feed on plant material, living or dead. The mouthparts are adapted for nipping, and these insects can do considerable damage in gardens and greenhouses. They are also disagreeable to have crawling around in the kitchen and bathroom. The young, which hatch from pearly eggs laid in clusters in soil, only slightly resemble the parents, and the change to the adult form is gradual.

Termites

In our region, termites are found mostly in stumps, logs, old boards, or wooden structures that are in contact with soil. One of our species, however, will build tubes of mud on concrete or stone in order to connect soil with wood. In spite of the damage they do, termites have earned the respect of biologists, for they are amazing insects. Their colonies operate with a caste system that usually consists of workers, soldiers, one or more kings and queens, and nymphs or young of any of the prospective specialized individuals. Workers lack wings and eyes, but have large heads, and their mouth parts are effective in excavating wood. They are responsible for feeding the kings and queens, as well as the young. Soldiers, which protect the colony, are also blind and wingless, but they have especially powerful jaws. As reproductive individuals of a new generation approach maturity, they develop wings. Eventually they fly away to look for decaying wood where they can start new colonies. Many of them are eaten by birds and other predators. The surviving males and females form pairs, break off their wings, and mate. The females become enlarged queens and produce many offspring.

Termites are unable to digest the cellulose of the wood they consume and depend on certain bacteria and protozoa to do this for them. If you have a microscope and can look at the contents of the digestive tract of a termite, you will see a teeming mass of organisms. The larger protozoa actually ingest particles of wood. The soluble products of digestion are shared by the microorganisms and the termites. These insects cannot live without their wood-digesting guests, and the latter depend on their termite hosts for a watery environment where they get what they need. The relationship represents a type of symbiosis called mutualism.

Our only termites belong to the genera *Zootermopsis* and *Reticulitermes,* and these are rather dissimilar in appearance as well as in their life styles. *Zootermopsis angusticollis* (fig. 112) is a relatively large species that restricts itself to wood and will extend its burrows into dry timbers.

The soldiers, about 2 cm long, are normally yellowish, with dark heads and large, black jaws. The prospective reproductive individuals reach a length of about 1.5 cm. One type is represented by nymphs that have wing pads and that eventually become transformed into long-winged males and females. These usually take to the air in early autumn, just after the first rains. If the reproductive individuals that have founded a colony die or are destroyed, nymphs of any type may become "precociously" sexually mature and take their place. These nymphs are eyeless; their wings never grow out; and they do not leave the colony. They become darker, and the females enlarge until they resemble typical queens.

In some kinds of termites the workers cannot become reproductive and thus constitute a separate caste. Because any of the young of *Zootermopsis* can be transformed into sexually functioning individuals if something happens to the founders of the colony, there essentially is no true worker caste.

Oversized nymphs of a strange type are sometimes numerous in colonies of *Zootermopsis.* They lack the wing pads of prospective "true" reproductive individuals and they are also eyeless. It is thought by some that they represent a foreshadowing of the evolution of the worker caste in these primitive termites. This is not probable, however, because when they are present they are the ones most likely to become reproductive and to succeed the founding queen or king if either or both should die.

Zootermopsis nevadensis should perhaps be mentioned, although it is less common in our region than in southern Oregon, California, and Nevada. It is so similar to *Z. angusticollis* that it may take an expert to tell them apart. *Zootermopsis nevadensis* is a little smaller, and the wings of reproductive individuals are rarely more than 20 mm long. (In *Z. angusticollis* the wings are regularly 23 to 25 mm long.)

Reticulitermes hesperus, though smaller than *Z. angusticollis,* is much more destructive. Its galleries are partly in the soil, partly in wood, and it will build tubes of earth and excrement to bridge over concrete or stone foundations. The activities of *Reticulitermes* above ground require moisture, and it helps its own cause by mixing its moist excrement with earth. A board or even a scrap of wood that has been embedded in soil for a year or two stands a good chance of being riddled by this pest. In any case, it is better to have it in the backyard than in the house.

The workers of *Reticulitermes* are grayish white, and the largest of them are about 6 mm long. The soldiers are a little larger and can be recognized by the shape of the head, which is about twice as long as wide. Reproductive individuals are nearly 1 cm long, including the wings, and decidedly darker than workers and soldiers. They generally make their flight in spring. Before the swarming period the colony will be made up of the usual workers and soldiers, but there will also be many eyeless nymphs with wing pads; these are the prospective reproductive individuals.

Tent Caterpillars

Tent caterpillars are larvae of certain moths and appear on deciduous trees and shrubs about the time the leaves unfold in spring. They associate in large numbers in silken webs. After eating their fill and reaching full size, the caterpillars pupate and become transformed into brown moths. These emerge in summer, and the females soon lay eggs in situations where the caterpillars will have plenty to eat when they hatch out.

The coast tent caterpillar, *Malacosoma californicum pluviale* (pl. 43), is the kind commonly found in our region. It reaches a length of about 3 cm, and its upper surface is marked by bright blue lines and orange spots; there are similar markings on the sides, but these are paler. In nature, *Malacosoma* focuses its destructive tendencies on willows, red alder, chokecherry, and ocean spray. For an encore, it will make a mess of a variety of cultivated plants, including apples, cherries, and roses.

Tent caterpillars are parasitized by larvae of certain wasps and flies. A little white spot on the head is the kiss of death left by a type of fly called a tachinid. The spot consists of a cluster of eggs, and the maggots that hatch from these will eventually devour the internal organs of the pupal stage.

Ground Beetles

The carnivorous ground beetles (pl. 43), belonging to the family Carabidae, are represented in our region by a number of species. In natural habitats they are generally found under logs and pieces of wood or bark lying on the ground, though at night they rove in search of prey. In gardens they are usually fairly common under boards, flower pots, and in similar situations. These beetles can move speedily to avoid being caught, but if escape is thwarted they emit a repugnant, volatile liquid. The odor varies from species to species, but almost always it seems related to that of vinegar. "Stink bug" is a name often applied to these beetles, though this is properly accorded only to certain true bugs. Most carabids are black, or close to it. They may be dull or shiny, and with or without an iridescent sheen. Their legs are long, and the large jaws are readily visible. Some of them have an hourglass figure because of the strong narrowing of the body between thorax and abdomen, but in others the constriction is minimal.

Carabids are friends of the gardener because their main ambition is to crush and eat other insects, as well as snails and slugs. Their nocturnal habits happily bring them into contact with cutworms and other insect pests that operate mainly at night. The larvae of carabids are also carnivorous. They are almost always blackish, like the adults, and look something like elongated sow bugs, though they have only three pairs of legs, limited to the anterior half of the body.

CENTIPEDES AND SIMILAR ARTHROPODS

Lithobius forficatus (pl. 43) is a European centipede with fifteen pairs of legs when it is full grown. It is usually some shade of brown or reddish brown and reaches a length of 3 cm. It hides under boards, bricks, flower pots, and the like. The female has a clever way of protecting her eggs. She covers them with a little mucus, then rolls them around to work in some soil. The mixture soon hardens into a firm coating.

Other true centipedes found in backyards are likely to be native species. Most of them will be small, slender types whose identification should be left to experts (of which there are very few!). Consult chapter 2 for descriptions of some larger types with twenty-three pairs of legs. These frequently turn up under boards and in woodpiles.

The so-called garden centipede, *Scutigerella immaculata* (fig. 113), is not a genuine centipede. It belongs to the Symphyla, a group of arthropods that are about as closely related to insects as to centipedes and millipedes. *Scutigerella immaculata* normally lives in soil, especially in tunnels that are left as roots of plants decay, but it is sometimes found under more or less permanent debris. It is a tiny white animal, not more than 7 mm long. There are twelve pairs of legs in the adult, and a pair of long antennae that seem never to stop moving. It is not as common in our region as in parts of California, but this is nothing to be sad about, for the garden centipede makes holes and burrows in sprouting seeds and seedlings, as well as in established plants. It is a serious pest of some crops.

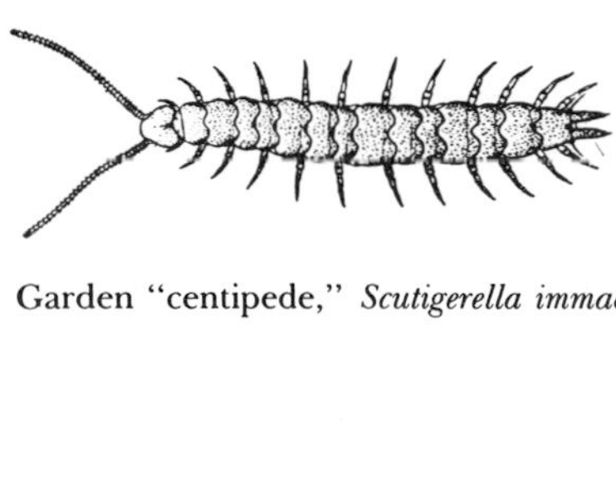

113. Garden "centipede," *Scutigerella immaculata*

SOWBUGS

Sowbugs are among the relatively few crustaceans that are successful in terrestrial environments. They belong to a group called the Isopoda, which has many marine representatives and a few in fresh water. Garden isopods, all introduced from the Old World, are primarily scavengers that feed on decaying vegetation, but they do sometimes pick away at young growth on plants and thus may become a nuisance, especially in greenhouses. Certain of them have a respiratory system much like that of insects: a system of fine tubes that run into the tissues from a few openings on the surface. Three species are rather regularly found in gardens, greenhouses, and vacant lots in the Northwest. Sometimes all of them turn up in the same yard. They will live under just about anything that fits tightly against the soil and gives them a comfortably moist environment.

The pillbug, *Armadillidium vulgare* (pl. 43), is the most distinctive of our sowbugs because of the way it can roll up neatly into a ball. The body is a little more than twice as long as wide, and the side margins are almost parallel for much of their length. The upper surface is shiny, and the color is generally an almost metallic blue-gray, although some lighter streaks or blotches may be present. The maximum length is not quite 1.5 cm.

Porcellio scaber (fig. 114) is about the same size as the pillbug, but it has a rough upper surface and is dull rather than shiny. The roughness is due to numerous little tubercles. The color is usually an almost uniform gray, but there are variants that are streaked or mottled. Neither this species nor the next can roll up into a ball.

Oniscus asellus (pl. 43) is our largest sowbug, occasionally reaching a length of nearly 2 cm. When mature, its upper surface is almost

114. Sowbug, *Porcellio scaber*

smooth and slightly glossy. Younger specimens, however, are dull and rough because of numerous small tubercles, especially near the head. The color is basically grayish brown, sometimes rather dark, but usually there are lighter spots or patches, the larger of which are most likely to be near the margins.

EARTHWORMS

The Northwest has an interesting fauna of earthworms. Some of the native species occur in upland soils; others are essentially aquatic, or at least limited to mucky situations. Several kinds introduced from the Old World have become abundant in gardens and fields, and where they have prospered, the native species have usually disappeared or become scarce. Only three of the more abundant imported species will be dealt with.

Just about everyone is familiar with the nightcrawler, *Lumbricus terrestris,* regularly found wherever man has settled. It reaches a length of more than 15 cm, and its color is a mixture of reddish brown and pink. It is the earthworm most commonly sold as fish bait, and may be gathered by digging in rich moist soil, by lifting boards, or by soaking a lawn in the evening and then waiting for the worms to emerge from their burrows. *Lumbricus rubellus* is a smaller and more nearly translucent species, but nevertheless decidedly reddish. It reaches a length of about 10 cm and is usually found along with the nightcrawler.

If there happens to be a manure pile in the yard, or a place where old lumber is lying around on decaying material, watch for *Eisenia foetida.* It is about the same size as *L. rubellus,* but is more slender and marked by closely spaced, dark red rings. *Eisenia foetida,* as its specific name implies, has a disagreeable odor, difficult to compare with that of any other foul smell.

SNAILS AND SLUGS

The climate of our region is conducive to the good health of several species of snails and slugs imported from the Old World. Unfortunately, nearly all of them are serious garden pests. They lay their whitish eggs, mostly about 3 to 5 mm in diameter, in clusters under boards and other objects that provide protection against desiccation. Commercial slug baits are effective in controlling these slugs, but it also helps not to have a lot of trash lying around.

The milky slug, *Agriolimax reticulatus* (pl. 42), is only about 5 cm long when fully extended, but it is as voracious as it is abundant. It is generally light brown or gray, with a little indistinct darker mottling; some specimens, however, are almost white. No matter which color phase happens to be eating your zinnias or baby lettuce, it will show a distinctive feature of the species: a milky slime, exuded copiously when the slug is irritated. But why irritate it? Just squash it. *Agriolimax laevis* is similar in size and appearance, but it is regularly brown, and its slime is clear.

Arion ater (pl. 42) is sometimes called the black slug, but it comes in a variety of colors. Locally, it is usually represented by a coal-black phase and a reddish brown phase that has an orange-red margin, with cross-streaks, around the foot. In Europe, however, there are a number of other color variants. *Arion ater* reaches a length of almost 15 cm and seems always to be ravenous. It is firm in texture, and tends to hump up when it is not actively crawling. The upper surface of the foot, behind the mantle, is strongly reticulated by a system of ridges and furrows. If you have to hate anything, let it be this slug, a cruelly destructive pest if there ever was one. Fortunately, it comes enthusiastically to slug baits.

Some smaller species of *Arion*—they are under 4 cm long—are also common in Northwest gardens. If you are annoyed by a little slug that has a dark lateral band on each side of the dorsal surface, your problem is probably either *A. circumscriptus* or *A. hortensis.* In the former the upper surface may be gray, yellowish orange, or reddish, but the dark lateral band on the right side is well above the opening to the lung; in *A. hortensis* the color of the upper surface is usually gray, and the lung opening is within the lateral band on the right side. Another species, *A. intermedius,* lacks lateral bands.

Limax maximus (pl. 42) is the most common and widespread species of its genus in Northwest gardens. It is mostly grayish brown, but the mantle is spotted with black and there are spots farther back as well. The length may exceed 10 cm. The opening to the lung, on the right side, is closer to the posterior end of the mantle than to its anterior end. (In species of *Arion* the reverse is true.)

The only introduced slug that seems not to be a vegetarian is *Testacella haliotidea.* This is an oddity, characterized by a very firm, nearly smooth body that is wider near the posterior end than elsewhere. On the back of the posterior half is a little external shell whose shape slightly resembles that of an abalone (hence the specific name, which alludes to *Haliotis,* the genus of abalones). The length may reach 5 cm. *Testacella* is commonly either grayish brown or pale yellow, although perhaps other color phases may be found in our region. The teeth on the radula—the ribbonlike structure that most land snails and slugs use for rasping away plant material—are barbed and used for impaling earthworms, which are swallowed whole.

Most of the shelled snails introduced into our region are either small, nondescript species found in greenhouses, or larger species that are still very restricted in distribution. A potentially serious pest in the Northwest is *Helix aspersa* (pl. 41), which has already taken much of the fun out of gardening in some parts of California. So far, it has been reported from only a few localities in Oregon and Washington, and every effort should be made to eliminate it. *Helix aspersa* is one of the snails used for food in Europe, and some of the colonies in North America can undoubtedly be traced to specimens that were intended for someone's supper but never got as far as the stove. Its streaked, brown shell reaches a diameter of nearly 3 cm, and the color of those portions of the body concerned with crawling around and eating is a pale, almost pearly, tan.

Small snails of the genus *Oxychilus* often congregate in greenhouses and under trash in backyards. Their shells are rather flat, uniformly brown, nearly transparent, and very glossy. In *O. alliarius* (pl. 41), which seems to be our most common species, the shell is rarely more than 7 mm in diameter. The animal is nearly black and smells strongly of garlic.

6

The Vertebrate Animals

Most of the plants and invertebrate animals covered in this guide have been discussed in connection with the habitats of which they are most typical. It is less practical to deal with the vertebrates in this way. Some birds and mammals move rather freely from one habitat to another, and there are amphibians that are terrestrial most of the time but that must go to water to breed. Furthermore, the number of reptiles and amphibians in our region is sufficiently small that it is possible to include substantially all of them, even those that are largely or totally aquatic.

The format for the treatment of vertebrates is not uniform, however. The only mammals covered are those that are likely to be seen, or those that leave telltale signs of their presence. The number of common or reasonably common birds is so large that it is only logical to let already published field guides provide actual descriptions and to concentrate here on helping a beginner narrow down the list of species to the ones he can confidently expect to find.

Amphibians

Amphibians are the most primitive vertebrates that have become successful on land. The class Amphibia includes the salamanders, frogs, and toads, all characterized by a skin that is rather soft and lacks scales. Usually the skin is also moist and smooth, although toads have a warty covering that may not be obviously moist, and one salamander in the region has a roughened skin. All of our frogs and toads lay their eggs in water to produce an aquatic tadpole stage with gills. Eventually hind legs appear, then front legs, and the little frog or toad moves onto land, even though it may remain close to water for the rest of its life. Certain of our salamanders have a similar life history, but some are strictly terrestrial. These do not have a tadpole stage; instead, the development that takes place within a fairly large egg leads directly to a little salamander.

Adult frogs, toads, and some salamanders have lungs, but they also breathe through the skin and mucous membranes of the mouth. The salamanders that are entirely terrestrial have no lungs, so their breathing must take place entirely through the skin and mucous membranes.

SALAMANDERS

Salamanders differ from frogs and toads in having long tails and moving on land by crawling rather than by hopping. In form, they superficially resemble lizards, but lizards are reptiles and have scaly skins. The more common species in our region are the Oregon salamander, western red-backed salamander, and rough-skinned newt. The first two are lungless and entirely terrestrial. The newt, however, has lungs, migrates to water to breed, and has an aquatic larval stage. It will be convenient to deal with all of our salamanders under two main headings that reflect this difference in life styles.

Lungless, Strictly Terrestrial Salamanders

Terrestrial salamanders live mostly under logs and under bark. As the habitat begins to dry out in late spring, they are usually forced to retreat into holes and burrows. They are not often seen between late May and October, except in very humid situations near the coast. The eggs of these salamanders, about the size of small peas, are laid in clusters in damp crevices in soil or wood, and the development of the embryos into little salamanders takes only a few weeks.

The Oregon salamander, *Ensatina eschscholtzii oregonensis* (pl. 44), is perhaps the most regularly encountered species of this group. The upper surface and sides are brown, usually with a tinge of orange; the underside is whitish or yellowish, with tiny black dots. The animal as a whole may have a rather translucent appearance, as if made of wax. The tail is cylindrical and distinctive in being markedly constricted at the base. The maximum length of the Oregon salamander is about 11 cm.

The western red-backed salamander, *Plethodon vehiculum* (pl. 44), is about the same length as *Ensatina* but more slender, and surprisingly agile when endangered. It has a continuous dorsal stripe that is generally bright pinkish brown but is sometimes tan, yellow, or a related color. The sides are usually brownish black with white dots. The lower surface is primarily bluish gray, but there are some yellowish or orange flecks which in some specimens cover a considerable area. In exceptional examples, the dorsal light stripe spreads down onto the sides and belly, so the animal is practically the same color all over.

Dunn's salamander, *Plethodon dunni,* closely resembles *P. vehiculum,* but its dorsal stripe is always some shade of yellow, greenish yellow, or tan. The main problem, then, is to distinguish it from specimens of *P. vehiculum* in which the dorsal stripe is tan or yellow. In *P. dunni* the stripe does not run to the tip of the tail as it does in *P. vehiculum.* It is usually peppered, however, with numerous dark spots, whereas *P. vehiculum* has only a few, widely scattered spots. The number of vertical grooves on each side of the body between the front and hind limbs provides another difference that will be helpful. In *P. dunni* there are typically fifteen, sometimes sixteen, grooves; in *P. vehiculum* there are typically sixteen, only occasionally fifteen or seventeen. The range of *P. dunni* extends from southwestern Washington to the Oregon–California border; and although it is occasionally found as far inland as the Willamette Valley, it is more abundant in the humid coastal region. It is usually very close to water, and sometimes actually immersed.

Van Dyke's salamander, *Plethodon vandykei,* is close to *P. vehiculum* and *P. dunni,* but can be distinguished from both because it has a distinct glandular swelling (parotoid gland) behind each eye. A broad dorsal stripe is generally present, and its color ranges from yellow to tan. Our subspecies is limited to Washington and has a spotty distribution: it is found in the Olympic Mountains, Willapa Hills (near Aberdeen and Grays Harbor), and on the west slope of the central Cascades. (Another subspecies is found in scattered localities in Idaho and Montana.)

All of the species of *Plethodon,* like most salamanders, have five toes on the hind foot. A salamander that could possibly be confused with one of them, but which has only four toes on the hind foot, is the Oregon slender salamander, *Batrachoseps wrighti.* It is found in the foothills of the Cascades, bordering the Willamette Valley, and also on the Oregon side of the Columbia River Gorge. It is rather uncommon. It reaches a length of about 10 cm and generally has a reddish median stripe on the otherwise dark brown upper surface; the stripe is sometimes gray or tan. The underside is dark and peppered with distinct white spots.

The clouded salamander, *Aneides ferreus* (pl. 44), is another slender species, reaching a length of about 13 cm. The coloration of the upper surface is usually dark grayish brown, marbled and mottled with yellowish gray, greenish gray, or some related light color. There may also be some white dots. The underside is normally dark gray. It is only fair to say, however, that the coloration is extremely variable, especially with respect to the proportion of light markings on the upper surface. This is the only one of our salamanders that has a real talent for climbing. It will work its way up trees and sometimes settle in hollows well above ground. The range of the clouded salamander is restricted to the area west of the crest of the Cascades, from northern California to the Oregon-Washington border; there are a few records for Vancouver Island, but this species seems to be missing from western Washington and the mainland of British Columbia.

Salamanders with Lungs, Either Permanently Aquatic or Breeding in Water

The rough-skinned newt, *Taricha granulosa* (pl. 45), spends more time in the water than any of our salamanders—except for the Olympic salamander and certain individuals of other species that fail to complete metamorphosis and are therefore obliged to remain permanently aquatic. *Taricha* may start heading for marshes, ponds, and lakes in late autumn or early winter, and frequently remains until June or July, long after the breeding season has ended, at least in the lowlands. Its migrations, especially the ones that take it to water, often involve large numbers and are perilous when there are roads to be crossed.

The rough-skinned newt reaches a length of about about 17 cm and is characteristically brown or blackish brown above, yellow or orange below. The skin of females, and of males while they are on land, is roughened by small bumps. After they have been in water awhile, the males develop a very smooth skin, and the tail becomes more expansive and more noticeably flattened. In addition, the orange color of the underside becomes more intense, and the region of the anus becomes swollen. This species lays its eggs singly, on submerged sticks or aquatic vegetation. The juveniles acquire both pairs of legs by late summer, when they are about 4 cm long.

The range of the rough-skinned newt extends from just south of San Francisco Bay to southern Alaska. In our area, it is found from the coast to moderate elevations on the west slope of the Cascades, but rarely the east slope. Two subspecies are recognized: *T. granulosa granulosa,* the northern rough-skinned newt, occupying the entire range of the species; and *T. granulosa mazamae,* the Crater Lake rough-skinned newt, found only in Crater Lake, Oregon.

The western long-toed salamander, *Ambystoma macrodactylum* (pl. 44), is perhaps second to the newt in abundance. It grows up to about 12 cm long and is a rather slender species. The tail is not flattened except near the tip. The color of the upper surface is on the whole blackish, but characteristically a greenish or yellowish stripe runs the full length of the body, starting at the back of the head. There are usually white dots on the sides. The underside is dark gray. In the autumn this species is often found under logs in wooded areas, but migration to ponds may begin by November. Breeding usually takes place in February (in the lowlands), and the eggs are laid in firm masses about 4 cm in diameter. Soon after their reproductive function has been completed, the adults move back onto land. As long as the woods remain moist, they may be found under logs; but as drier weather comes on they must retreat into holes. The larvae may grow sufficiently in one season to lose their gills and become terrestrial by the end of summer, but at higher altitudes they probably routinely spend another year in the water.

Ambystoma macrodactylum macrodactylum is the only subspecies likely to be found within the range covered by this book. In the coastal part of the mainland of northern British Columbia, however, the northern long-toed salamander, *A. macrodactylum krausei,* replaces it; *krausei* is also found in the mountains of mainland British Columbia and in mountain meadows on the eastern slope of the Cascades of eastern Washington and Oregon. In the extreme southern part of western Oregon, the subspecies *sigillatum* replaces *A. macrodactylum macrodactylum.*

The brown northwestern salamander, *Ambystoma gracile* (pl. 44), is not quite so graceful as its species name implies. It is almost uniformly blackish brown, although there may be some reddish tones on the head and tail. The length is up to nearly 20 cm, and a distinctive feature of this species is the swelling, called the parotoid gland, on each side of the head behind the eye. In general, the habits of the northwestern salamander are similar to those of the long-toed salamander, but it is less likely to be found very far from water. This species lays astonishingly large egg masses, sometimes 10 cm in diameter. The larvae generally metamorphose at the end of the second summer, when they are about 6 cm long. Some specimens, because of their age, their response to a hormone produced by the thyroid gland, and environmental conditions, may fail to metamorphose; but although they retain gills and never leave the water, they become sexually mature and breed.

The subspecies *A. gracile gracile* ranges from northern California well into British Columbia, but is limited to the region west of the Cascades. In the northern part of the mainland of British Columbia, it is replaced by *A. gracile decorticatum,* characterized by some light flecks on the upper surface, as well as by three joints (instead of two) in the fourth toe of the hind foot.

The Pacific giant salamander, *Dicamptodon ensatus,* is the largest terrestrial salamander in the world. It is a pudgy species that may reach a length of slightly more than 25 cm. Its coloration is on the whole dark. The upper surface and sides are brown, gray, or purplish gray, with irregular splotches of black; at least some of the splotches may be arranged as crumpled rings or in networklike patterns. The underside is generally lighter. *Dicamptodon* is rarely found far from water, either streams or lakes. While out of water, it hides under logs, under little "overhangs" at the edges of streams, and in similar situations. Eggs are laid one at a time, and the larvae normally leave the water at the end of their second summer, when they are about 15 cm long. As in the case of the northwestern salamander, a certain percentage of specimens in some populations fail to metamorphose properly. They remain completely aquatic, but continue to grow and eventually reach sexual maturity. They retain the external gills, sharply flattened tail, and relatively small legs characteristic of older larvae.

The Olympic salamander, *Rhyacotriton olympicus,* is found in springs and streams coming down from the Coast Range, Olympic Mountains, and Cascades (especially on the Oregon side of the Columbia River Gorge). When encountered, it is either completely submerged or among rocks in situations where water percolates freely. It is a small species, rarely longer than 6 cm. The posterior half of the tail is strongly flattened. Just behind their hind legs, on the underside of the body, males have two lobes which are broad and abruptly cut off. Most specimens from Washington and northern Oregon belong to the subspecies *olympicus* (pl. 45). They are usually brown above, with white dots on the sides; the underside is yellowish orange with scattered black markings. Specimens from the southern half of Oregon and northern California generally fit into the subspecies *variegatus.* They are typically olive or olive brown above and have darker markings instead of white spots; the underside is greenish or yellowish, with considerable black mottling. The ranges of the two subspecies overlap to some extent in Oregon and the extreme southern part of Washington, and some specimens cannot definitely be assigned to one subspecies or the other. The gills characteristic of the larval stage are not lost until the salamander has grown almost to full size. The food consists of a wide variety of small aquatic invertebrates, including insects and crustaceans.

FROGS AND TOADS

The Pacific treefrog, *Hyla regilla* (pl. 45), is by far the most abundant tailless amphibian of our region. In the early spring it congregates in open ponds and swamps to breed, and the croaking of the males fills the air almost every night for several weeks. The call, repeated about every two or three seconds, usually sounds something like "wreck-it." As spring wears on, the chorus grows weaker, and by May the breeding ponds are quiet except for an occasional misplaced croak. Many of the treefrogs leave the water soon after the mating season has ended.

The females lay little clusters of eggs on sticks, grass stems, or other vegetation in shallow water. Tadpoles ready to be transformed are small—only about 2 cm long—and begin to sprout legs and to resorb their tails by August or September. In the late summer or early fall, when the little frogs are leaving the water, large numbers of them are sometimes seen crossing roads.

Adult treefrogs are about 4 cm long and are characterized by a white-bordered dark streak running through each eye. The color as a whole varies, depending on the background, for this species can change from green to brown or gray. There are typically some dark blotches on the back and on the legs. The fingers and toes are tipped by little pads that enable treefrogs to cling to a surface as slick as glass.

The northern red-legged frog, *Rana aurora aurora* (pl. 45), prefers streams, ponds, and marshes that lie in wooded areas. It often sits on the bank, just one leap away from water. It is up to about 10 cm long and is characterized by a well-developed dorsolateral fold starting behind the eye and running for about two-thirds the length of the trunk. The eardrum is smaller than the eye. The upper surface and sides are usually reddish brown, with a few dark spots or blotches. The outer surfaces of the legs are also spotted, blotched, or banded, but the background color of the limbs is less inclined to be reddish. The underside of the belly and inner surfaces of the legs are suffused by a pretty shade of pinkish red. This is the reason for the specific name, which alludes to the dawn. The red-legged frog has a very characteristic odor, too—something like that of a wet rubber balloon.

Rana aurora aurora is a practically voiceless frog, though it generally utters a squeak or "pip" when it makes its frightened leap into water. In the lowlands it lays its eggs in early spring, but the breeding season may be held up a bit at higher elevations. The tadpoles grow legs and leave the water near the close of their second summer.

The spotted frog, *Rana pretiosa,* is represented in our region by one subspecies, and specimens of this may be quite similar to those of the red-legged frog because the color of the belly and lower surfaces of the legs is usually orange or salmon. The blotches on the upper surface often have light centers (while those on the red-legged frog do not). The maximum size does not often exceed 10 cm. One foolproof way to tell them apart is to pull the hind leg forward and check the position of the heel with respect to the nostrils. If it does not reach the nostrils, the specimen in hand is almost certainly a spotted frog, because in the case of the red-legged frog the heel reaches at least to the nostrils, and sometimes beyond them. The spotted frog is uncommon in our area, but is found in the Willamette Valley of Oregon and in the Puget Trough in Washington. Its habits are much like those of the red-legged frog.

A frog closely related to both of the last two species is the Cascades frog, *R. cascadae* (pl. 45). It is limited to meadows and ponds at elevations of about 1000 m (approximately 3300 feet) and higher in the Olympic Mountains and Cascades. The color of the upper surface is brownish, with very distinct black spots on the back. The underside is slightly yellowish. The length attains 7 cm. In the lower reaches of its altitudinal range, it may mix with *R. aurora* and *R. pretiosa* but is not likely to be confused with either of these.

The foothill yellow-legged frog, *Rana boylei,* is found in the extreme southern portion of the Willamette Valley, then extends southward to central and southern California. It has poorly defined dorsolateral folds compared with the three species just described. The upper surface is usually gray, olive, or brown, with or without some small, blackish spots; the belly and undersides of the legs are a rather clear yellow. The length reaches 7 cm.

The bullfrog, *Rana catesbeiana* (pl. 45), was introduced into California over a hundred years ago and is now widely distributed west of the Rocky Mountains. It reaches a length of about 20 cm. The upper surface and sides are usually greenish or olive, and there are typically some darker spots on the forelegs and several darker crossbands on the hind legs. There may also be spots on the back. The underside is on the whole light—generally almost white—but is marbled with gray. Two distinctive features of this species are the large eardrum—its diameter is at least as large as that of the eye—and the rather conspicuous skin-fold above and behind the eardrum. The bullfrog is found in swamps and lakes characterized by ample shallow-water vegetation, but not densely shaded.

The male bullfrog's superb calls—"jug-a-rum . . . jug-a-rum"—enrich the night air all through the breeding season. The eggs are laid in late spring, in floating masses. The tadpoles reach a length of about 15 cm. They may develop into little frogs at the end of the second summer of growth, but sometimes require a third summer before they are ready to try their first leap on land.

The green frog, *Rana clamitans,* is another eastern species that seems to be hanging on in a few localities in British Columbia (mostly around Victoria and Vancouver) and in Washington close to the Canadian border. The coloration and large eardrum of the green frog make it resemble the bullfrog more than any of our native species. It is smaller, however, lacks a fold above and behind the ear, and has a dorsolateral fold that runs for about two-thirds the length of the body.

The boreal toad, or northwestern toad, *Bufo boreas boreas* (pl. 46), is a subspecies of the western toad. It lives in burrows of mammals or under rock piles, or it may work itself into loose sand. A favorite habitat in our region seems to be a boulder-strewn area, not far from a stream. Characteristic features include a conspicuously warty skin and a large oval gland (parotoid gland) behind each eye. The coloration is variable, but is usually gray or greenish, with the warts being tinged with reddish brown and spotted and edged with black.

This species, our only true toad, breeds in water, as do all of our tailless amphibians. The adults head for swamps, sluggish creeks, and lakes in early spring. The females deposit their eggs in long strings of jelly, which are draped over aquatic vegetation or applied directly to the bottom. The tadpoles grow to a length of about 5 cm, but after growing legs and resorbing their tails, the baby toads are scarcely 1 cm long. They leave the water at the end of the summer or in early autumn, and may temporarily be abundant underfoot and on roads.

The tailed frog, *Ascaphus truei* (pl. 46), resembles the treefrog, for it is about the same size and has a dark line running through the eye. Its skin is rougher than that of the treefrog, and it lacks toe pads. The male has a short taillike appendage for copulation, so that it looks as though it has not completed metamorphosis. This is not a true tail, for the one opening that serves as anus, as well as for exit of kidney wastes and sperm, is at its tip. Some distinctive features characteristic of both sexes are the vertical pupil of the eye and the lack of any obvious eardrum. The upper surface and sides are light reddish brown, ocher, or gray, generally suffused with some dark pigment. The underside is usually yellowish white, but a pinkish tinge may be present, especially on the throat and legs.

The tailed frog is the only member of its family found outside of New Zealand. Though its geographic distribution extends from northern California to British Columbia, it is almost restricted to boulder-strewn streams coming down from the mountains. It lays its eggs in the autumn, attaching them in what look like strings of beads to the lower surfaces of rocks. The tadpole is unusual in having a sucking disk around the mouth, an adaptation enabling it to hang onto rocks in a swift current.

Reptiles

Reptiles include the lizards, snakes, and turtles. All have lungs and scaly skins, and in turtles there is also a shell into which the animal can withdraw. Most of our reptiles lay eggs that are protected from drying by parchmentlike shells, and the young hatch as small versions of their parents. In some snakes and lizards, however, the eggs are retained within the body of the mother until the babies are ready to be born.

In reptiles, as in amphibians, the temperature of the body fluctuates with that of the environment. During cold weather, activity is curtailed or arrested. Although reptiles are evolutionarily more advanced than amphibians, they are more severely limited by low temperatures. Some of our amphibians migrate to their breeding places in late winter, long before any lizards, snakes, or turtles have warmed up enough to crawl out of their holes.

LIZARDS

West of the Cascades, the variety of lizards is poor. Only one species is widely distributed: the northern alligator lizard, *Gerrhonotus coeruleus principis* (pl. 46), ranges from northern California to British Columbia, including the southern portion of Vancouver Island. It is also found in some areas east of the Cascades. The alligator lizard is large, often attaining a length of 25 cm; the tail accounts for more than half of this, unless the specimen in hand happens to be one that has lost its tail and is in the process of growing a new one. The scales are fairly smooth and the legs sprawl. This is not a lizard that keeps its belly well off the ground and runs straight ahead; its movements are sinuous, almost snakelike. The coloration varies, but the upper surface and sides are usually a mixture of gray, brown, and olive, with some of the scales being wholly or partially black. There may be a broad streak of brown or tan running down the back. The underside is gray, sometimes with narrow darker lines.

The alligator lizard is typically found under rocks or logs in fairly exposed situations, or under old boards in backyards and junkpiles. It feeds largely on insects. When captured, it is ready to bite; but although its jaws are strong, its teeth are too small to do much damage. Fat females found in late summer are expectant mothers. They give birth, in August or September, to several fully formed little ones that must start right away to look after themselves.

Another alligator lizard is occasionally encountered in western Oregon (but not close to the coast), along the Columbia River Gorge in both Oregon and Washington, and along the eastern base of the Cascades not far from the Columbia River. This species, *G. multicarinatus scincicauda,* the Oregon alligator lizard, can be distinguished from the northern alligator lizard because its eyes are to a large extent yellow, instead of almost completely dark. In addition, it generally has distinct crossbands on the back and upper side of the tail; about a dozen of these are spaced between the level of the ear and the hind legs. In the northern alligator lizard there are no distinct crossbands on the back, although there may be aggregates of dark scales, and on the sides there are dark scales that do nearly form regular bands. The Oregon alligator lizard is the larger of the two species and sometimes reaches a length of 30 cm.

The western skink, *Eumeces skiltonianus* (pl. 46), has scales that are so smooth that the body surface is almost glassy. The tail is longer than the rest of the body, and the movements are snaky, much like those of an alligator lizard. The total length rarely exceeds 18 cm. In younger individuals the tail is bright blue, and the cream-colored dorsolateral stripe on each side of the head and body contrasts sharply with the darker background of the upper surface and sides. There is a narrow and less well-defined light stripe on the lower part of each side, scarcely separated from the pale gray color of the belly by flecks of dark pigment. In older specimens the tail generally shows only a tinge of blue or bluish gray, and the dorsolateral light stripes are not as sharp as they are in younger individuals. During the breeding season, in spring, there may be an orange suffusion on the head (especially the chin) and on the tail.

The skink is most likely to be found in ravines and on hillsides where rocks are abundant, or where there are both rocks and logs. The only subspecies we have *(skiltonianus)* is found through much of Oregon, although it avoids the north coastal section; it is absent from the western portions of Washington and British Columbia. East of the Cascades it is widespread in Oregon and Washington, and just barely gets into British Columbia. It feeds primarily on insects and other terrestrial arthropods, including spiders and sowbugs. Its tail is readily detached from the rest of the body, and any skink that may be the lucky survivor of an unhappy experience with a predator will probably have a new tail that is shorter than normal and not nearly so beautiful as the original. A tough old skink has perhaps had to replace its tail more than once.

The only other lizard in our region is the northwestern fence lizard, *Sceloporus occidentalis occidentalis* (pl. 46). From central and northern California its range extends through much of western Oregon except for the north coastal area. It is abundant on both sides of the Columbia River Gorge and in some portions of Washington just east of the Cascades; in western Washington, however, it has been reported from only a few localities. The fence lizard is a rough-scaled species and can run straight forward with its belly well off the ground. It reaches a length of about 15 cm. The coloration of the upper surface and sides is usually a complicated mixture of gray, brown, and some darker pigment organized into a pattern of blotches and bars. There are also ill-defined, small patches of blue, turquoise, or greenish blue. The underside of the throat is bright blue, tinged with green, and this same color prevails on both sides of the belly. The blue is especially bright in males. The midline and most of the rest of the lower surface is gray, although there may be orange tints on the legs. Fence lizards do actually get up on rail fences and fence posts, and their claws enable them to climb efficiently. They are most regularly found in exposed areas where there are plenty of rocks, or both rocks and old, weathered logs. When a fence lizard is frightened, it generally heads for cover; but if you are patient and just wait awhile, it will probably reappear to take stock of the situation. Then it may do a few push-ups, a regular feature of this lizard's behavior. The food of the fence lizard consists mostly of insects and spiders.

SNAKES

The most common and widely distributed snake in our region is the northwestern garter snake, *Thamnophis ordinoides* (pl. 47). It is almost ubiquitous in the lowlands, and is found in the mountains at elevations of 1000 m (about 3300 feet) or a little higher. The length does not often exceed 60 cm. The coloration varies so much that a beginner at identifying snakes may think that almost every specimen he finds belongs to a different species. In most individuals there is a dorsal stripe of cream, yellow, orange, or red; but this stripe may be weak or missing altogether. Lateral stripes, if present at all, are rarely distinct. The background color of the upper surface and sides is usually dull black or brown, often tinged with blue or green. The underside is generally slate gray or olive gray, but in some specimens it is yellowish; some black markings may be present.

The northwestern garter snake is usually found in fields, meadows, and brushy areas, and sometimes in woods. It is common in gardens, especially those with rock walls. This is primarily an upland species, and even specimens found close to water are not likely to dive in to escape; they usually head for cover. It eats enough slugs, including destructive introduced types, to be helpful; but it also consumes earthworms, frogs, and salamanders. When handled, it rarely tries to bite, but it has anal glands that discharge a foul-smelling secretion. It may also let loose its excrement. So don't pick one up just before a picnic lunch, unless you have a bar of soap and some scented hand lotion.

All species of garter snakes bear their young alive. In August or September, fat females give birth to little snakes that resemble their mothers but are only about the size of a large earthworm.

The other species of garter snakes found west of the Cascades are the common garter snake, *T. sirtalis,* and the western terrestrial garter snake, *T. elegans.* Both typically have a distinct, light dorsal stripe and a reasonably distinct lateral stripe on each side, and both are fairly large, occasionally exceeding a length of 1 m. They can be separated rather reliably, however, on the basis of the fact that in *T. sirtalis* there are seven scales constituting the upper lip on each side of the head, whereas in *T. elegans* there are eight. Both species are represented in our region by two subspecies.

The common garter snake is largely limited to situations where there is water close by. When frightened, it is more inclined to start swimming than to head for the brush, and it is apt to bite when handled. Being primarily aquatic, it eats fish, frogs, tadpoles, and other animals found in water. It also takes what it can get on land: toads, worms, slugs, and even small mammals and nestling birds. Specimens found around salt water may go onto the beach or into tidepools to look for food.

The red-spotted garter snake, *T. sirtalis concinnus* (pl. 47), is the subspecies found in western Oregon as far south as Coos Bay, and occasionally in the most southern part of western Washington. The top of the head is reddish, and there is generally considerable red between the dorsal and lateral stripes. The dorsal stripe involves about half of the width of the row of scales on each side of the middorsal row.

The Puget Sound red-spotted garter snake, *T. sirtalis pickeringi,* is found on Vancouver Island, in the coastal region of southern British Columbia, and throughout western Washington. The top of its head is usually dark, and the dorsal stripe, nearly white, is very distinct but so narrow that it typically involves just one scale row. As in the red-spotted garter snake, considerable red is worked into the dark areas between the dorsal and lateral rows.

Our two subspecies of the western terrestrial garter snake are well separated west of the Cascades. The wandering garter snake, *T. elegans vagrans,* is found in the southern portion of Vancouver Island, on the mainland of British Columbia, in the San Juan Archipelago, and elsewhere in the Puget Trough. It does not occur along the coast of Washington, however. Its dorsal and lateral stripes are usually whitish yellow or light brown, and the background color between the stripes may be either rather light with small blackish blotches or almost black with scattered flecks of a whitish color. This subspecies is not as terrestrial as its name implies. It may spend a lot of its time on land, but it loves water and is said to go into tide pools occasionally to hunt food. It eats fishes, frogs, tadpoles, lizards, snakes, small mammals, and even birds, as well as a variety of invertebrates, especially slugs and worms. It will usually try to bite when handled, as well as defecate and discharge the secretion of its anal glands.

The mountain garter snake, *T. elegans elegans,* ranges from California to about as far north as Salem, Oregon, but it is absent from the coastal strip. Its dorsal and lateral stripes are yellow or orange-yellow and are separated by wide black bands with small whitish flecks. This subspecies is also primarily aquatic, though perhaps a little less so than *T. elegans vagrans.*

The northwestern ringneck snake, *Diadophis punctatus occidentalis* (pl. 46), is a pretty little thing. The color above is typically brown, olive brown, or bluish brown. The vermilion on the belly is carried into a ring behind the head. The body is slender, and the scales are very smooth. The length rarely exceeds 40 cm. The ringneck snake is not often observed crawling in the open and must be looked for under rocks, logs, or boards. Where there is one, there may be several. This species feeds on a variety of small animals, including insects, worms, lizards, and other snakes. When handled, it may produce an ill-smelling (and undoubtedly bad-tasting) secretion. The way it coils its tail, when disturbed, to show off the orange-red underside is probably a warning to predators that a mouthful of snake is a mouthful of misery. This species is so attractive that we must lament its absence from much of our region. It is fairly widespread in western Oregon, but it barely gets into Washington. In both Oregon and Washington, however, its distribution includes the area of the Columbia River Gorge.

The sharp-tailed snake, *Contia tenuis* (pl. 47), is another secretive species. It has been reported from the Puget Sound region, from certain islands of the San Juan Archipelago, and from several localities in Oregon and Washington along the Columbia River Gorge and the area just east. It occurs in the Willamette Valley, and from there it ranges south into much of California. The sharp-tailed snake is aptly named, for the tail is almost spinelike. This species feeds to a large extent on slugs, and the tail, thrust into the ground, helps the snake to cope with its prey. The teeth are admirably adapted for their work; they are long and directed backward, so that a slug is not likely to slip back out of the mouth. The color above is usually reddish brown or grayish brown, and the underside is cream-colored, with some black crossbars. The scales are relatively smooth. A large specimen is about 25 cm long.

The Pacific rubber boa, *Charina bottae bottae* (pl. 47), is an unprepossessing relative of the large boas and pythons of tropical regions. The members of this group have a little clawlike structure, especially evident in males, on each side of the anus. This is a remnant of a hind limb, a reminder that snakes have evolved from reptiles that had legs. The rubber boa is found through much of our area. It is most likely to be encountered in open woods or in rocky areas that are interrupted by woods. In the spring, when the rubber boa first comes out of hibernation, it may be seen sunning itself in an exposed place, but otherwise it tends to be secretive and to limit its activity to the morning and evening. Because of its drab coloration and sluggishness, it is easily overlooked.

The common name of this species is appropriate. The scales are small and smooth, so the snake does almost appear to be made of rubber. Another good name for it is "two-headed snake" because its tail is so blunt that it resembles the head. The color of the upper surface and sides ranges from olive brown to blackish brown, and the underside is generally yellowish. The length rarely exceeds 60 cm. This snake feeds largely on lizards and mice, which it kills by constriction, after the fashion of its tropical kin. The two to several young are born alive.

The Pacific gopher snake, or bull snake, *Pituophis melanoleucus catenifer* (pl. 47), is found in the Willamette Valley and elsewhere in western Oregon, and there are a few reports of what is probably the same subspecies in western Washington. (East of the Cascades, gopher snakes range northward into British Columbia, but these belong to a different subspecies, *P. melanoleucus deserticola.*) The gopher snake regularly surpasses a length of 1 m, and specimens larger than 1.5 m are occasionally seen. The back is strikingly marked with a series of dark brown blotches, and there are smaller blotches or spots along the sides. The background color is usually yellowish or grayish.

This species does actually eat gophers, as well as a variety of other rodents, small rabbits, birds, bird eggs (which it swallows whole), lizards, and perhaps other animals. It kills by squeezing its prey within its coils. In spite of the fact that it has an appetite for some animals that are more helpful than destructive, it is a friend that should be protected. When handled, the gopher snake may bite with conviction, but generally it is more anxious to escape. Sometimes it will puff itself up and hiss menacingly. It may also vibrate its tail, rather effectively mimicking a rattlesnake.

The western yellow-bellied racer, *Coluber constrictor mormon,* is our swiftest snake, and seemingly the most intelligent. When it flees, it acts as though it has the locations of safe hiding places memorized. Its speed and agility make it a hard snake to capture, and even if caught, it does not give up. It will almost always sink its razor-sharp teeth into your hand. If you hold it up for a close look, keep your nose out of its way!

The yellow-bellied racer is olive brown or grayish brown above, pale yellow underneath. The body form is very slender and the length may exceed 1.5 m. The scales are rather smooth. This species is frequently encountered east of the Cascades, where it may occur together with the striped whipsnake, *Masticophis taeniatus.* West of the Cascades it is uncommon, and its northward distribution stops at a point about half-way between Portland and Seattle. It feeds on rodents, lizards, and a variety of other small animals. Although its species name is *constrictor,* it does not really constrict. After it captures its prey, it swallows it directly, or pins it down with loops of the body until it can work it deeper into the mouth and throat. This species, like other racers, often climbs up into bushes and trees.

The most beautiful snake found in the Pacific states is the California mountain kingsnake, *Lampropeltis zonata* (pl. 47). From California its distribution extends into southern Oregon as far as Roseburg, and a few specimens have been found in Washington along the eastern part of the Columbia River Gorge. Its occurrence in the Northwest is thus extremely limited and discontinuous. The color pattern consists of alternating red and white rings separated from one another by black rings; the snout and top of the head are also black. The length rarely exceeds 60 cm. There is no need to confuse this little jewel with the venomous coral snakes (the closest of which is found in Arizona); on the latter, each red ring is preceded and succeeded by a white ring, so the black rings separate consecutive sequences of white-red-white. The mountain kingsnake is partial to open woods and brushy areas. It is a constrictor that feeds on other snakes, lizards, small mammals, and young birds that have not left the nest.

The common kingsnake, *L. getulus,* is a larger species, up to more than 1 m long. It is characterized by ivory rings alternating with black or blackish brown rings. The outlines of the rings are often much less regular than in the mountain kingsnake. The distribution of one subspecies, *L. getulus californiae,* reaches northward to the area around

Roseburg, but for all practical purposes this fine snake is outside our range. It is famous for eating rattlesnakes, which it kills by constriction. But it also consumes other snakes, lizards, frogs, and nestling birds. It is most likely to be found in fairly open areas where there is some brush.

If you are afraid of being bitten by a venomous snake, you will be comforted by the fact that throughout most of the range covered by this book, there are no venomous snakes at all. The northern Pacific rattlesnake, *Crotalus viridis oreganus* (fig. 115), has a wide range extending from central California to British Columbia, but in the Northwest it is restricted almost completely to the region east of the Cascades. It does occur in southern Oregon, between the coast and the Cascades, and there are scattered colonies on some of the rocky buttes in the Willamette Valley, as far north as Monroe and Lebanon. From Salem north, all of our region is free of rattlesnakes. Even where there are rattlesnakes, the danger of being bitten is minimal. The idea of killing them, unless they are close to settlements where there are children, is abhorrent to most naturalists. These snakes are a part of the balance of nature, and they help to hold down populations of some rodents that might otherwise become too numerous.

Rattlesnakes are characterized by a nearly triangular head, set off

115. Northern Pacific rattlesnake, *Crotalus viridis oreganus*

from a rather heavy body by a slender neck. At the tail end there is a rattle consisting of one or more units. The number of units is not a reliable guide to the age of a rattlesnake; one is normally added each time the snake sheds its skin, and young specimens that are growing rapidly may put on two to four units in a year. Also, a portion of the rattle can be broken off. When a rattlesnake uses its rattle, it may make it really whir, or just give it a flick or two. Rattlesnakes are confident animals that often hold their ground when approached. They capture small mammals and birds, and sometimes lizards, by striking from a coiled position. The hollow fangs that conduct the venom are directed backward when the mouth is closed, but swing forward during the act of striking. Rattlesnakes belong to a group of snakes that have a pit on each side of the head, between the nostril and eye. The pit contains an organ sensitive to temperature changes and is thus useful for locating warm-bodied prey. The eye of a rattlesnake is distinctive in having a vertical pupil. All species bear their young alive.

The northern Pacific rattlesnake is just one subspecies of the western rattlesnake, whose range extends eastward to Kansas, Nebraska, the Dakotas, and even western Iowa. The length is generally no more than 1 m, and specimens close to the maximum size—about 1.5 m—are rare. The coloration is variable, but in our region the upper surface is usually mostly either gray, brown, or blackish, with a series of darker blotches that almost touch one another. This snake is normally found where there are rock formations that offer good hiding places. In the spring, after it has emerged from hibernation, it may be observed sunning itself close to the den where it has overwintered. After becoming really active again, it may range widely. In the heat of the day, it is likely to seek the shade of bushes.

TURTLES

There are only two freshwater turtles in our area, and they are easy to tell apart. The painted turtle, *Chrysemys picta* (pl. 48), has yellow lines on the head, neck, and legs. If the turtle is out of the water, sunning itself, these markings can be seen from a distance. There is also a red mark just behind the eye. The upper part of the shell—called the carapace—is basically dark olive or nearly black, but at least some of the individual shields have a yellow margin on their front border, and there may be yellow lines elsewhere on the shields. The lower part of the shell—the plastron—is strikingly marked with a symmetrical, dark figure that looks as if it were taken from a Rorschach test. In larger specimens the background for the figure is dingy yellow, but in young individuals it is bright orange or red. The shell of this species commonly reaches a length of 20 cm and may be a bit larger. The painted turtle has a wide range in central and eastern North America and just barely gets into our region. From eastern Oregon and Washington, it comes down the Columbia River Gorge into the general vicinity of Portland and the northern half of the Willamette Valley. It also occurs in the southern half of Vancouver Island, but elsewhere west of the Cascades there are only a few scattered reports of its occurrence. In any case, in those areas where both of our turtles may be expected, the painted turtle is the one more likely to be found. The diet of both species is diversified. They eat some plant material, as well as insects, crustaceans, worms, molluscs, small fishes, tadpoles, and other animals.

In the northwestern pond turtle, *Clemmys marmorata* (pl. 48), there are no bright yellow lines on the head, neck, and legs, but usually there are darker markings, some of which may be organized into a network-like pattern. The carapace is dark olive, or blackish brown, typically with broken darker streaks radiating outward from near the center of the individual shields. The plastron is mostly dingy yellow, but there are usually some dark blotches, especially in the central portion. The carapace of a large specimen is about 20 cm long. From California and southwestern Oregon, the range of this species runs northward down the Willamette Valley to the area around Portland, and there are some records for the Puget Sound region in Washington and for the coastal portion of British Columbia.

Occasionally, other turtles turn up. These are former "pets," released by their owners into the nearest pond or lake.

Birds

The birds of our region are so well covered by inexpensive field guides that duplication of information available in these is unwarranted. The more useful references on birds of the western states, as well as some helpful booklets on birds of specific areas, are listed in the bibliography. The beginner who hardly knows one bird from another, however, runs the risk of identifying a common species as some rare visitor, or perhaps as a species that is not likely to be seen west of the Cascades. In connection with this problem, it should be mentioned that some local chapters of the Audubon Society publish handy checklists of all birds known to be found near certain cities, with notations that help the novice appreciate that certain species are seasonal, apt to be seen only while in migration, or rare or "accidental."

The treatment of birds in this book is simplified still further. First of all, waterfowl and shore birds are excluded. No rare species are mentioned, and a good many birds that advanced bird watchers can expect to recognize on a thorough foray are omitted. The list provided includes most of the common land birds found in our region. This is not to say that the beginner will not see others, but it is likely that of the first ten birds he encounters, at least nine will be on the list. Actually, the first ten birds a person learns will probably be the hardest. The next ten will come a bit more easily. Until one has looked carefully at a variety of birds, he probably will not have a good idea of their relative sizes. Most birds are larger than they look from a distance. As soon as one fixes in his mind the size of a warbler, a song sparrow, a robin, and a crow, he is well on his way.

To help a beginner learn the "top twenty," some names on the list are marked with an asterisk (*). If you study the characteristics of these in advance, there is a good chance that you will see half of them in one morning in the field. Of course, this depends to some extent on where you go and what season it is. But let us assume that it is winter and that you visit a place where deep woods give way to brush and then to a large, cleared field, so that a variety of habitats are represented. In late spring and summer, most of the same birds will still be there, but there will also be a number of species that have moved into the area to breed. Those that may most confidently be expected are marked with a dagger (†).

In reading ahead on birds, and in actual field study, it is essential not only to pay attention to size, form, and distinguishing marks of the male and female but also to begin learning the habits, call notes, and songs. If you see, in a coniferous forest, a tiny brown bird with a straight, sharp bill and a tail that looks as if most of it had been trimmed off, it is almost certainly a winter wren. But it helps to know that the winter wren is not likely to be seen except in a coniferous forest, that it moves about close to the ground, and that its long, drawn-out song sounds like a squeaky tricycle. After you have a little experience, all the "little brown birds" will not look alike anymore.

The birds listed are arranged in the same sequence as in the checklist of the American Ornithological Union, followed in most field guides.

Permanent Residents
(will be seen in approximately the same numbers at all seasons)

* Red-tailed hawk	* Brown creeper
Bald eagle	Dipper
Sparrow hawk	* Winter wren
Ruffed grouse	Bewick's wren
California quail (introduced)	* Robin

Ring-necked pheasant (introduced)
Killdeer
Screech owl
Belted kingfisher
* Common flicker (including the red-shafted flicker)
* Hairy woodpecker
* Downy woodpecker
* Steller's jay
* Northwestern crow
Black-capped chickadee
* Chestnut-backed chickadee
* Common bushtit
* Red-breasted nuthatch
White-breasted nuthatch
* Golden-crowned kinglet
Cedar waxwing
Starling (introduced)
Yellow-rumped warbler (including Audubon's warbler)
* House sparrow (introduced)
Western meadowlark
Red-winged blackbird
* Brewer's blackbird
* Purple finch
Pine siskin
* Rufous-sided towhee
* Dark-eyed junco (including the Oregon junco)
* Song sparrow

Winter Residents
(generally observed only between October and March or April)

* Varied thrush
Hermit thrush
Ruby-crowned kinglet

Late Spring and Summer Residents
(generally observed only between April and September)

Turkey vulture
Band-tailed pigeon
Mourning dove
† Rufous hummingbird
Western wood pewee
† Olive-sided flycatcher
† Violet-green swallow
Tree swallow
Barn swallow
Cliff swallow
† Swainson's thrush
† Orange-crowned warbler
Yellow warbler
MacGillivray's warbler
Yellowthroat
† Wilson's warbler
Brown-headed cowbird
Western tanager
† American goldfinch
† Chipping sparrow
† White-crowned sparrow

Mammals

The mammals, like birds, have warm blood maintained at a constant temperature. The insulating body covering consists of hair instead of feathers. They regularly bear their young alive (the only exceptions are the duckbill platypus and anteater of Australia) and nurse their young with milk produced by mammary glands. This combination of characteristics sets them apart from all other vertebrates.

Most mammals are nocturnal, or at least highly secretive. It would be impractical, in a book like this, to deal with more than a few common species. Most of the ones included are those that are often seen in the open, that burrow in lawns or cultivated ground, or that are likely to be found in a house, barn, or cabin in the woods.

RODENTS

The rodent group has the largest representation in our region. It includes all of the kinds of mice, rats, gophers, and squirrels, as well as the beaver, mountain beaver, and porcupine. Rodents have a single pair of sharp incisor teeth at the front of each jaw, but no canine teeth ("eye teeth"). Thus there is quite a gap between the incisors and the assemblage of premolars and molars that are toward the rear of the jaws. The incisors, used for gnawing—and all the rest of the teeth, too—grow out as fast as they are worn down.

There is little doubt that the mammal most in evidence—even if not often actually seen—is the white-footed mouse, or deer mouse, *Peromyscus maniculatus* (fig. 116). It has several geographic subspecies in our region. This rodent, characterized by proportionately large ears,

116. White-footed mouse, *Peromyscus maniculatus*

reaches a total length of about 15 cm, the slender tail accounting for half of this. The upper surface and sides of the head and body are brown or grayish brown, and the lower surface is usually almost white. The feet and underside of the tail are likewise white. It nests in holes in trees, in or under logs, in piles of brush, and of course in attics, overstuffed furniture, and boxes of stored linen. It is often confused with the house mouse. Out in the country, and even in the suburbs, the white-footed mouse just happens to be the species that lives in houses. One may have to move all the way into the city to get the real house mouse, *Mus musculus* (fig. 117), imported from the Old World. The house mouse has appreciably smaller ears, and although the underside of the head and body is lighter, it is not white; the lower surface of the tail is about the same color as the upper surface.

The white-footed mouse is usually gentle, and if held by the tip of the tail it is less inclined than the house mouse to turn back and bite. It lives on a wide variety of seeds, fruits, and other plant material, and also on insects and other animal matter. Coastal populations make use of crabs and molluscs. What they eat in houses depends on the menu thoughtfully provided for them.

The nests of *Peromyscus* are made mostly of plant fibers. These mice usually produce at least two litters a year, sometimes four, and the

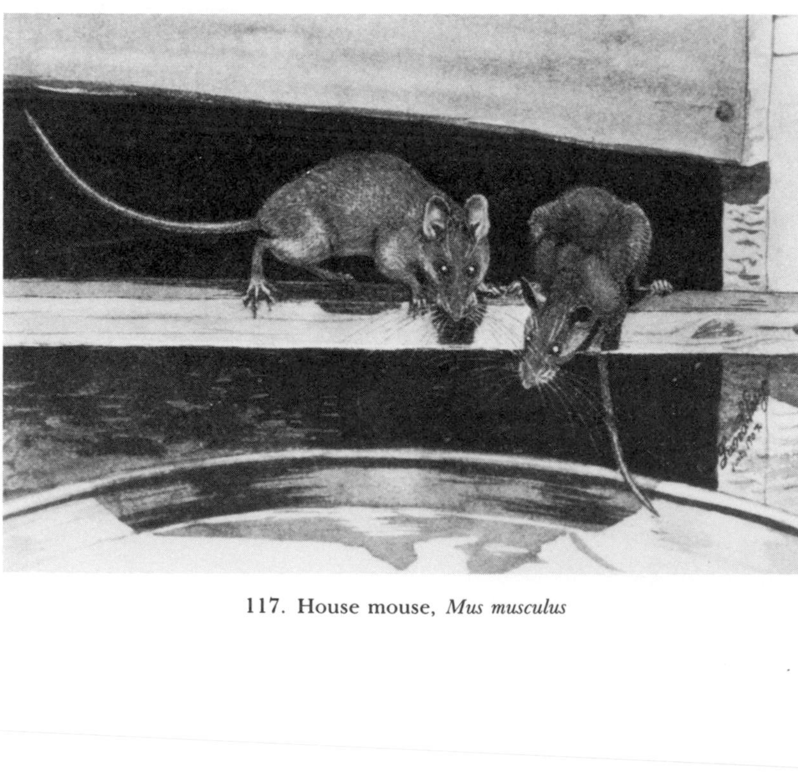

117. House mouse, *Mus musculus*

number of young in a litter ranges from two to eight. We would soon be overrun by them if they were not preyed upon by owls and other carnivorous animals. Many of the bones seen in owl droppings once belonged to *Peromyscus.*

The voles, or field mice, belong to the genus *Microtus* (fig. 118). There are several species and subspecies in our area, and it would be too complicated to separate them here. As a group, they are fat little mice, generally about 15 or 20 cm long, with a tail shorter than the

118. A vole, *Microtus*

body proper, and with relatively small ears. They do not make a habit of entering cabins. They live in underground runways, either in open, grassy areas or under fallen logs, depending on the species and local situations. Once in a while, turning over a large plank that has been undisturbed for a long time will expose the burrows of some kind of vole. Voles are primarily vegetarians that consume stems, roots, bulbs, and tubers. Certain species do considerable damage to garden plants and commercial crops, generally attacking them underground.

A pocket gopher is about the size of a rat, but it has a short tail. In this respect, and also because it has small ears, it resembles a large vole. The eyes are proportionately small, and the brownish gray fur is short and very dense. Like certain other rodents, pocket gophers have external cheek pouches lined with fur, which they use to store food in temporarily. Our most common species, *Thomomys talpoides,* reaches a total length of about 20 or 22 cm, the tail making up just a little less than a third of this. There are several subspecies of *T. talpoides* in our region, and some of them are local and ill-defined. Pocket gophers do not occur in the San Juan Archipelago or in any part of British Columbia that falls within the range covered by this book, but they are fairly abundant around the south end of Puget Sound and in much of western Oregon. The strange Mima Mounds found in a prairie not far from Olympia, Washington, have been interpreted as huge gopher hills, but these deformities have probably been formed in some other way.

Pocket gophers develop rather complex underground burrows. Certain of the tunnels in a system terminate at the surface, where the earth is pushed out to form a nearly fan-shaped pile. (A mole hill is usually more like a volcano, because the dirt is pushed straight up, rather than to one side.) As a gopher extends its tunnels, it comes across roots, bulbs, and other plant material that it will stuff into its cheek pouches and carry to the chamber where it stores up food. A gopher will also crawl out of its burrow and help itself to leaves, stems, and seeds. Any activity above ground is almost strictly nocturnal.

Pocket gophers are animals of open grasslands and prairies, not of forested areas. Under natural circumstances, where they do not compete with man or mess up his lawns, they are on the whole beneficial, for they cultivate the soil, thus encouraging the growth of vegetation that helps prevent rapid run-off and erosion.

At any time of the year, one can almost count on seeing the Douglas squirrel, or chickaree, *Tamasciurus douglasi.* This is a delightful little rodent, with entertaining antics. It will probably be heard before it is seen. The sound it makes is hard to describe, but it slightly resembles a semiexplosive rush of air, as when a tire is suddenly deflated. After encountering you face to face, the squirrel continues to scold, retreat, and come back to scold some more.

The Douglas squirrel reaches a total length of about 30 cm, of which the tail accounts for about two-fifths. It varies in color, depending on the subspecies and the season, but in general the upper surface and sides of the body proper are brown and the undersurface is orange-buff or buff in summer, paler (and with a little gray) in winter. A vague darker line on each side separates the colors of the upper and lower surfaces. The tail is fairly bushy, darker above than below. In winter the ears are usually tufted.

The Douglas squirrel eats a variety of plant material, especially seeds and berries. Its nests, mostly in holes in dead trees, are lined with moss and strips of cedar bark. Generally the female produces a single litter each year.

On Vancouver Island, and on the mainland of British Columbia well north of Vancouver Island, the Douglas squirrel is replaced by the red squirrel, *T. hudsonicus.* The upper surface and sides of this species are gray or brown, with a reddish tinge that is most marked on the top of the body. The lower surface is white or grayish white, never orange-buff or buff as in the Douglas squirrel.

The Townsend chipmunk, *Eutamias townsendii,* is found over most of the range of the Douglas squirrel, but it hibernates rather soundly in late autumn and winter. Females, which are slightly larger than males, reach a total length of about 28 cm, almost half of which is taken up by the somewhat bushy tail. The color of the upper surface is basically brown, but there are five lengthwise dark stripes on the body; three of these are distinct on the head. The dark stripes are separated by pale stripes. The underside is whitish. The tail is dark brown above, grayish brown below. The Townsend chipmunk consumes a variety of seeds, nuts, and berries. It is found almost throughout western Oregon and Washington, but it barely gets into the mainland portion of British Columbia and is absent from Vancouver Island and the San Juan Archipelago. There are, in fact, no chipmunks at all on Vancouver Island and in the San Juan Archipelago.

The northwestern chipmunk, *E. amoenus,* is a species with a wide distribution in the region east of the Cascades. It is represented by just one subspecies (*felix*) in the western part of the mainland of British Columbia along the Strait of Georgia, and in certain portions of western Washington. It is, in general, a chipmunk of mountain slopes, but it does occur in the lowlands in situations where mountains rise up abruptly not far from the shoreline. In general, *E. amoenus* and *E. townsendii* occupy mutually exclusive areas; the latter is the common one in most of our region, although it drops out near Vancouver. *Eutamias amoenus* is slightly smaller, the females not quite reaching a length of 25 cm. Some of the pale stripes are much lighter and more distinct than in *E. townsendii.*

The western gray squirrel, *Sciurus griseus,* is our largest species, with a total length of about 55 cm; the tail constitutes slightly less than half of this. The upper surface and sides are silvery gray, and the belly is nearly white. This is an impressive squirrel, found in almost all of western Oregon and in the Puget Trough about as far north as Tacoma. Like the Douglas squirrel, it is a tree-loving species, but it is more often found in extensive oak woods than in coniferous forests. Acorns seem to constitute its principal food resource.

The tree squirrel that comes for peanuts in city parks is usually the eastern gray squirrel, *S. carolinensis* (fig. 119), which has been introduced. It is larger than the Douglas squirrel, smaller than the western gray squirrel, and has a very bushy tail. The upper surface of the body proper is generally gray or dark gray, usually with a little brown worked in; the underside ranges from gray to nearly white. This squirrel eats about all of the seeds and fruits it can get, and also buds and leaves. It usually nests in holes in trees, producing one or two litters a year. Cats and other predators, as well as competition for food, keep the populations at more or less stable levels.

119. Eastern gray squirrel, *Sciurus carolinensis*

The eastern fox squirrel, *S. niger,* has been introduced in a few places. It is about the same size as the eastern gray squirrel or a little larger, and the coloration of its upper surface is similar. The underside, however, is usually decidedly reddish. When this is not the case, it may be difficult to tell the fox squirrel from the eastern gray squirrel without looking into its mouth. (Don't try it!) The fox squirrel has four big teeth near the rear of each side of the jaw; the eastern and western gray squirrels both have five.

The Beechey ground squirrel, *Otospermophilus beecheyi* (pl. 48), is sometimes called the "gray digger." The range of this rodent in western Oregon is extensive, and it is found in the southern part of western

Washington. It is almost completely restricted to open areas, and prefers somewhat rocky hillsides. Some of the largest colonies will be found along the eastern portion of the Columbia River Gorge and foothills of the eastern slope of the Cascades just north and south of the river. It is believed that this particular ground squirrel spread into Washington sometime after the turn of the century.

The ground squirrel reaches a total length of about 45 cm, the tail constituting decidedly less than half of this. The upper surface of the body, behind the head, is brownish or blackish gray, marked with obvious whitish speckles. The underside is buff. The head lacks the spots, and the tail is dark gray above, buff below.

The ground squirrel digs extensive burrows, usually on sloping ground. The burrows angle downward at first, then level out. Some of them may run for 2 m. They often branch, and a system of runways may have more than one opening at the surface. The dirt pushed out of the burrows is well worn by ground squirrels going in and out of their holes. These rodents use elevated places as watch towers and pass high-pitched barks from one to another to keep the colony on the alert when predators or intruders show up.

Their food consists of bulbs, roots, seeds, nuts, green shoots, and just about any other kind of plant material, as well as insects. They are capable of doing considerable damage to crops. The young, born in litters of several, usually emerge from the burrows in June, when they are a few weeks old. They stick close to their mothers until they are at least half-grown. In some areas the ground squirrel hibernates; but where the weather is mild, it seems to be reasonably active even in winter.

RABBITS AND HARES

Rabbits and hares are rather similar to rodents in many respects, but their hind legs are much longer than the forelegs, and they have a total of six incisor teeth—four in the upper jaw and two in the lower. The incisors of the upper jaw are in tandem, a smaller tooth being located directly behind each of the ones in front. Hares are larger than rabbits, and most of them have especially long ears. The more basic differences between them, however, are found in the skeleton.

The varying hare, *Lepus americanus,* is also called the snowshoe hare and snowshoe rabbit. Its length, including the short tail, is up to about 45 cm, and the hind feet of a large specimen may be more than 12 cm long. For a hare, it has relatively short ears, only about 7 cm long. This species occurs almost throughout our region, except on Vancouver Island and in the San Juan Archipelago; but it is largely nocturnal and not often seen. Instead of burrowing, as some hares do, it forms little nests in situations where it is protected by brush or roots. In western Oregon and Washington, and on the mainland of British Columbia south of the Fraser River, the subspecies represented is *washingtonii.* It is typically dark brown in summer, slightly paler in winter. The subspecies *cascadensis,* which ranges northward and eastward from the area around Vancouver, is a little brighter and more colorful in summer than *washingtonii,* and is characterized by a reddish or rusty tint in the fur. Still farther north and farther east, a paler subspecies (*pallidus*) prevails. Both of the last two subspecies may turn white by the time snow has begun to fall in earnest.

The black-tailed jackrabbit, *Lepus californicus,* is a rarity in our region, but it is occasionally seen in the Willamette Valley. This is a grayish hare, with a tail that is black above. The total length may reach 60 cm, and the ears in a large specimen are about 13 cm long. This species prefers open spaces, but it does get into brushy areas. It is to a considerable extent nocturnal, but it is not altogether inactive in the daytime. Where it is common, as in some parts of California and in areas east of the Cascades, it may lie out on the grass, protected by nothing more than its coloration—and by its prodigious speed when finally forced to run.

The brush rabbit, *Sylvilagus bachmani,* is a little fellow found in western Oregon, but apparently not farther north. The total length is just a little over 30 cm, and the ears are about 6 or 7 cm long. The area under the tail is white, and that makes it one of the "cottontails." (If you find a rabbit of this type in western Washington or western British Columbia, it will almost certainly be the eastern cottontail, *Sylvilagus floridanus,* which has been introduced. It is not yet really abundant.) The brush rabbit prefers situations where there is a dense growth of shrubs, but it will move out into an open area to graze. It is most likely to be seen in the early morning or evening, but is also active through the night.

The rabbit that has just about taken over San Juan Island is *Oryctolagus cuniculi* (fig. 120), the European species from which domesticated breeds originated. It was first turned loose many years ago—perhaps before the turn of the century—and has brought untold suffering to farmers, gardeners, and tender-hearted drivers. One soon learns that it is safer not to swerve to avoid running over a rabbit that has leaped onto the roadway. This species digs deep burrows for protection and nesting. It is to a large extent nocturnal, but there is rarely a shortage of rabbits on San Juan Island in broad daylight.

120. European rabbit, *Oryctolagus cuniculi*

Mature specimens, with a total length of about 50 cm, have ears close to 10 cm long. The color is generally grayish above, with some blackish hairs, and often with a slightly reddish patch on the fore part of the back. Some specimens are almost as black as any domesticated breeds, and occasionally mottled individuals are noted; but these probably can be traced to stocks released in the last thirty or forty years. The European rabbit may be getting a foothold on a few other islands of the Archipelago, and it has at times been introduced in British Columbia.

This pest will eat almost any plant that is not poisonous or disagreeable; and where the population is dense and food especially scarce, it will test things that it might otherwise not try. Daffodils and peonies are among the very few plants that are substantially immune to its depredations. The population on San Juan Island shows some natural fluctuations, and many rabbits are carted away by hunters. There seems to be little chance, however, that the European rabbit will disappear in the near future. The best thing that can be said for it is that it provides food for humans, as well as for owls, hawks, eagles, and other predators.

HOOFED MAMMALS

Deer and elk belong to the same group of mammals as sheep, goats, pigs, and cattle. The prong-horned antelope and mountain sheep, found in certain other areas of the Northwest, also fit here. All of these animals have two hooves on each foot, and they are herbivores that graze on low vegetation or browse on tender twigs of shrubs and trees.

The deer of our region is the Columbian blacktail deer, *Odocoileus hemionus columbianus.* (East of the Cascades, the mule deer, *O. hemionus hemionus,* prevails.) It varies considerably in size, depending on the habitat. Specimens seen in the islands of the San Juan Archipelago, for instance, are on the average smaller than those of mainland areas not far away. The height, at the shoulders, of a large mature male will be about 90 cm, and the weight more than 90 kilograms (200 pounds). Small specimens are about 75 cm high and weigh only a little more than 45 kilograms (100 pounds). Mature females are slightly smaller than the males.

The coloration varies according to season. In winter it is brown tinged with red or gray, and generally there is some black worked into the fur. The tail is decidedly black except for its basal portion, and there is no extensive white rump patch. (In the mule deer, only the tip of the tail is black; the rest of it is very light, and there is a large white rump patch.) The chest is brown; but the belly, inside surfaces of the legs, and a patch on the throat are almost white. As summer approaches, the body coloration shifts toward buff with a reddish tinge, but without any black. Fawns are some shade of brown with light spots, but already show the tail coloration characteristic of adults, although the pigmentation is not as strong.

The antlers of a full-grown male fork twice, so that there are four nearly equal points, in addition to a nearly basal point ("eye guard") on each antler. The antlers are normally shed near the beginning of spring, and then replacement gets underway. In late summer the male rubs his new antlers on bushes and trees to remove the "velvet" and to polish them up.

Deer browse on a wide variety of shrubs and trees (including conifers), and also softer plants. In winter they tend to remain in deep coniferous woods, and deer of the mountains may move down into the lowlands where food is more plentiful in cold weather. This species mates in autumn, and the fawns are born in spring. Whether there are one, two, or three in the litter depends to a considerable extent on the age and nutritional state of the female. The Columbian blacktail deer may live for more than ten years (animals about twenty years old have been reported), but the average life span is probably much less.

CARNIVORES

The order Carnivora includes skunks, raccoons, bears, and weasels, as well as dogs and cats. A good sign that a particular mammal is a carnivore is the presence of a large, pointed canine tooth on each side of the upper jaw. This is a handy invention for biting murderously and for tearing away at flesh and bone.

The two skunks in our region are the only mammals with a color pattern consisting entirely of black and white. The striped skunk, *Mephitis hudsonica,* has just two white stripes. They diverge from a single stripe on the back of the head and run to the base of the tail. The spotted skunk, *Spilogale gracilis* (fig. 121), has several stripes, not all of which are strictly lengthwise, and some of which are not continuous. The striped skunk is, in general, more widespread and more common. It is also larger, reaching a total length of about 70 cm; the spotted skunk is rarely larger than 50 cm. But both know how to manufacture the volatile oil for which they are famous. This is secreted by glands next to the anus.

121. Spotted skunk, *Spilogale gracilis* (photographed in Woodland Park Zoo, Seattle)

Skunks live in burrows, either their own or those dug out by other mammals. The striped skunk is the one more likely to long for a more civilized life and to move into the crawl space under a house or into an old barn; it is sometimes seen in broad daylight. In general, however, skunks are animals of the night. They hunt rodents, birds and bird eggs, reptiles, amphibians, and insects and other invertebrates; they will also eat flesh of dead animals, as well as fruits. The young are born in the spring.

The raccoon, *Procyon lotor* (fig. 122), reaches a total length of about 1 m, but about one-third of this is tail. Its body is mostly brownish gray,

122. Raccoon, *Procyon lotor*

but the face is distinctively marked with a black mask, and the tail has several black rings. Raccoons are generally plentiful in wooded areas, but they are more likely to be seen in areas where they are used to being pampered. There are campgrounds and communities where they show up at dusk (if not earlier) for hand-outs, and later on rattle the garbage cans for an encore. When it comes to food, their tastes are catholic, ranging from fish, frogs, and aquatic invertebrates to reptiles, birds, eggs, land snails, fruits, and other plant material. If a saltwater beach is handy, they will forage for crabs, snails, fish, and other meaty things. The habit of washing food before eating it does seem to be characteristic of some really wild raccoon populations, but the amenity is dispensed with wherever pork chop bones or Kentucky fried chicken is on the menu. If you and your children like to feed raccoons, be sure you do not let them eat directly from your fingers. Their eyesight seems to be good, but many an overeager raccoon has been known to miss the mark. If you must tempt fate, make sure first that you can get to a doctor right away and that the premiums on your health insurance are paid up. Raccoons climb well and can run with considerable agility. Their hideouts are usually hollow trees or burrows dug out under roots. The young are born in spring, and a large female may have several babies in a litter.

BATS

In these marvelous mammals, the forelimbs are modified as wings, the fingers being much elongated to serve as a framework on which the thin membrane of skin is stretched. The tail and hind limbs are connected by a similar membrane. All of our bats feed on insects caught in flight. The ease and agility with which they maneuver in darkness is due in part to their system of echo-location. The high pitched sounds they emit are reflected from solid objects and inform the bat of its position with respect to these objects; they also help the bat to locate insects.

There are several species of bats in our region, and most of them are very much alike. The most common and most widely distributed species, and the one most inclined to collect in attics, is the little brown bat, *Myotis lucifugus*. Just one subspecies, *alascensis* (pl. 48), occurs in our range, but it is everywhere. It is dark brown in color, and its wingspread is about 25 cm. This bat, like all other species in our region, feeds on insects that it catches in flight, and in one evening a single specimen may eat enough to equal about a quarter of its own weight. Most specimens migrate out of our region for the winter.

The big brown bat, *Eptesicus fuscus,* is fairly common in western Oregon and Washington, but barely gets into southern British Columbia. It is rusty red, with blackish ears, and has a wingspread of about 30 or 35 cm. A bat of this size, observed feeding before dark, will almost certainly be of this species.

POUCHED MAMMALS

The American opossum, *Didelphis marsupialis virginiana* (fig. 123), is the only North American representative of the group to which kangaroos and almost all other mammals of Australia belong. It is a native of the southeastern United States, but seems to be getting on very well in some sections of the Northwest where it has been introduced. In certain places, it is often seen crossing roads at night.

The opossum is almost as large as a cat, having a total length of 75 or 80 cm, of which two-fifths is taken up by the tail. The female has a fur-lined abdominal pouch, and the young, born in a very unfinished state, crawl up into this, find a nipple, and hang on tightly for a few weeks. The face of an opossum is pointed, and the body is covered with long, coarse hair; the tail is hairless. The color of the fur is mostly gray, but the face is whitish.

Opossums are not fussy about what they eat. Their diet includes fruits, insects, other mammals, eggs, and young birds. It is unfortunate

123. American opossum, *Didelphis marsupialis virginiana*

that they were brought to our region, for they compete with, and destroy, some native animals.

INSECTIVORES

Insectivores include moles, shrews, and shrew-moles, characterized by rather long, sensitive noses and numerous, evenly spaced teeth; the teeth are all much alike, even if some are larger than others and may have two cusps. Eyes, if present, are covered with skin and scarcely visible. These relatively primitive mammals feed mostly on insects, sowbugs, worms, and snails, but some take a certain amount of plant material.

In moles and shrew-moles, the front feet are much enlarged and specialized for digging, and there is no external ear. In shrews the front feet are no larger than the hind feet, and there is a small external ear.

The moles are the largest of our insectivores: mature animals are regularly more than 15 cm long. The tail is thick, almost hairless, and less than a quarter of the total body length. The fur is soft and velvety, and the color is usually nearly black. There are two species in our region: the coast mole (*Scapanus orarius,* pl. 48) and the Townsend mole (*S. townsendi*). The former is not often more than 18 cm long; the latter is regularly 20 or 22 cm long. Otherwise, they are fairly similar and have comparable habits. Both make burrows just under the surface of the ground in relatively open areas, such as pastures, fields, and lawns. The burrows are so shallow that their presence can often be established by the way the soil is raised and cracked. Periodically along their burrows, moles throw up volcanolike piles of earth. As they burrow, they consume worms, insects, and a certain amount of plant material; however, they do not concentrate on bulbs, roots, stems, and leaves the way pocket gophers do. The damage they cause in gardens is caused in part by their burrowing so close to plants that the roots are disturbed and exposed to air.

Moles have barely noticeable eyes. These are covered by skin and probably are useless as far as vision is concerned. Anyway, these animals stay in their burrows almost all of their lives.

The shrew-mole, *Neurotrichus gibbsii* (pl. 48), has a total length of about 10 or 11 cm. The tail accounts for a little more than a quarter of this and shows a rather prominent constriction at its base. The dark, slate-colored fur is on the whole short, but on the tail there are some moderately long bristles. The eyes, covered by skin, are scarcely visible. The shrew-mole is most abundant in shaded ravines where there are alders and maples. It digs burrows resembling those of moles, mostly right under the layer of humus on the forest floor. A shrew-mole will leave its burrow and walk over the ground to hunt for food, tapping with its snout all the time. It eats a variety of insects, worms, and other invertebrate animals, as well as some plant material.

There are several species of shrews (pl. 48) in our region, and no effort will be made to tell them apart. They are all members of the genus *Sorex.* Few of them are more than 13 or 14 cm long, and the length of some does not exceed 11 or 12 cm. As a group, the shrews are hot-blooded and short-lived, burning themselves out in a year or so. Their metabolism is so high that they literally must feed almost continuously to stay alive. Some species maintained in the laboratory were found to consume meat at the rate of three times their own weight each hour. Our species seem to eat a variety of insects and other invertebrates, and at least occasionally take seeds and other plant material. Shrews live just under the layer of leafmold and moss on the forest floor and develop complex runways. They will leave the burrows at night, and sometimes even during the day. In fact, shrews that have died in their tracks are among the more commonly observed mammals in woodland situations. Certain of our species are called water shrews because they are to some extent aquatic.

Glossary

ALTERNATE. With a single leaf or branch arising at a particular level on a stem

ANNUAL. A plant that flowers and produces seed the first year, then dies

ANTHER. The portion of a stamen in which pollen is produced

AXIL. The apex of the angle between a stem and a leaf, where a branch or flower may originate

BIENNIAL. A plant that normally lives two years, producing flowers and seeds in the second year

BLADE. The broadened portion of a leaf, sometimes divided into separate leaflets (as in a clover)

BLOOM. A whitening, in the form of a fine, waxy powder, on leaves or fruits

BRACT. A modified leaf situated just below a flower or flower cluster

CALYPTRA. In mosses, a delicate cap, sometimes hairy, that covers all or part of the spore-producing capsule (it may be shed early in the development of the capsule or persist until the capsule is nearly mature)

CALYX. The collective term for the sepals of a flower

CAPSULE. In mosses, the structure within which spores are produced; in flowering plants, a type of fruit that consists of more than one seed-producing chamber and that cracks open when dry

CATKIN. A condensed spike of flowers that lack petals, as found in willows, birches, and alders

COROLLA. A circle of petals, whether they are united or not

CRUSTOSE LICHEN. A lichen that forms a thin encrustation on rock, wood, or bark

DECIDUOUS. Applied to plants that drop their leaves in autumn

DISK FLOWER. One of the tubular flowers constituting the central portion of the flower head of a daisy or similar plant

ESCAPE. A garden plant that has become established in the wild

FOLIOSE LICHEN. A lichen that consists largely of leaflike expansions

FRUTICOSE LICHEN. A lichen that consists to a considerable extent of upright stalks, usually branched

GAMETOPHYTE. The sexual generation of a plant, usually alternating with the spore-producing generation (sporophyte)

GEMMA (pl. GEMMAE). In certain liverworts and mosses, small buds by which the sexual generation (gametophyte) reproduces vegetatively

HAIR-POINT. A hairlike prolongation of the leaf of a moss

HERBACEOUS. Applied to plants that are soft, rather than woody

INFLORESCENCE. A cluster of flowers

INTERNODE. The portion of a stem between points where leaves or branches originate

ISIDIUM (pl. ISIDIA). A small outgrowth from the surface of some lichens; it may eventually fall away and develop into a new plant

LEAFLET. In a compound leaf (as of a clover), one of the separate divisions of the blade

OPPOSITE. With leaves or branches situated directly opposite one another on the stem

PANICLE. A flower cluster, usually elongated, in which the side shoots are branched

PEDUNCLE. The stalk of a flower (when the flowers are grouped in an inflorescence, the term peduncle is applied to the main stalk and PEDICEL to the stalks of the individual flowers)

PERENNIAL. A plant that lives for more than two years

PETAL. One of the inner set of leaflike structures of a flower, usually white or brightly colored

PETIOLE. The stalk of a leaf

PINNATE. With two rows of opposite branches or leaflets, thus organized like a feather

PISTIL. The part of a flower concerned with seed production (the pistil, sometimes augmented by tissue adjacent to it, develops into a fruit)

PISTILLATE. Referring to a flower that has one or more pistils but no stamens; also referring to a plant that has only pistillate flowers, or to a catkin or inflorescence composed of pistillate flowers

RACEME. An elongated flower cluster in which the individual flowers arising from the peduncle have stalks (pedicels) of approximately equal length

RAY FLOWER. A flower of the type found at the margin of the disk of a daisy, with the corolla drawn out into what resembles a single petal (but is in fact composed of several fused petals)

RHIZOID. In lower plants, a fine, rootlike outgrowth

RHIZOME. A creeping underground stem

ROOTSTALK. An underground rootlike stem that sends up new shoots each year

RUNNER. A slender, prostrate stem that lies at the surface of the ground, rooting and forming new plants at intervals

SAPROPHYTE. A plant that lives on decaying organic matter

SEPAL. One of the outer set of leaflike structures of a flower (when petals are also present the sepals are usually green, but when petals are absent the sepals are generally some other color)

SOREDIUM (pl. SOREDIA). In certain lichens, a minute reproductive body consisting of algal cells and fungal filaments (soredia originate beneath the surface but erupt to the outside, usually in powdery or granular clusters)

SPATHE. A bract, often brightly colored, that partially or almost completely encloses a flower cluster, as in a calla lily or skunk cabbage

SPOROPHYTE. The spore-producing generation of a plant, usually alternating with the generation that reproduces sexually (gametophyte)

STAMEN. The part of a flower concerned with production of pollen

STAMINATE. Referring to a flower that has stamens but no pistils; also referring to a plant that bears only staminate flowers, or to a catkin or inflorescence composed of staminate flowers

STIGMA. The sticky tip of the pistil of a flower, on which pollen lands

STIPULE. A leaflike outgrowth of the basal portion of the petiole of a leaf

STOLON. A stem that creeps along at the surface of the ground, rooting and forming new plants at intervals (a "runner")

STYLE. The slender stalk that connects the stigma of a pistil with the portion that will eventually enlarge to form the fruit (a distinct style is often lacking)

THALLUS. The body of a lower plant such as a fungus, alga, moss, or liverwort

References

All of the works listed deal at least to some extent with plants and animals of our region. Some of them, of course, serve a much wider area. These references will be helpful in providing additional information concerning the species covered by this book, as well as descriptions and illustrations of hundreds of others that could not be included. Most of them have bibliographies that will lead the student to specialized accounts, including those published in scientific periodicals. Works that have been almost completely superseded by recent publications are not listed.

A few of the books are marked with an asterisk (*) to indicate that they are known to be out of print. They are cited because they are still important, even though they are no longer available from their publishers. It should be possible to locate them in larger public libraries and in libraries of most colleges and universities in the Northwest.

It is important to realize that not all of the books included in this bibliography are fully up-to-date and without flaws. Even the most scholarly of books will beg for revision within a year after it is published. The state of our knowledge with respect to a particular group of animals or plants must also be considered. For instance, the birds of the United States and Canada are so well known that it is unlikely that a species not previously reported will turn up, except as a stray from Europe, Asia, or somewhere else. This cannot be said of many other groups. Yet even the names of birds are sometimes changed in accordance with new findings concerning the extent to which a species varies, or the extent to which it interbreeds with what has been thought to be a separate species. It may take a few years for a recommendation adopted by the American Ornithological Union to be assimilated into guidebooks. In the case of groups such as fungi, lichens, millipedes, centipedes, and earthworms, there are yet undescribed species, and our understanding of some species that have been given names is imperfect. Many changes in names and characterizations must be expected as progress is made toward the development of comprehensive monographs.

On the basis of what has just been said, it can be seen that not all of the references dealing with a particular group will be equally useful or in agreement with one another. Some books are more technical and more complete than others, and some are more recent than others. The newest treatise does not necessarily make older works obsolete. A good case in point is the literature on lichens of our region. The guidebook of Hale (1969), which covers much of North America, is essentially up-to-date in nomenclature, but it hardly touches crustose lichens. The works of Fink (1935) and Howard (1950) deal with crustose types, but the nomenclature for these, and for foliose and fruticose lichens as well, needs to be revised. Howard's book is especially valuable because it gives the localities where lichens found in the state of Washington have been collected. Clearly, then, it is advisable to refer to more than one book, and to use caution in relying on what seem to be the best parts of each.

Animals

MAMMALS

Banfield, A. W. F. *The Mammals of Canada.* Toronto and Buffalo: University of Toronto Press, 1974.

Barbour, R. W., and W. H. Davis. *Bats of America.* Lexington: The University Press of Kentucky, 1969.

Burt, W. H., and R. P. Grossenheider. *A Field Guide to the Mammals.* Boston: Houghton Mifflin, 1964.

Cowan, I. McT., and C. J. Guiguet. *The Mammals of British Columbia.* 5th ed. Handbook 11, British Columbia Provincial Museum, Victoria, 1973.

Ingles, L. G. *Mammals of the Pacific States—California, Oregon, and Washington.* Stanford, Calif.: Stanford University Press, 1965.

Larrison, E. J. *Washington Mammals, Their Habits, Identification, and Distribution.* Seattle: Seattle Audubon Society, 1970.

Maser, C., and R. M. Storm. *A Key to Microtinae of the Pacific Northwest (Oregon, Washington, Idaho).* Corvallis: Oregon State University Bookstores, 1970.

BIRDS

Gabrielson, I. N., and S. G. Jewett. *Birds of Oregon.* Corvallis: Oregon State College Press, 1940. (Reprinted, 1970, as *Birds of the Pacific Northwest,* by Dover Publications, New York.)

Guiguet, C. J. *The Birds of British Columbia. (1) Woodpeckers; (2) Crows and Their Allies.* 3rd ed. Handbook 6, British Columbia Provincial Museum, Victoria, 1969.

———. *The Birds of British Columbia. (4) Upland Game Birds.* Handbook 10, British Columbia Provincial Museum, Victoria, 1955.

———. *The Birds of British Columbia. (7) Owls.* 2nd ed. Handbook 18, British Columbia Provincial Museum, Victoria, 1969.

———. *The Birds of British Columbia. (8) Chickadees, Thrushes, Kinglets, Pipits, Waxwings, and Shrikes.* Handbook 22, British Columbia Provincial Museum, Victoria, 1964.

(Other handbooks in this series deal with waterfowl and shorebirds.)

Jewett, S. G., W. P. Taylor, W. T. Shaw, and J. W. Aldrich. *Birds of Washington State.* Seattle: University of Washington Press, 1953. (Paperback edition, 1968.)

Larrison, E. J., and K. G. Sonnenberg. *Washington Birds. Their Location and Identification.* Seattle: Seattle Audubon Society, 1968.

Marshall, D. B. *Familiar Birds of Northwest Forests, Fields and Gardens.* Portland: Oregon Audubon Society, 1973.

Peterson, R. T. *A Field Guide to Western Birds.* Boston: Houghton Mifflin, 1961.

Pough, R. T. *Audubon Western Bird Guide.* New York: Doubleday, 1957.

Robbins, C. S., B. Bruun, H. S. Zim, and A. Singer. *Birds of North America.* New York: Golden Press, 1966.

AMPHIBIANS AND REPTILES

Carl, G. C. *The Amphibians of British Columbia.* Handbook 2, British Columbia Provincial Museum, Victoria, 1966.

———. *Reptiles of British Columbia.* 3rd ed. Handbook 3, British Columbia Provincial Museum, Victoria, 1968.

Stebbins, R. C. *Amphibians and Reptiles of Western North America.* New York: McGraw-Hill, 1954.

———. *A Field Guide to Western Reptiles and Amphibians.* Boston: Houghton Mifflin, 1966.

INSECTS

Borror, D. J., and R. E. White. *A Field Guide to the Insects of America North of Mexico.* Boston: Houghton Mifflin, 1970.

Ehrlich, P. R., and A. Ehrlich. *How to Know the Butterflies.* Dubuque, Iowa: Wm. C. Brown, 1961.

Essig, E. O. *Insects and Mites of Western North America.* 2nd ed. New York: Macmillan, 1958.

Hatch, M. H., et al. *The Beetles of the Pacific Northwest.* University of Washington Publications in Biology, vol. 16 (issued in 5 parts). Seattle and London: University of Washington Press, 1953–71.

Helfer, J. R. *How to Know the Grasshoppers, Cockroaches, and Their Allies.* Dubuque, Iowa: Wm. C. Brown, 1953.

Jacques, H. E. *How to Know the Beetles.* Dubuque, Iowa: Wm. C. Brown, 1951.

———. *How to Know the Insects.* 2nd ed. Dubuque, Iowa: Wm. C. Brown, 1947.

Klots, A. B. *A Field Guide to the Butterflies.* Boston: Houghton Mifflin, 1951.

Needham, J., and M. J. Westfall. *A Manual of the Dragonflies of North America (Anisoptera) Including the Greater Antilles and the Provinces of the Mexican Border.* Berkeley and Los Angeles: University of California Press, 1955.

Pyle, R. M. *Watching Washington Butterflies.* Seattle: Seattle Audubon Society, 1974.

Swain, R. B. *The Insect Guide: Orders and Major Families of North American Insects.* New York: Doubleday, 1948.

SPIDERS

Kaston, B. J., and E. Kaston. *How to Know the Spiders.* Dubuque, Iowa: Wm. C. Brown, 1953.

LAND MOLLUSCS

Pilsbry, H. A. *Land Mollusca of North America (North of Mexico).* 2 vols., issued in 4 parts. Monograph 3, Academy of Natural Sciences of Philadelphia, 1939–48.

INTRODUCED ANIMALS (VERTEBRATES AND INVERTEBRATES)

Carl, G. C., and C. J. Guiguet. *Alien Animals in British Columbia.* 2nd ed. Handbook 14, British Columbia Provincial Museum, Victoria, 1972.

PLANTS

GENERAL FLORAS

(These usually include ferns, fern allies, conifers, and flowering plants.)

Gilkey, H. M. and L. J. Dennis. *Handbook of Northwestern Plants.* Corvallis: Oregon State University Bookstores, 1973.

Hitchcock, C. L., and A. Cronquist. *Flora of the Pacific Northwest.* Seattle and London: University of Washington Press, 1973.

Hitchcock, C. L., A. Cronquist, M. Ownbey, and J. W. Thompson. *Vascular Plants of the Pacific Northwest.* University of Washington Publications in Biology, vol. 17 (issued in 5 parts). Seattle and London: University of Washington Press, 1955–69.

Peck, M. E. *A Manual of the Higher Plants of Oregon.* 2nd ed. Portland, Ore.: Binfords and Mort, 1961.

TREES AND SHRUBS

Baerg, H. J. *How to Know the Western Trees.* Dubuque, Iowa: Wm. C. Brown, 1955.

Bowers, N. A. *Cone-Bearing Trees of the Pacific Coast.* 7th printing (enl.). Palo Alto, Calif.: Pacific Books, 1965.

Garman, E. H. *Guide to the Trees and Shrubs of British Columbia.* 5th ed. Handbook 31, British Columbia Provincial Museum, Victoria, 1973.

Gilkey, H. M., and P. L. Packard. *Winter Twigs: A Wintertime Key to Deciduous Trees and Shrubs of Northwestern Oregon and Washington.* Corvallis: Oregon State University Press, 1962.

Mosher, M. M., and K. Lunnum. *Trees of Washington.* Extension Bulletin 440, Washington State University, 1974.

Peattie, D. C. *A Natural History of Western Trees.* Boston: Houghton Mifflin, 1953.

Randall, W. R., and R. F. Keniston. *Manual of Oregon Trees and Shrubs.* Corvallis: Oregon State University Bookstores, 1968.

Ross, C. R. *Trees to Know in Oregon.* Extension Bulletin 697, Oregon State University, 1966.

Sudworth, G. B. *Forest Trees of the Pacific Slope.* U. S. Department of Agriculture, Forest Service, 1908. (Reprinted 1967, with a list of nomenclatorial changes and a foreword, by Dover Publications, New York.)

WILDFLOWERS, INDIVIDUAL GROUPS OF FLOWERING PLANTS, AND AQUATIC PLANTS

Clark, L. J. *Wild Flowers of British Columbia.* Vancouver: Evergreen Press, 1973.

Hitchcock, A. S. *Manual of the Grasses of the United States.* 2nd ed., revised by A. Chase. U.S. Department of Agriculture, Miscellaneous Publication no. 200. Washington, D.C., 1951.

Hubbard, W. A. *The Grasses of British Columbia.* Handbook 9, British Columbia Provincial Museum, Victoria, 1969.

Larrison, E. J., G. W. Patrick, W. H. Baker, and J. A. Yaich. *Washington Wildflowers.* Seattle: Seattle Audubon Society, 1974.

Munz, P. A. *Shore Wildflowers of California, Oregon and Washington.* Berkeley and Los Angeles: University of California Press, 1964.

Rickett, H. W. *Wild Flowers of the United States,* volume 5: *The Northwestern States* (in 2 parts). New York: McGraw-Hill Book Co., 1971.

Steward, A. N., L. J. Dennis, and H. M. Gilkey. *Aquatic Plants of the Pacific Northwest; with Vegetative Keys.* 2nd ed. Corvallis: Oregon State University Press, 1963.

Szczawinski, A. F. *The Orchids of British Columbia.* 2nd ed. Handbook 16, British Columbia Provincial Museum, Victoria, 1969.

———. *The Heather Family (Ericaceae) of British Columbia.* 2nd ed. Handbook 19, British Columbia Provincial Museum, Victoria, 1970.

Szczawinski, A. F., and G. A. Hardy. *Guide to Common Edible Plants of British Columbia.* Handbook 20, British Columbia Provincial Museum, Victoria, 1969.

Taylor, T. M. C. *The Lily Family (Liliaceae) of British Columbia.* 2nd ed. Handbook 25, British Columbia Provincial Museum, Victoria, 1973.

———. *The Rose Family of British Columbia.* Handbook 30, British Columbia Provincial Museum, Victoria, 1973.

———. *The Pea Family (Leguminosae) of British Columbia.* Handbook 32, British Columbia Provincial Museum, Victoria, 1974.

———. *the Figwort Family (Scrophulariaceae) of British Columbia.* Handbook 33, British Columbia Provincial Museum, Victoria, 1974.

WEEDS

Gaines, X. M., and D. G. Swan. *Weeds of Eastern Washington and Adjacent Areas.* Davenport, Wash.: Camp-Na-Bor-Lee Association, 1972.

Gilkey, H. M. *Weeds of the Pacific Northwest.* Corvallis: Oregon State College, 1957.

FERNS AND FERN ALLIES

Frye, T. C. *Ferns of the Northwest.* Portland, Ore.: Binfords and Mort, 1934.

Taylor, T. M. C. *The Ferns and Fern Allies of British Columbia.* Handbook 12,

British Columbia Provincial Museum, Victoria, 1963.

———. *Pacific Northwest Ferns and Their Allies.* Toronto: University of Toronto Press, 1970.

MOSSES AND LIVERWORTS

Conard, H. S. *How to Know the Mosses and Liverworts.* Dubuque, Iowa: Wm. C. Brown, 1956.

*Frye, T. C., and L. Clark. *Hepaticae of North America.* University of Washington Publications in Biology, vol. 6 (issued in 5 parts). Seattle: University of Washington, 1937–47.

Harthill, M., and I. O'Connor. *Common Mosses of the Pacific Coast.* Healdsburg, Calif.: Naturegraph Publishers, Inc., 1975.

Lawton, E. *Moss Flora of the Pacific Northwest.* Nichinan, Miyazaki, Japan: Hattori Botanical Laboratory, 1971.

Schofield, W. B. *Some Common Mosses of British Columbia.* Handbook 28, British Columbia Provincial Museum, Victoria, 1969.

MUSHROOMS AND OTHER LARGER FUNGI

Bandoni, R. J., and A. F. Szczawinski. *Guide to Common Mushrooms of British Columbia.* Handbook 24, British Columbia Provincial Museum, Victoria, 1964.

McKenny, D. E. *The Savory Wild Mushroom.* 2nd ed., revised by D. E. Stuntz. Seattle and London: University of Washington Press, 1971.

Miller, O. K. Jr. *Mushrooms of North America.* New York: E. P. Dutton, 1972.

Smith, A. H. *The Mushroom Hunter's Field Guide.* 2nd ed. Ann Arbor: University of Michigan Press, 1963.

———. *A Field Guide to Western Mushrooms.* Ann Arbor: University of Michigan Press, 1975.

LICHENS

Fink, B. *The Lichen Flora of the United States,* completed for publication by Joyce Hedrick. Ann Arbor: University of Michigan Press, 1935.

Hale, M. E., Jr. *How to Know the Lichens.* Dubuque, Iowa: Wm. C. Brown, 1969.

*Howard, G. E. *Lichens of the State of Washington.* Seattle: University of Washington Press, 1950.

Index

Bold-face numerals refer to pages on which text figures are located. If two or more subspecies or varieties of a species are mentioned in the text, the Latin names of these are omitted from the index.